beloved brands

table of contents

Strategic Thinking and Analytics

Brand Positioning

Brand Plans

Marketing Execution Decisions

Brand Toolkit and Marketing Training programs

How the beloved brands playbook can work for you

It takes a fundamentally sound marketer to figure out how to win with brand love in this crazy cluttered world of brands. The fundamentals of brand management matter more now than ever.

Today's marketers have become so busy, as they run from meeting to meeting, they have become a little overwhelmed and confused. They have no time to think. Marketing has become about 'get stuff done,' never taking the time to stop and ask if it is the right stuff to do.

To build a relationship, you must genuinely court your consumer. To move your consumer from stranger to friend and onto the forever stage, you need to think all the time. With the focus on access to big data, marketers are drowning in so much data they do not even have the time to sort through it all to produce the analytical stories that help to make decisions. Marketers are so overwhelmed by the breadth of media choices and the pressure to be everywhere that the quality of the execution has suffered.

If marketers do not love the work they create, how can they ever expect the consumer to love the brand? My goal in writing this book is to make you a smarter brand leader so your brand can win in the market. I know your role and the challenges you face. I have been in your shoes. I will share everything I have learned in my 20 years in the trenches of brand management. I want to help you be successful. This book is intended as an actionable "make it happen" playbook, not a theory or opinion book.

The fundamentals of marketing matter

When I see marketers jump straight to tactics, I know they are missing the underlying issues hurting their brand.

Without taking enough time to think strategically, marketers fail to build on their brand's core strength, create a bond with consumers, win competitive battles, or improve the business situation of the brand. Our Strategic ThinkBox tool pushes marketers to capture the unique circumstances before taking action.

When brands make the mistake of trying to be everything to anyone, the brand ends up being nothing to everyone.

Without a clearly defined brand positioning, the brand never establishes the desired reputation with consumers. With a lack of clarity, all execution teams lacks direction, so the brand messaging ends up random and confusing to consumers. Marketers should never allow competitors to define the brand because they certainly won't like how they define the brand. We will show how to define the target market and turn product features into consumer benefits, with a balance of functional and emotional benefits.

When marketers try to do too many things in their plan, none of their ideas end up with enough resources to make the impact they expect.

Marketing plans that fail to make firm decisions spread their limited resources across so many tactics that none of the ideas create a big enough impact to make a difference. With a lack of vision, the plan meanders and confuses those who work behind the scenes of the brand. We will show how to build your plan with a brand vision, purpose, values, key issues, strategies, and execution plans.

When the marketing execution is not organized and aligned to the strategy, everyone operates in silos, and the consumer sees a disjointed, confused brand.

Brand communication, new product innovation, and the sales team never benefit from working together. Consumers get frustrated by the disjointed execution, and they never feel connected to the brand. Our playbook teaches everything that marketers need to know about writing a creative brief, giving valuable feedback for better work, and making decisions on marketing execution.

When marketers don't go deep enough on analytics, they speak with random opinions not connected to the reality of what's happening in the marketplace.

They miss out on understanding the consumer trends, competitive dynamics, evolving technologies, shopper channels, and brand performance. The problems fester, and competitors steal the untapped opportunities. As a result, the brand positioning, marketing plans, and execution are not good enough. You owe your business a deep-dive business review at least once a year. We show how to lead a deep-dive business review that looks at five areas: the marketplace, consumers, channels, competitors, and the brand.

Consumer business models

Alcoholic Beverages

Consumer Packaged Goods

Retail

Health & Beauty

Technology

Product verticals

Personal Services

Transportation

Vertical search

Direct To Consumer

Destination/Tourism

Financial Services

Restaurants

Automobiles

Image / Fashion Brands

Telecommunications

We will show you how the best marketers think, define, plan, inspire, and analyze

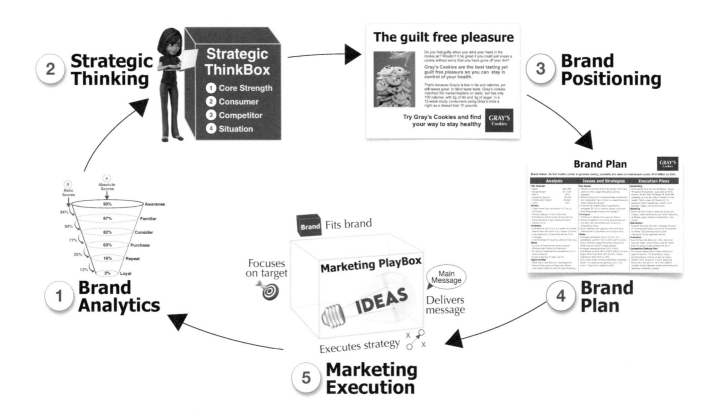

1. How to analyze your brand's performance

Too few marketers take the time to dig into data analytics. There is no value in having access to data if you are not using it to discover meaningful insights. The best brand leaders can tell strategic stories through analytics. I will show you how to create a deep-dive business review, looking at the marketplace, consumers, competitors, channels, and brand. I will teach you how to turn your analysis into a presentation for management, showing the ideal presentation slide format. I will also provide a Finance 101 for Marketers, giving you every financial formula you need to run your brand.

In our section on how to analyze the brand's performance, you will learn how to:

- ✓ Analyze the marketplace your brand plays in
- ✓ Assess your consumers
- ✓ Assess the retail channels you sell through
- ✓ Analyze the competitors
- ✓ Analyze the health and wealth of your brand
- ✓ Use 60 of the best analytical questions to ask
- ✓ Bring the analysis together to summarize the drivers, inhibitors, threats, and opportunities
- ✓ Know the financial formulas for compound CAGR, price increases, COGs. and ROI
- ✓ Prepare a deep-dive business review presentation

2. How to think strategically

Too many marketers are so busy that they do not even have time to think. The best brand leaders do the necessary critical strategic thinking to find ways to win in the market. Strategic thinking is an essential foundation, forcing marketers to ask big questions that challenge and focus brand decisions.

I will show you four ways to enhance your strategic thinking, using the brand's core strength finder, consumer strategy, competitive strategy, and situational strategy. You will learn how to set a vision for your brand, focus your limited resources on breakthrough points, take advantage of opportunities you see in the market, find early wins to leverage to give your brand a positional power to drive growth and profits for your brand.

In our section on strategic thinking, you will learn how to:

- ✓ Use five elements of smart strategic thinking.
- ✓ Engage our ThinkBox 360-degree strategic thinking model to trigger new questions
- ✓ Build everything around your brand's core strength
- ✓ Think strategically to tighten your brand's bond with consumers
- ✓ Think strategically to win the competitive battles you face
- ✓ Think strategically within your brand's current situation
- ✓ Write strategic objective statements for each of the four strategies

3. How to define your brand positioning

Too many marketers are trying to be everything to anyone. This strategy is the usual recipe for becoming nothing to everyone. The best brand leaders target a specific motivated consumer audience and then define their brand around a brand idea that is interesting, simple, unique, motivating, and ownable.

I will show you how to write a winning brand positioning statement with four essential elements: target market, competitive set, main benefit, and reason to believe (RTB). You will learn how to build a brand idea that leads every touchpoint of your brand, including the brand promise, brand story, innovation, purchase moment, and the consumer experience. I will give you the tools for how to write a winning brand concept and brand story.

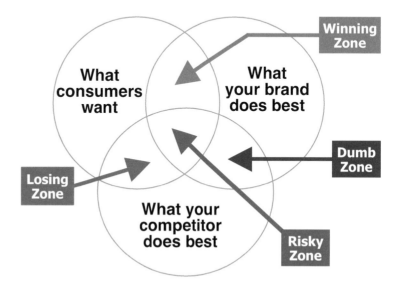

In our section on defining your brand, you will learn how to:

✓ Write brand positioning statements
✓ Define your target market, with insights, enemies, and need states
✓ Define consumer benefits, both functional and emotional
✓ Brainstorm brand support points and claims
✓ Understand relationship between the brand soul, brand idea and brand reputation
✓ Develop your brand idea
✓ Write brand concept statements
✓ Turn your brand concept into a brand story
✓ Use the brand positioning and brand idea to build your internal brand credo

4. How to write brand plans

Too many marketers focus on a short-term to-do list, not a long-term plan. The best brand leaders write brand plans that everyone in the organization can follow with ease, including senior management, sales, R&D, agencies, and operational teams.

I will teach you how to write each element of the brand plan, including the brand vision, purpose, values, goals, key Issues, strategies, and tactics. Real-life examples will give you a framework to use on your brand. You will learn to build execution plans including a brand communications plan, innovation plan, and in-store plan.

In our section on how to write brand plans, you will learn how to:

✓ Use five strategic questions as an outline for your entire plan
✓ Write an inspirational brand vision statement to frame your brand plan
✓ Develop a brand purpose and brand values
✓ Summarize your brand's situation analysis
✓ Map out the key issues your brand faces
✓ Write smart, brand strategy objective statements to build around your brand's core strength
✓ Write smart, consumer brand objective strategy statements
✓ Write smart, competitor-driven brand objective strategy statements
✓ Write smart, situational brand strategy objective statements
✓ Focus tactics to ensure a high return on effort
✓ Write specific execution plans for brand communications, innovation, and in-store
✓ Develop a profit statement, sales forecast, goals, and marketing budget for your plan
✓ Use an ideal one-page brand formats for the annual brand plan and long-range strategic roadmap

5. Marketing execution decisions

Too many marketers are becoming task-masters and step over the line into execution. The best brand leaders need to inspire experts to produce smart and creative execution. I will provide tools and techniques for judging and making decisions on creative advertising from your agency.

For judging execution, I use the ABC's tool, believing the best executions must drive Attention (A), Brand link (B), Communication (C) and Stickiness (S). I will provide a checklist for you to use when judging executions, then show you how to provide direction to your agency to inspire and challenge great execution.

In our section on how to lead the marketing execution, you will learn how to:

✓ Understand the crucial role of the brand leader in getting great creative execution
✓ Be the brand leaders who can successfully manage the 10 stages of the advertising process
✓ Write a brand communications plan
✓ Turn the brand communications plan into a creative brief
✓ Leverage smart and bad examples of the creative brief
✓ Use the ABC's advertising decision-making tool
✓ Give inspiring feedback on advertising that pushes for great work
✓ Build your media planning with six media questions
✓ Align media choices with where consumers are most willing to engage with your brand

What you get from the Beloved Brands playbook?

In the past two decades, what makes brands successful has changed, and you must change with it. You will learn the fundamentals of managing your brand, with brand love at the core. I will show you how to improve your thinking to unleash your full potential as a brand leader.

You will learn how to **think, define, plan, execute,** and **analyze**, and I provide every tool you will ever need to run your brand. You will find models and examples for each of the four strategic thinking methods, looking at core strength, competitive, consumer, and situational strategies.

To define the brand, I will provide a tool for writing a brand positioning statement as well as a consumer profile and a consumer benefits ladder. I have created lists of potential functional and emotional benefits to kickstart your thinking on brand positioning. We explore the step-by-step process to come up with your brand idea and bring it all together with a tool for writing the ideal brand concept.

For brand plans, I provide formats for a long-range brand strategy roadmap and the annual brand plan with definitions for each planning element. From there, I show how to build a brand execution plan that includes the creative brief, innovation process, and sales plan. I provide tools for how to create a brand calendar, and specific project plans.

To grow your brand, I show how to make smart decisions on execution around creative advertising and media choices. When it comes time for the analytics, I provide all the tools you need to write a deep-dive business review, looking at the marketplace, consumer, channels, competitors and the brand. Write everything so that it is easy to follow and implement for your brand.

You will learn everything you need to know so you can run your brand. We have translated most of our brand tools into brand management templates in downloadable PowerPoint presentations that you can purchase at **beloved-brands.com** My brand promise is to help make you smarter so you can realize your full potential in your brand management career.

graham

Graham Robertson

Founder and CMO of Beloved Brands Inc.
graham@beloved-brands.com

Why being a beloved brand matters

Do you love it?

When I was a VP of marketing, I remember when one of my brand managers brought in an awful print ad for my approval. I looked at this boring ad, wondering where to begin my feedback. It was apparent he saw this ad as a mere task on his to-do list. I sensed he had no passion for the work. I sat there for 3-4 minutes and tried to think of something to challenge him. It was so awful I had no advice on how to make it better.

So I asked one of the best questions I have ever asked, "Do you love it?" He said, "No, not really." I gently passed the ad back and said, "Bring me back something you love."

While I hope it was an excellent lesson for him, it was an even more significant lesson for me. My passion has always driven my work. I wanted to see a passion inside everyone on my team.

It was the first time I asked someone, "Do you love it?" but it indeed would not be the last. I began asking that same question to everyone who entered my office. I asked it of myself when I had to make a decision.

We can never settle for O.K. Each time we reject O.K., the work gets better. It makes our expectations higher. When you have to love your work, you will fight for it, with your agency, your boss or anyone in the way. No longer can we think about consumers in a strictly functional or logical way.

The best brands of today, like Tesla, Apple, Starbucks, Nike, Dove or Airbnb have found a way to capture the imagination of their consumers and take them on a journey of delightful experiences that fosters a deeper emotional and lasting relationship.

The best brands win because of the passionate and lasting love they have established with their most cherished consumers

Brands must treat their most cherished consumers with the respect that establishes trust, enabling consumers to open up to a point where they replace thinking with feeling. The logic of demand evolves into an emotional state of desire, needs become cravings and repeat purchases progress into rituals and turn into a favorite moment in the day. Consumers transform into the most outspoken and loyal brand fans and ambassadors.

Old-school marketing no longer works, but the fundamentals of brand management matter more now than ever

The old logical ways of marketing no longer work in today's world. These brands feel stuck in the past, talking about gadgets, features, and promotions. They will be friend-zoned by consumers and purchased only when the brand is on sale. The best brands of the previous century were little product inventions that solved small problems consumers did not even realize they had until the product came along. Old-school marketing was about bold logos, catchy jingles, memorable slogans, side-by-side demonstrations, repetitive TV ads, product superiority claims, and expensive battles for shelf space at retail stores. Every marketer focused on how to enter the consumer's mind.

Old-school marketers learned the 4Ps of product, place, price, and promotion. It is a useful start, but too product-focused, and it misses out on consumer insights, emotional benefits, and consumer experiences.

The Crest brand knew that the "Look, mom, no cavities!" TV ads annoyed everyone, yet they also knew it stuck in the consumer's brain. No one cared how nice the Tide logo looked, as long as it stood out on a crowded grocery shelf. The jingle "Plop, plop, fizz, fizz, oh what a relief it is" was often repeated to embed itself in the consumer's memory bank. The side-by-side dish detergent advertising that showed spots on the wine glass of a competitor, to shame consumers into using Cascade. Brands that continue to follow only a logical play will fail miserably in today's emotion-driven marketplace.

New-school brands need to build a passionate and lasting love for their consumers

How can brand leaders replicate Apple's brand lovers who line up in the rain to buy the latest iPhone before they even know the phone's features? I see Ferrari fans who paint their faces red every weekend, knowing they will likely never drive a Ferrari in their lifetime. There are the 'Little Monsters' who believe they are nearly best friends with Lady Gaga.

It was amazing to witness 400,000 outspoken Tesla brand advocates who put $1,000 down for a car that did not even exist yet. I love the devoted fans of In-N-Out Burger who order animal-style burgers off the secret menu. Every brand should want this type of passion and power with their consumers.

The way consumers make decisions has changed

It takes a smart strategy to balance the rational and emotional management of the brand-to-consumer relationship. These beloved brands are so exceptional because of how well they treat their most loyal consumers. They make them feel loved.

The consumers of today must be won over. They are surrounded by the **clutter** of 5,000 brand messages a day that fight for a glimpse of their attention. That is 1.8 million per year or one message every 11 waking seconds. Consumers are **continuously distracted**—walking, talking, texting, searching, watching, replying—and all at the same time. They glance past most brand messages all day long. Their brain quickly rejects boring, irrelevant, or unnecessary messages. Brands must capture the consumer's imagination right away, with a brand idea that is simple, unique. It must create as much excitement as a first-time encounter.

Consumers are **tired of being burned** by broken brand promises. Once lied to, their well-guarded instincts begin to doubt first, test second, and at any point, they will cast aside any brand that does not live up to the original promise that captured them on the first encounter. A brand must be worthy of love. The best brands of today have a soul that exists deep within the culture of the brand organization.

Brands must be **consumer focused.** The brand's purpose must be able to explain why the people who work behind the scenes of the brand come to work every day so energized and ready to over-deliver on the brand's behalf. This purpose becomes a firm conviction, with inner motivations, beliefs, and values that influences and inspires every employee to want to be part of the brand. This brand conviction must be so firm that the brand would never make a choice that directly contradicts their internal belief system. Consumers start to see, understand, and appreciate the level of conviction with the brand.

Brands must listen, observe, and start to know the thoughts of their consumer before they even think it. Not only does the brand meet their functional needs, but the brand must also heroically beat down the consumer's enemy that torments their life, every day.

The brand must show up consistently at every consumer touchpoint, whether it is the promise the brand makes, the stories they tell, the innovation designed to impress consumers, the happy purchase moments or the delightful experiences that make consumers want to tell their friends the brand story. The consumer keeps track to make sure the brand delivers before the consumer is willing to commit. Only then will the consumer become willing to open up and trust the brand.

The integrity of the soul of the brand helps tighten the consumer's unshakable bond with that brand. Brands have to do the little things that matter, to show they love their consumer. Every time the brand over-delivers on their promise, it adds a little fuel to the romance.

Over time, the brand must weave itself into the most critical moments of the consumer's lives, and become part of the most cherished stories and memories within the consumer's heart. In today's cluttered brand world, the pathway to brand success is all about building relationships with your most cherished consumers.

A brand idea must be interesting, simple, unique, inspiring, motivating, and own-able. The brand idea must attract and move consumers

The first connection point for consumers with a brand is that moment when they see a brand idea worth engaging the brand. The brand almost jumps off the shelf, grips the audience's attention to itself on a TV ad, or compels consumers to click on a digital ad. The brand has to generate interest very quickly.

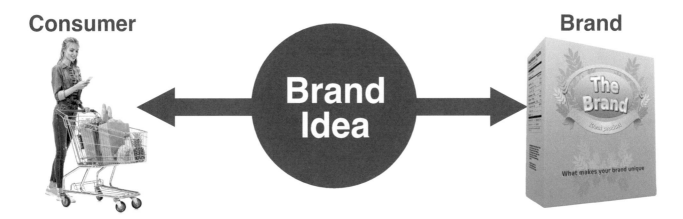

When the brand idea is **interesting** and **simple**, it helps the brand gain quick entry into the consumer's mind, so they want to engage and learn more about the brand. With the consumer bombarded by 5,000 brand messages every day, the brand only has seven seconds to connect or else consumers will move on.

That is why the brand idea should be **unique** and **ownable** to stand out amid the clutter, and the brand can see enough rich potential to build their entire business around the idea. The idea should **inspire** the team working behind the scenes to deliver amazing consumer experiences. The idea must be **motivating** to consumers, so the brand can move consumers to see, think, feel, or act in positive ways that benefit the brand.

A brand idea must have enough **longevity** to last 5 to 10 years and enough flexibility to show consistency no matter what media options you choose. The idea must provide a common link across the entire product line-up. Everything you do should deliver the brand idea.

The brand has to show up the same way to everyone, no matter where it shows up. Even as the brand leader expands on the idea, whether telling the brand story over 60 seconds, 30 minutes or over the lifetime of the brand, it must tell the same story.

When the idea works best, the most far-reaching sales rep, the scientist in the lab, the plant manager or the customer service rep must all articulate the brand idea, in the same way, using the same chosen words. Every time a consumer engages with the brand, they must see, hear and feel the same brand idea. Each positive interaction further tightens their bond with that brand.

Use your brand idea to organize everything you do

As a brand leader, you have **five consumer touchpoints** to align and manage, including the brand promise, brand story, product innovation, the path to the purchase moment, and the overall consumer experience. The brand idea map shows you how to invest in and align all five consumer touchpoints.

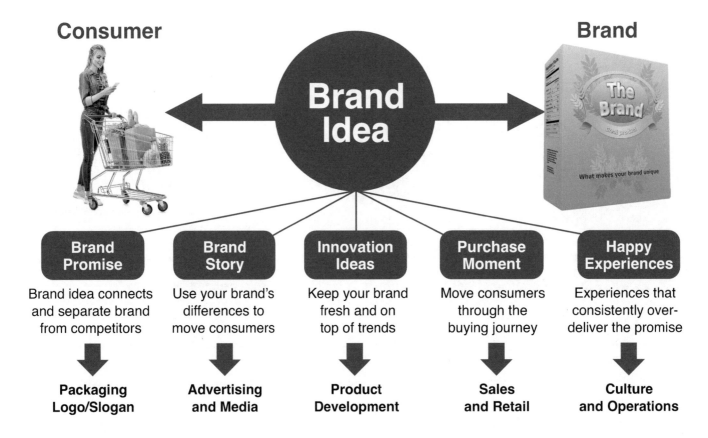

- The **brand promise** connects with consumers and separates your brand from competitors. The promise must position the brand as interesting and unique, utilizing brand positioning work to define the target market, the balance of functional and emotional benefits, along with key support points.

- The **brand story** helps the brand stand out from the pack and gain the consumer's consideration for purchase. The brand idea must push consumers to see, think, feel, or act differently than before they saw the brand message.

- **Innovation** must help the brand stay on top of the latest trends in technology, consumer need states, distribution, and competitive activity. A brand cannot stand still. The brand idea should act as an internal beacon to help inspire the product development team to come up with new ways to captivate consumers.

- The **purchase moment** transforms the awareness and consideration into a purchase. The brand idea ensures everyone along the path to purchase delivers the same brand message, using retail and selling strategies to influence consumers.

- Create **consumer experiences** that overdeliver the promise, driving repeat purchase, and future consumer loyalty. When you partner with HR, the brand idea inspires the culture and organization, influencing hiring decisions, service values, and motivation of the operations teams who deliver the experience.

It takes a strategic mind to figure out brand love

To show the differences in how consumers feel about a brand as they move through five stages, I created the **brand love curve**. It defines consumers' feelings as unknown, indifferent, like it, love it and onto the beloved brand status.

For **unknown** brands, the strategic focus should be to stand out so consumers will notice the brand within a crowded brand world. For **indifferent** brands, the strategy must establish the brand in the consumer's mind so they can see a clear point of difference.

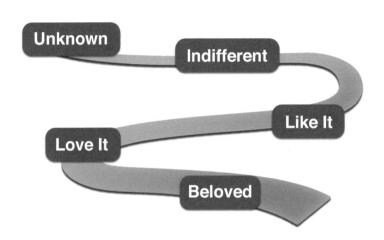

At the **like it** stage, the strategy is to separate the brand from the pack, creating happy experiences that build a trusted following. At the **love it** stage, the focus shifts to tugging at heartstrings to tighten the bond with the most loyal brand fans. At the **beloved brand** stage, the strategic challenge is to create outspoken, loyal brand fans who are willing to whisper to their friends on the brand's behalf.

Necessary ingredients to create brand love

- **Everything must be about the consumer:** You need to know your consumers as well as you know your brand. Dig deep to understand and appreciate the consumer insights, enemies, and needs. Emphasize consumer benefits, not features. Since consumers always wonder, "What's in it for me?" communicate what they get from you and talk about how your brand makes them feel.
- **Dare to be different:** Your brand needs to stand out as being better, different, cheaper, or else your brand will not be around for very long. Be the brand that defines your unique value, rather than adding more clutter to the mountain of clutter.
- **Build everything you do around your brand idea:** Your brand idea is the first point of connection and creates a lasting impression. The brand idea is the reason consumers first buy. Every time your brand delivers, the bond tightens just a little more. Whenever you fail to deliver, the consumer goes into doubt mode, wondering if they will stay with your brand.
- **Breakthrough focus.** You must focus your brand's limited resources to key breakthrough points you believe will tighten the bond with your consumers, putting the brand in a more powerful position to drive higher profits. You have to know your consumer, know what your brand stands for, and be willing to focus on the strategies that will pay back in building the brand.
- **Passion matters:** You must exhibit incredible passion in the marketing execution, consistently focused on surprising your consumers, to become one of their favorite brands. Always remember "I love it" is the highest bar you can set for achieving great work. If you do not love the work, how can you ever expect your consumer to love your brand?

Brand love generates brand power

The tighter the bond a brand creates with its consumers, the more powerful the brand will become with all stakeholders. Think of brand love as stored energy a brand can unleash in the form of power into the marketplace. You can use that power with consumers, competitors, new entries, employees, influencers, media, suppliers, and channel partners.

These beloved brands command power over the very **consumers** who love them, as consumers feel more and think less. These consumers pay price premiums, line up in the rain, follow the brand as soon as it enters new categories, and relentlessly defend the brand to any attackers. They cannot live without the brand.

Beloved brands have power over **channel customers**, who know their consumers would switch stores before they switch brands. Stores cannot stand up to the beloved brand; instead, they give the brand everything in negotiations. The beloved brand ends up with stronger store placement, better trade terms, and better promotions from retail partners.

Consumers
Brand fans think less and feel more

Competitors
Gain a positional per and change momentum

Channels
Use retailers to gain a competitive advantage

New Entries
Reduce their impact and create a failure

Suppliers
Get them to cut costs or terms.

Brand Power

Employees
Engaged, motivated, outspoken culture.

Media
Leverage paid, earned, search, social or home

Influencers
Get outspoken brand fans to influence others

The **competitors**, whether current competitors or new entries, cannot match the emotional bond the beloved brand has created with their brand fans. The beloved brand has a monopoly on emotions, making the consumer decisions less about the actual product and more about how the experience makes consumers feel. Unless a new brand has an overwhelming technological advantage, it will be impossible to break the emotional bond the consumer has established with the beloved brand.

The beloved brand also has power over the **media** whether paid, earned, social, or search media. With paid media, the beloved brand gets better placement, cheaper rates and they are one of the first calls for possible brand integrations. The beloved brand is considered newsworthy, so they earn more free media via mainstream media, expert reviews, bloggers and user-generated content.

Being a famous, beloved brand helps bypass the need for **search engine optimization (SEO)**. The beloved brands become part of the conversation, whether it is through social media or at the lunch table at work. Beloved brands can use their homepage website to engage their most loyal users, inform the market of upcoming changes, allow consumers to design their version of the brand and then sell the product directly to brand lovers.

Suppliers serve at the mercy of the beloved brand. The high volumes drive efficiencies of scale that drive down production costs, backing the supplier into a corner before they offer up most of those savings. Plus, the supplier becomes willing to give in, so that they can use the beloved brand as a selling tool for their supplier services to other potential brands.

Beloved brands even have power over **employees**, who want to be part of the brand. They are brand fans, who are proud to work on the brand. They embody the culture on day 1 and want to help the brand achieve success.

The beloved brands have power over **key influencers**, whether they are doctors recommending a drug, restaurant critics giving a positive review or salespeople at electronics shops pushing the beloved brands. These influencers become fans of the beloved brand and build their own emotions into their recommendations.

Brand love means brand profits

With all the love and power the beloved brand generates, it becomes easy to translate that stored power into sales growth, profit, and market valuation. Here are the eight ways a brand can drive profits:

1. Premium pricing
2. Trading up on price
3. Lower cost of goods
4. Lower sales and marketing costs
5. Stealing competitive users
6. Getting loyal users to use more
7. Entering new markets
8. Finding new uses for the brand.

Beloved brands can use higher prices and lower costs to drive higher margins

Most beloved brands can use their loyal brand lovers to command a premium price, creating a relatively inelastic price. The weakened channel customers cave in during negotiations to give the brand richer margins. Satisfied and loyal consumers are willing to trade up to the next best model. A well-run beloved brand can use their high volume to drive efficiency, helping to achieve a lower cost of goods structure.

Not only can beloved brands use their growth to drive economies of scale, but suppliers will cut their cost to be on the roster of the beloved brand. The beloved brand will operate with much more efficient marketing spend, using their power with the media to generate lower rates with plenty of free media. Plus, the higher sales volumes make the beloved brand's spend ratios much more efficient. The consumer response to the marketing execution is much more efficient, giving the brand a higher return on investment.

Beloved brands use higher shares of a bigger market to drive higher volume

The beloved brands use their momentum to reach a tipping point of support to drive higher market shares. They can get loyal users to use more, as consumers build the beloved brand into life's routines and daily rituals.

It is easier for the beloved brands to enter new categories, knowing their loyal consumers will follow. Finally, there are more opportunities for the beloved brand to find more uses to increase the number of ways the beloved brand can fit into the consumer's life.

Eight ways a brand can drive profits

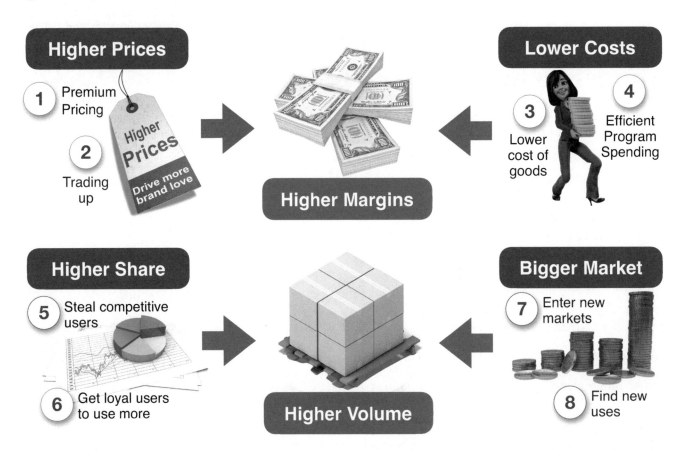

How to use strategic thinking to help your brand win

Strategic thinkers see questions before they see solutions.

Ever hear someone say, "That's a good question." It usually means someone has just asked an interruptive question designed to slow everyone's thinking so they reflect and plan before they act. The strategic thinking side of marketing is logical and has to map out a range of decision trees that intersect by imagining how events will play out in the future. The risk of being only strategic is that if you think too long, you may spiral around, unable to decide. Moreover, you may miss an opportunity window.

Opposite to a strategic thinker is the instinctual thinker who jumps in quickly to find answers before they even know the right question. Their brains move fast; they use emotional impulses and intuitive gut feel. They want action now and get easily frustrated by delays. They believe it is better to do something than sit and wait around. They see strategic people as stuck running around in circles as they try to figure out the right question. Instead, these instinctual leaders choose emotion over logic. While a "make it happen" attitude gets things done, if they go too fast, their actions may solve the wrong problem.

Brand leaders must be both strategic and intuitive. Learn to change brain speeds. Slow down the thinking when faced with challenging issues and move quickly with your best instincts on execution.

We will explore our strategic ThinkBox for how to come up with the best key questions facing your brand. And we will then use our five elements of strategy - vision, investing resources to solidify capabilities, focused opportunity, market impact, and performance result - to structure brand strategy statements.

Our Strategic ThinkBox and Marketing PlayBox

I want to introduce you to my **ThinkBox** concept, which I have borrowed from sports. Using a ThinkBox forces you to consider everything you are facing before taking the shot. For instance, in golf, look at any lakes or bunkers in the way, the wind condition, or how well you are playing that day and then, decide on your shot strategy. As you move to a **PlayBox**, visualize the ideal shot, think and feel your way through the mechanics of your swing, and trust you are making the right shot. Avoid over-thinking the strategy during the execution.

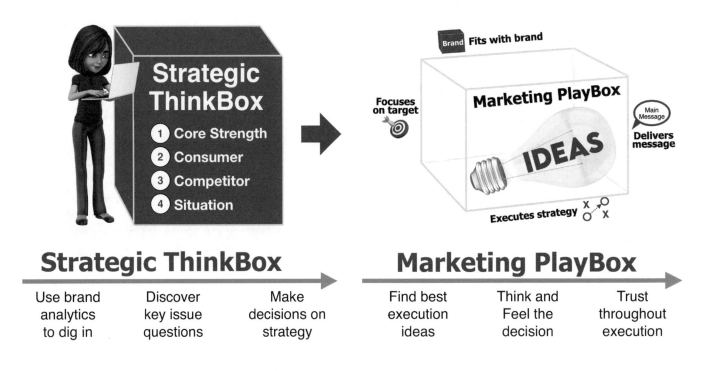

In managing your brand, you should use our **Strategic ThinkBox**, to get a 360-degree view of the situation before taking action. Consider your brand's core strength, your bond with your consumers, your brand's competitive position, and your brand's business situation.

Once you have completed your thinking, use the Marketing PlayBox to keep your marketing execution focused on the target, fit with the brand, delivers the brand message, and execute the strategy. The Marketing PlayBox allows you to use your instincts to find the best execution ideas and to think, feel, and trust your way through the execution. More on the PlayBox later in the book.

The four questions in our Strategic ThinkBox

As I created the Strategic ThinkBox, I made it so that each of the four questions uses a forced choice to make decisions, where you must focus on only one possible answer for each question.

1. What is the **core strength** that will help your brand win?
2. How tightly connected is your **consumer** to your brand?
3. What is your current **competitive** position?
4. What is the current business **situation** your brand faces?

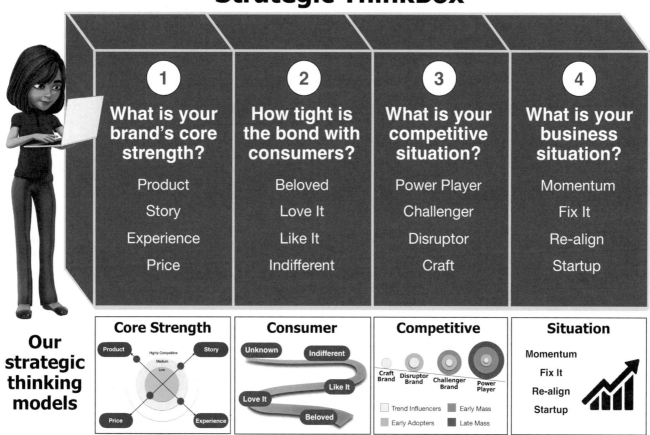

1. Start with your brand's **core strength**. Think of your core strength as your brand's superpower or secret sauce that separates you from other brands. Is it your product, brand story, consumer experience, or price? Your core strength steers your entire strategy, including the brand messages and the focus of your investment. In the next chapter, I show a unique process for how to choose your brand's core strength and then show you how to write smart, strategic objective statements around your core strength.

2. Next, you have to look at your **consumer strategy.** Start by determining where your brand currently sits on the brand love curve, whether your brand is unknown, indifferent, like it, love it, or at the beloved stage. The goal is to tighten the bond with your consumer and move them from one stage to the next. In a later chapter, I will show you how to use brand funnel data, the voice of the consumer, and market dynamics to determine where your brand sits on the brand love curve. I will outline clear game plans for each stage.

3. Regarding the **competitive strategy**, you must choose from one of four different types of competitive situations you find your brand operating within. The dominant leader in the category is the power players, who take a competitive defensive stance. The challenger brands have gained enough power to battle head-to-head with the market leader. The disruptor brands have found a space so different they can pull consumers away from the significant category players. Craft brands aggressively go against the category with a niche target market and a niche consumer benefit. They are small and stay far away from the market leaders. Each competitive situation leads to different strategy choices.

4. A brand must look at the **situational strategy**, which starts with understanding your brand health by looking at both internal and external factors. Choose one of four potential situations: whether you keep the momentum going, face a business turnaround situation, realign everyone behind a strategy, or your brand is a start-up. Each situation leads to distinct strategies and leadership styles to deploy.

How our Strategic ThinkBox works

Coke

Coke's core strength is its brand story, as told over the past hundred years. It links the Coke brand to the virtues of enjoying life, using brand stories around refreshing, happiness, and the real thing. Coke even invented our current visualization of the modern-day Santa. The brand has a long-standing and tight connection with consumers.

Even with recent sales declines, Coke remains a beloved brand with a loyal following of brand fans. Concerning the cola market, Coke remains the power player brand over Pepsi. However, Coke faces a complicated situation because the sugar version of the cola market is rapidly declining as consumers shift to healthier beverage alternatives.

Most recently, bottled water has passed the cola category in dollar sales. Coke needs to realign and make some tough choices. The original Coke is no longer the hero of the portfolio, in decline for the past few years. The growth comes from Coke Zero, Diet Coke, or other beverages within the portfolio. Can Coca-Cola grow Coke Zero faster than the original Coke's declines? Coke needs a turnaround strategy to determine a sustaining pathway to grow over the next ten years. The brand should face the reality of the category declines, and the path to success would involve reducing Pepsi's market presence and eliminating some of the smaller brands in the category.

Tide

Tide is a product-led brand that should continue pushing its "superior clean" message to consumers. The brand has a tight bond with consumers. While Tide is not the most outwardly emotional brand, it has earned a long history of consumer trust. Tide is the dominant power-player brand in the laundry category, owning superior stain cleaning. They have successfully neutralized competitive attacks regarding fresh scents or new formats. Tide should continue to exert its power against competitors and retailers.

Regarding its current situation, Tide needs to keep the momentum going. The 2018 Super Bowl's "It must be a Tide ad" was remarkable. It is my first time wanting to see another Tide ad.

The National Football League (NFL)

The NFL is one of the best experience-led brands on the planet. It is a beloved brand with passionate fans who have turned the NFL into a power player that dwarfs the other North American sports leagues.

The NFL generates significantly higher ticket sales, merchandise sales, and TV viewership than the combined efforts of the next three most significant sports—baseball, basketball, and hockey.

While the brand remains compelling, many recent high-profile scandals and a dramatic change in viewing habits among youth have triggered a need for a realignment for the NFL.

The NFL needs to step back and refuel the brand love to keep the consumer bond strong. The NFL must also work hard to maintain its status, especially as the brand hits a potential plateau. They may create a global brand as they find success by generating new fans in the UK and Germany.

Facebook

Although Facebook is primarily a consumer-facing brand, its revenues come from B2B media sales. Facebook is an idea-led brand and the dominant power player, willing to bully any competitor who threatens it.

In terms of its bond with customers, eight years ago, Facebook was on the verge of becoming a beloved brand. Facebook's arrogance and hunger for even more power have eroded its trust with users, putting its future B2B media revenues at risk. They keep copying every new player. However, they have yet to come up with an answer for TikTok.

There remains doubt about how Facebook will handle privacy, political interference, and concerns over the accuracy of its audience numbers – uncertainty that continues to cloud Facebook's trust.

Mark Zuckerberg must be more forthcoming and honest in portraying his brand. The question Facebook should focus on is how to tighten its bond with users.

Looking at its business situation, Facebook appears to have peaked, with recent revenue declines and layoffs. Their stock price is plummeting. Facebook needs to regain its trust because the most significant risk to its arrogance is the threat of government regulations that would severely cut into future revenues.

Use our Strategic ThinkBox tools to engage, trigger, and debate

Putting each of the four answers together starts to map out the overall strategic direction where you should focus. When writing the brand plan, you should map out a specific key issue question for each of the four strategic questions in your ThinkBox.

Over the next few chapters, I will continue going in-depth on these strategies. And I will introduce various thinking tools for each question. Try them with your team. Our strategic tools won't give you the answers. They help start a debate. From there, I hope you spend time figuring out the most challenging, interruptive questions facing your brand.

Five elements of smart strategic thinking

Slow down and organize our thoughts with five elements of strategic thinking, including the vision, investment in solidifying capabilities, focused opportunity, market impact, and performance result. The five elements create a flywheel to keep investing behind to fuel growth toward the vision.

Set a vision of what you want

Set aspirational goal, anchored by your current situation. Then identify key issues by asking questions.

(A) Invest in capabilities to deliver the strategy

Invest in the brand's core strength, build consumer bonds, challenge competitor positioning, and address situational opportunities.

(D) Performance result that pays back

Shift in power propels the vision, drives results, and paves the way for stronger consumer bonds, brand strength, and profitability.

(B) Focused accelerator to propel strategy

Focus limited resources on distinct opportunities arising from market dynamics like consumer trends, influencers, competitors, or new tech and channels.

FOCUS

We write brand strategy statements using our

A + B + C + D

(C) Market impact tipping point

Leverage early win to shift market momentum. Advance consumer journeys, boost brand reputation, or strengthen consumer bonds.

Your vision acts as a magnet to pull everyone toward your ideal future.

A vision sets aspirational stretch goals for the future linked to a clear result or purpose. It should steer everyone who works on the brand to focus on finding ways to create a bond with your consumers that will lead to power and profit beyond what the product alone could achieve. Imagine it is five or ten years from now, and you wake up in the most fantastic mood. Visualize a perfect future and write down the most critical milestones you must achieve. Consider words that will inspire, lead, and steer your team toward your vision. If the vision is too close to your current situation, it will have no impact. If the vision is impossible, it will fail to connect with the team.

The key issues define what is in the way of achieving your aspirations.

Brands must examine the gap between the current trajectory and their aspiring vision. We use interruptive questions that frame the issues regarding what is in the way of achieving what you want. By raising those issues early on, you can focus the team on the significant problems to solve on the pathway to the stated vision.

* Roger Martin "Playing to win"

A. Invest in building capabilities to deliver the brand strategy.

Invest your limited resources—money, people, time, and partnerships—in strategic programs that will build the capabilities to help close the gap between your current projection and the aspirational vision. From a brand viewpoint, align your investment to reinforce the brand promise, communicate the brand story, close the deal at the purchase moment, launch new product innovation, or create an ideal consumer experience.

These investments line up to deliver a brand's consumer touchpoints so that you will tighten the bond with consumers. The investment will result in a more powerful, faster-growing, and profitable brand.

1. **Consumer Knowledge.** Know your consumer better than your competitors know them. Focus on those who are most motivated by what you offer. Discover the consumers' moments of accelerated needs, enemies, and insights. Leverage data to understand what it takes to move consumers along their purchase journey.

2. **Brand Promise.** Build brand positioning around your brand's core strength, whether you lead with the product, story, consumer experience, or price. Combine the ideal functional and emotional benefits to create a brand idea that is unique, simple, ownable, inspiring to employees, and motivating for consumers. Use the brand idea to organize everything you do.

Invest in building capabilities to deliver the strategy

1. Consumer knowledge

2. Brand promise

3. Brand communications

4. Purchase moment

5. Innovation

6. Consumer experience

7. Operations strengths

8. Brand culture

3. **Brand Communications.** Use creative communications to capture attention, link to the brand, communicate the message and stick with consumers. Invest in media to attract, inform, close, service, and delight consumers when they are most open to moving along their purchase journey.

4. **Purchase moment.** Invest in people to inform, close, and service consumers, through retail with merchandising, assortment, promotions and shelf space, or with content to drive DTC or e-commerce.

5. **Innovation.** Invest in continuously exploring new products and services to stay fresh with consumers and differentiate your brand. Inspire ideas, test, and deliver product extensions, improvements, new formats, brand stretching, game-changing technology, and blue ocean exploration.

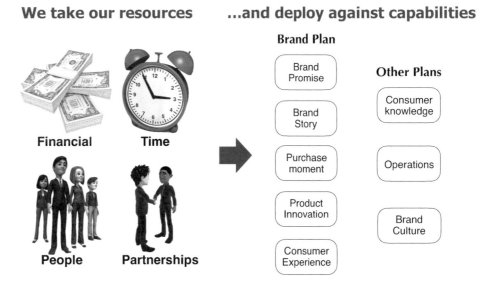

We take our resources

Financial   Time

People   Partnerships

...and deploy against capabilities

Brand Plan

Brand Promise

Brand Story

Purchase moment

Product Innovation

Consumer Experience

Other Plans

Consumer knowledge

Operations

Brand Culture

6. **Consumer Experience.** Alignment of the brand story that creates consumer desire with your employees' delivery of a consumer experience that exceeds the consumer's expectation. Operations, sales, and innovation must work together, and each understands their specific role in bringing the brand idea to life.

7. **Operations strengths.** Use operations to create a competitive advantage that beats competitors based on speed, flexibility, cost, and simplicity through the production process, ingredients, quality, sourcing, forecasting, supply, shipping, servicing, tracking, financial management, and measurement.

8. **Brand culture.** Use an internal rallying cry that reflects your brand's purpose, values, and motivations. It must inspire, challenge, and guide your people to provide their greatness on behalf of the brand. It is the quality of your people that drives the success of your brand.

B. Focused accelerator to propel strategy

Identify who you are talking to and whether you will focus on new category consumers, competitive consumers, or current consumers.Then, look for a trend accelerator that is already happening in the market that can accelerate your strategy, whether that means you focus your limited resources on a distinct opportunity you have identified based on a potential change in market dynamics such as consumer trends, influencer opinions, competitors, new technology or channels.

Many marketers struggle to focus

Myth 1: The belief that your brand will get bigger if you have a broader target market.

✓ **Reality:** Marketers must act like investment managers, not cost centers. We must invest in those consumers who are the most likely to respond to our marketing. Others will tell you light buyers are essential. But that doesn't mean you invest in them. If they are light buyers before your marketing and light buyers after, you just wasted your precious investment. Find the consumers most motivated by what you offer and use your marketing investment to move them in ways that generate more profit than the original investment. Invest over the long term to build the target over time.

Myth 2: The second myth to becoming a more prominent brand is to believe a brand stands for everything. Some brands try to say everything possible, hoping the consumer hears anything.

✓ **Reality:** A brand must stand for something with a backbone and conviction. Trying to be everything to anyone ends up with a brand that is nothing to everyone.

Myth 3: The belief that your brand will achieve higher sales if you try to be everywhere in every sales channel or every possible media option.

✓ **Reality:** You can't spread your limited resources so thin that nothing has an impact. The costs become prohibitive by trying to be everywhere, and you will drain the brand's profitability. A brand must earn its physical and mental availability, not just mindlessly trying to buy it. Brand success leads to increased distribution points, and brand profit leads to the increased investment that allows you to increase the breadth of your brand message.

Every brand has limited financial, time, people, or partnerships resources. Marketers always face the temptation of unlimited choices, whether in the potential target market, brand messages, strategies, or tactics. The smartest marketers limit their choices to match up to their limited resources, to focus on those that will deliver the highest return.

When you focus, five amazing things happen to your brand:

1. **Stronger return on investment (ROI):** When you focus your dollars on a distinct breakthrough point, with an ideal target, message, and media, you will see the most positive and efficient response in the market.
2. **Better return on effort (ROE):** You must make the most efficient use of your limited people resources. Find the Big Easy! Focus on the ideas with the most significant impact that is the easiest to execute. Avoid those ideas that are small and difficult to implement. While you may not always have the data to calculate your ROI, you should have the instinct to figure out your return on effort (ROE).
3. **Stronger reputation:** When you limit your audience and brand message, you will have a better chance to own that reputation among that core target audience.
4. **More competitive:** As you grow, your brand will start to create a space in the market, and you can use your core base of brand fans to defend against others from entering your space.
5. **More investment behind the brand:** When you show up as an investment manager who delivers profitable business results, your CFO will provide more money to keep doing what you are doing. Even with increased resources, you must take the same focused approach.

C. Breakthrough market impact to create a tipping point

A smart strategy turns an early breakthrough win into a shift in momentum, positional power, or tipping point where you begin to achieve more in the marketplace than the resources you put in.

Many underestimate the need for an early win. You need a crucial breakthrough point where you start looking at a slight momentum shift toward your vision. While there will always be doubters to every strategy, the results of the early win provide compelling proof to show everyone the plan will work, helping change the doubters' minds —or at least keep them quiet.

Strategy can isolate where you want to move your target

Strategy can tighten the target's bond with the brand

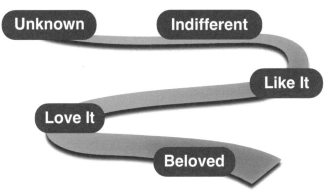

The magic of strategy happens through leverage, where you can use the early win as an opening or a tipping point where you start to see a transformational power that allows you to make an impact and achieve results in the marketplace. A smart strategy should trigger the consumer to move along the buying journey from awareness to buy and onto loyalty, and it can help tighten the consumer's bond with the brand.

D. Achieve a performance result that pays back

The shift in positional power in the marketplace moves your brand toward your vision and creates a future pathway to building a consumer bond, brand power, and brand profitability. A brand can become powerful compared to the consumers they serve, the competitors they battle, the channels they sell through, the suppliers who make the products or ingredients, the influencers in the market, any media choices, and the employees who work for the brand. We explored these eight sources of power in the opening chapter.

You can drive **profit** through premium pricing, trading consumers up on price, finding a lower cost of goods, using lower sales and marketing costs, stealing competitive users, getting loyal users to use more, entering new markets, or finding new uses for the brand.

In the opening chapter, we explore eight ways a brand can add to its profitability.

For a brand strategy to work, what pays off in the marketplace must pay off in brand power or business results.

Power		**Profit**		
Gain a competitive advantage		New to category	Competitive users	**Penetration drives share and revenue**
Tighten the bond with consumers	**Harnessed power leads to future growth**	Higher usage from current consumers	Higher share of requirements	**Usage drives share and revenue**
Added distribution presence		Get consumers to pay price premiums	Trade up to higher priced items	**Higher prices drives margins**
Improve service through employees		Cross sell existing items	Get loyalists to follow brand to new categories	**Expand market size**

Our Strategic ThinkBox defines a brand's key issues

The key issues and strategies are the guts of your strategic plan. Take all your thinking on your brand and start organizing the best strategic questions and answers.

The key issues answer, **"Why are we here?"** Take the summary findings of the deep-dive analysis. Draw out the significant issues that are in the way of achieving your stated brand vision. Our methodology for finding key issues is to return to our **Strategic ThinkBox** with my four strategic questions.

Our Strategic ThinkBox ensures you take a 360-degree view of your brand—your brand's strength, consumer bond, competitive dynamic, and business situation. With each of these four questions, you need to decide on your main answer and see if your investments, communications, and execution deliver on that answer.

What is your competitive situation?

What is your business situation?

How tight is the bond with consumers?

What is your brand's core strength?

Strategic ThinkBox

1. Core Strength
2. Consumer
3. Competitor
4. Situation

1. What is your brand's core strength?

What is your brand's super power? Here is the game I have created to help you choose your brand's core strength. Using the diagram to the right, start with four chips. You must place one chip where you believe you have the highest competitive advantage to win. Then put two chips at the medium level that backs up and supports the core strength. Finally, the game forces one chip to be at the low end, almost a throwaway weakness that will not be part of the strategy.

It is a great game to try with your team, as it creates a great debate among your team members.

Once you dig in, here are the questions you should be asking. Is your core strength the product, story, experience, or price? Are your capabilities lined up to deliver? Is your investment lined up with building capabilities that support your core strength? What has paid off or not? Are you communicating your core strength? Are you using your strength to move consumers? What is working well? What needs fixing?

Core Strength

Product — Highly Competitive — Medium — Low — Story
Price — Experience

We will use our fictional **Gray's Sporting Goods** brand as our example to demonstrate how we use this tool. Gray's started 50 years ago as a product-led brand, evolving to a consumer experience-led brand. What began as fitting centers are now interactive zones. With new sports experiences like TopGolf or e-sports, Gray's sees a future with interactive in-person versions of e-sports. We need to invest in innovation to drive CX communication to drive traffic. With many brand fans, now is the time to unleash that passion for the brand and create a community. We know once they engage in interaction, they are more likely to buy.

Playing with this tool helps conclude that Gray's needs to shift from a product-led brand to a more consumer-experience led. Can we create experience zones for consumers to play, compete and win?

2. How tight is the bond with consumers?

To replicate how brand building matches up with building a relationship, I created the brand love curve, which outlines how consumers move through five stages: unknown, indifferent, like it, love it, and onto the beloved brand status.

Who is the consumer target, what is your knowledge and insights about them, and how do they match the brand's main benefits? Then ask where your brand is on our brand love curve; is your brand unknown, indifferent, liked, loved, or beloved? Many times, you may have groups of consumers at different stages. Which capabilities do you need to invest in to tighten the brand's bond with consumers? What does the funnel indicate? Penetration, frequency?

Consumer

Gray's Sporting Goods is the beloved power player in the sporting goods category. Our loyalty has been tested this year with Sports World's EDLP pricing strategy, and they are pulling away our loyal consumers just as they are about to purchase. We must give our most passionate brand fans more reason to love us, rewarding them with what they love best—participating, competing, and winning through sports. We believe the power of sports can transform lives.

Playing with this tool for Gray's makes me conclude that we need to figure out how to leverage our most passionate brand fans to tighten the bond with them.

3. What is your competitive situation?

A winning brand positioning statement matches what consumers want with what your brand does best, always better than your competitors. I will outline four types of competitive brand strategy situations: the power player, challenger, disruptor, and craft brands. You must identify and choose one competitive situation, which best fits where you are today, and where you want to go next.

Competitive

To start, figure out the unique positioning space your brand can win. Look at the intensity of competition and decide if your brand is the power player, challenger, disruptor, or craft brand. Should you be attacking or defending? Are you winning the battles, whether investment, messages, innovation, retail, or location?

Continuing with **Gray's Sporting Goods**, the most significant competitive issue is the attack by Sports World (SW) on the pricing of the big three sports (football, baseball, basketball). With flat sales in the big three sports, we want to avoid a price war. However, SW's taking away business at the convert-to-purchase stage. We need to fight back to assert our power but then figure out how to raise the prices. For Gray's, we need to exert our power by attacking back to regain our share lost due to Sports World's EDLP on the big three sports.

4. What is your business situation?

Before moving towards a plan, you must fully understand your situation. Each year, conduct a deep-dive business review to assess the health of your branded business. A smart brand strategy is a smart business strategy. You are running a live business that needs to drive sales, manage costs, and produce profits. You must address the competitive and consumer factors you face to ensure your great strategic thinking is stable around you.

This thinking creates four distinct situations your brand could face: Fuel the momentum, Fix it, Realignment, or a Start-up. Dig in on the wealth of the brand by looking at market share, sales, and profits. Then look at the brand's health by looking at the reputation, distribution, and pipeline. Do you see significant gaps that need fixing: message, distribution, innovation? What are the current drivers and inhibitors? Future opportunities and threats?

For **Gray's Sporting Goods**, the sales are flat in our core business as youth participation shifts from traditional sports to e-sports. While the interactive zones within our stores are a good start, do we need to go even further to enter into the e-sports business through acquisition, partnership, or innovation? No significant threats, but flat business results put us at risk of attack. Playing with this tool for Gray's makes me question whether we must explore realigning the brand to open up interactive zones and virtual esports. Do we acquire, partner, or build from scratch?

Situation

Momentum

Fix It

Re-align

Startup

Summarize what's happening with each of the four areas

After looking at all four of the Strategic ThinkBox questions, we need to narrow down to a conclusion statement for each of the four ThinkBox questions. For Gray's Sporting Goods, the four conclusions are:

1. **Core Strength:** Gray's aims to transition from a product-led brand to a story-led brand by establishing experiential zones where customers can engage in play, competition, and winning opportunities.

2. **Consumer Bond:** Gray's should harness the power of their loyal brand fans to strengthen the emotional attachment and fortify the bond.

3. **Competitive Situation:** The analysis suggests that Gray's needs to exert its power by attacking SportsWorld to regain our share lost due to Sports World's EDLP on the big three sports.

4. **Business Situation:** While sales are flat, how kids play sports is shifting to more experiential and e-sports. Gray's to explore creating interactive zones in the short term and whether to enter into virtual/e-sports. Gray's needs to explore whether to acquire, partner, or build from scratch.

Transforming the thinking into key issue questions

360° ThinkBox Questions

(1) What is the core strength your brand can win on?

(2) How tightly connected is your Consumer to your brand?

(3) What is your current competitive position?

(4) What is the current business situation your brand faces?

Gray's Sporting Goods Key Issues

(1) How do we transform our fitting centers into experiential zones within our stores?

(2) How do we connect on an emotional level with our most beloved brand fans?

(3) What pricing strategy leverages our power to regain our growth in the top 3 sports?

(4) How do we explore a significant entry for Gray's into virtual or e-sports?

Make sure you find the right level of the key issue

Keep asking the key question until it gets better. Tweak. Challenge. Debate. Refine. Perfect.

- **Too low:** How do we get consumers to use more coupons? In this example, the key issue is too specific and tactical. It needs to be more significant to set up a strategic solution.
- **Too high:** How do we become the #1 brand? This key issue is too general and too broad of a question to lead to a pinpointed, strategic solution. It is more suited to a question on brand vision.
- **Just right:** How do we drive usage among loyal consumers? With this example, the key issue does an excellent job of addressing an obstacle in the way of the vision. It is big enough to leave sufficient room to explore various strategic solutions.

Once you nail the key issue question, move on to the planning stage, and build a brand strategy statement that answers the question. The better the key issue question, the better the strategy.

Ideal structure for the vision, key issue, and strategy statement

Let's look at how to turn your smart strategic thinking into writing a strategic objective statement that can provide specific marching orders to everyone working on the brand. The vision is the aspirational target five to ten years from now. The key issue examines the gap between aspiration and current projection and asks what is in the way. Write a strategy statement to answer the key issue.

We want our process to cover all five elements of smart strategic thinking. Above, you can see the brand vision and key issue statement we developed through our Strategic ThinkBox. The vision covers the first strategic element. Next, you need a strategy statement to cover the remaining four other strategic elements: A) program investment, B) focused accelerator, C) market impact, and D) performance result.

Here's how that brand strategy statement includes all four remaining elements:

A. **Build capabilities to deliver the vision:** The investment in capabilities to deliver the strategy whether you are building the brand promise, brand story, purchase moment, product innovation, and consumer experience. These crystal-clear marching orders to the team leave no room for doubt, confusion, or hesitation. In this example, the strategic capability is to **"Communicate Gray's new "sports transform lives" positioning."**

B. Focused Accelerator: The breakthrough point where the brand will exert pressure to create a market impact. In this example, the focused accelerator "involves our strong base of brand fans."

C. **Market impact:** Achieves a specific desired market impact with a stakeholder you will attempt to move, whether it is consumers, sales channels, competitors, or influencers. In this example, the desired market impact is to **"tighten their bond with Gray's"**

D. **Performance result:** Drive a specific performance result linked to the market impact, making the brand more powerful or profitable. In this example, the result is to **"drive traffic into stores."**

Turn your thinking into brand strategy statements

Our unique strategic model will force you to pick answers to build a strategy statement with marching orders for those who follow your plan. As you build your brand plan, I recommend you use these four elements of smart strategy statements to ensure you structure and demonstrate your great thinking.

Strategic Writing

Brand Vision: To transform Gray's to an interactive sports destination to help our customers play, compete, and win

Key Issue in the way of achieving that vision: How do we connect on an emotional level with our brand fans?

Strategic Objective Example:

(A) **Building Capabilities:** Communicate Gray's new "transform lives " positioning

(B) Focused Accelerator: to involve our strong base of brand fans

(C) **Market Impact:** to tighten their bond with Gray's

(D) **Performance result:** and drive traffic into stores

Writing your brand strategy statements

Using the cheat sheet for brand strategy statements: start by investing in capabilities, then choose the target and focused accelerator. For the market impact, will you attract, inform, close, service, or delight consumers? What do you want them to do? For performance results, choose one of four ways to get more powerful or wealthier by pushing penetration, frequency, pricing, or entering new markets.

Brand Strategy = (A) **Building Capabilities** + (B) **Focused Accelerator** + (C) **Market Impact** + (D) **Performance Result**

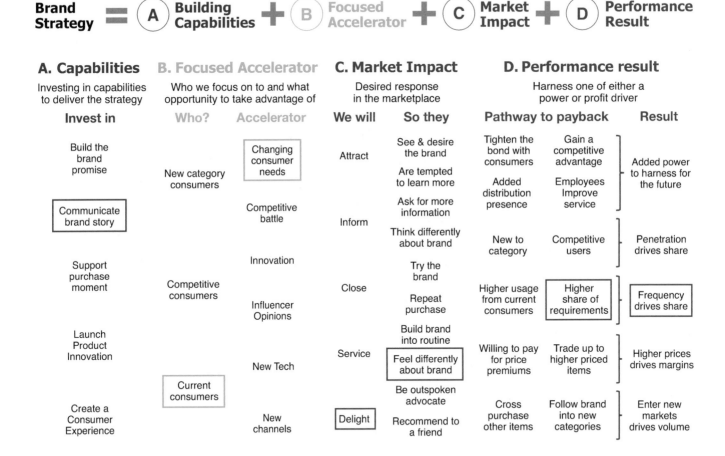

A. Capabilities

Investing in capabilities to deliver the strategy

Invest in

- Build the brand promise
- Communicate brand story
- Support purchase moment
- Launch Product Innovation
- Create a Consumer Experience

B. Focused Accelerator

Who we focus on to and what opportunity to take advantage of

Who?

- New category consumers
- Competitive consumers
- Current consumers

Accelerator

- Changing consumer needs
- Competitive battle
- Innovation
- Influencer Opinions
- New Tech
- New channels

C. Market Impact

Desired response in the marketplace

We will

- Attract
- Inform
- Close
- Service
- Delight

So they

- See & desire the brand
- Are tempted to learn more
- Ask for more information
- Think differently about brand
- Try the brand
- Repeat purchase
- Build brand into routine
- Feel differently about brand
- Be outspoken advocate
- Recommend to a friend

D. Performance result

Harness one of either a power or profit driver

Pathway to payback

- Tighten the bond with consumers — Gain a competitive advantage
- Added distribution presence — Employees Improve service
- New to category — Competitive users
- Higher usage from current consumers — Higher share of requirements
- Willing to pay for price premiums — Trade up to higher priced items
- Cross purchase other items — Follow brand into new categories

Result

- Added power to harness for the future
- Penetration drives share
- Frequency drives share
- Higher prices drives margins
- Enter new markets drives volume

Structuring your brand strategy statement

Communicate Gray's new 'sports transform lives' positioning **(A)** to involve our strong base of brand fans **(B)** to delight and tighten their bond with Gray's **(C)** to drive high share of requirements and drive frequency **(D)**.

How to conduct a deep-dive business review to uncover brand issues

Too many marketers are not taking the time to dig in on the analytics. There is no value in having access to data if you are not using it. The best brand leaders can tell strategic stories through analytics.

Conduct a deep-dive business review at least once a year on your brand. Otherwise, you are negligent of the brand, where you are investing all your resources. Dig in on the five specific sections—marketplace, consumers, channels, competitors and the brand—to draw out conclusions to help set up your brand's key issues, which you answer in the brand plan.

1. **Marketplace:** Start by looking at the overall category performance to gain a macro view of all significant issues. Dig in on the factors impacting category growth, including economic indicators, consumer behavior, technology changes, shopper trends, and political regulations. Also look at what is happening in related categories, which could impact your category or replicate what you may see next.
2. **Consumers:** Analyze your consumer target to better understand the consumer's underlying beliefs, buying habits, growth trends, and critical insights. Use the brand funnel analysis and leaky bucket analysis to uncover how they shop and how they make purchase decisions. Try to understand what they think when they buy or reject your brand at every stage of the consumer's purchase journey. Uncover consumer perceptions through tracking data, the voice of the consumer, and market research.
3. **Channels:** Assess the performance of all potential distribution channels and the performance of every major retail customer. Understand their strategies, and how well your brand is using their available tools and programs. Your brand must align with your retail customer strategies.

4. **Competitors:** Dissect your closest competitors by looking at their performance indicators, brand positioning, innovation pipeline, pricing strategies, distribution, and the consumer's perceptions of these brands. To go even deeper, you can map out a strategic brand plan for significant competitors to predict what they might do next. Use that knowledge within your brand plan.

5. **Brand:** Analyze your brand through the lens of consumers, customers, competitors, and employees. Use brand funnel data, market research, marketing program tracking results, pricing analysis, distribution gaps, and financial analysis. Focus on managing your brand's health and wealth.

Analysis of Consumers & Channels

How tight is the bond with consumers?

Competitive Analysis

What is your competitive situation?

Financial Analysis

What is your business situation?

Analysis of market & brand

What is your brand's core strength?

Strategic ThinkBox

1 Core Strength
2 Consumer
3 Competitor
4 Situation

6. **Summarize** analysis to set up the key issues to tackle in your brand plan:

- **What's driving growth?** The top factors of strength, positional power, or market inertia, which have a proven link to driving your brand's growth. Your plan should continue to fuel these growth drivers.

- **What's inhibiting growth?** The most significant factors of weakness, unaddressed gaps, or market friction you can prove to be holding back your brand's growth. Your plan should focus on reducing or reversing these inhibitors to growth.

- **Opportunities for growth:** Look at specific untapped areas in the market, which could fuel your brand's future growth, based on unfulfilled consumer needs, new technologies on the horizon, potential regulation changes, new distribution channels, or the removal of trade barriers. Your plan should take advantage of these opportunities in the future.

- **Threats to future growth:** Changing circumstances, including consumer needs, new technologies, competitive activity, distribution changes, or potential barriers, which create potential risks to your brand's growth. Build your plan to minimize the impact of these risks.

We offer **brand template**s you can use to run your brand. We include PowerPoint templates for strategic brand plans, marketing plans, deep-dive business reviews, brand positioning presentations, and creative briefs. For more information: **https://beloved-brands.com/brand-management-templates/**

1. The marketplace review

A. First, look at the trend line for both **sales dollars** and **sales units**. Compare growth rates with the local economy or other similar categories. In this case, we see more dramatic double-digit growth rate swings between +19% and -13.5%. Compare the growth rates of dollars and units to see if there are differences.

Overall Category Sales

	2015	2016	2017	2018
Sales Dollars	878	760	791	803
% change	+19.1%	-13.5%	+4.8%	-0.7%
Units	134.0	117.5	119.5	122.7
% change	+28.3%	-12.35	+1.7%	+2.7%
Avg Price	$6.55	$6.47	$6.62	$6.54
% change	-6.4%	-2%	+3.1%	-1.9%

A
B

B. Then look at the trend line on **price** and compare it to inflation rates. In this case, the price has seen minor swings, which are less dramatic than volume swings.

C. The next critical dimension to look at is the **regional** performance. Start by understanding the size of each region and their relative growth rates. The combined size and growth rate may influence your investment in each region.

D. Then look at the **relative size of each region**. Two ways to view the region is the share of the national business or use a development index relative to population or a bigger category (e.g. cereal to grocery).

Regional Category Sales Performance

	Northeast	Midwest	South	West
Regional Sales Dollars	350	50	100	302
Regional % change	+12%	-3%	+3%	-11%
Share of Nat'l Business	44%	6%	12%	38%
Development Index to pop	115	75	122	97
Brand Share	22%	9%	27%	23%
% brand growth	-2.4%	+11%	+2%	-1.9%

C
D
E

E. Finally, look at your **brand's performance within each region**. While this is still the macro category, it is useful to get a read on how your brand is doing at the macro level of the regions.

This process will help you decide on the regional activity, which either continues to drive growth or closes gaps that might exist. As a good practice, whenever you see a trend line, come up with the factors driving the category growth and the factors holding the category back. For each of the years, explain the major events and factors, which could explain the ups and downs.

There are many other aspects of the marketplace you should look at, including product formats (e.g., size, flavors, etc.), distribution channels, benefit segments, or competitors. With each element, look for breaks in the data to tell a story on the category. Each element adds to the story.

Use a **PEST analysis** of the macro trends impacting the category through political, economic, social, and technology trends.

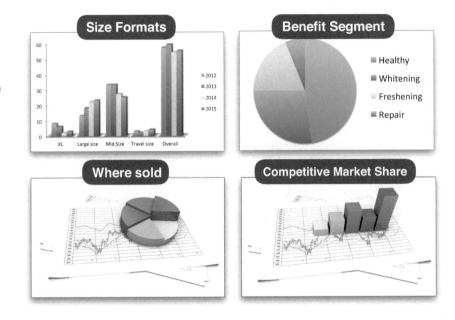

- The **political** elements look at changes in regulatory, tax codes, trade restrictions, or the political climate, which could restrict or enhance your business. Consider local, national, or even international trends.

- Summarize **economic factors**, such as GDP growth, employment, inflation, interest rates, wages, interest rates, and foreign exchange rates. Understand how your brand reacts to any critical economic factors.

- **Social** trends include demographics, consumer mindset changes, the use of media, or behavioral changes.

- **Technology** trends include advancements in the category, new scientific discoveries, formats, product deliveries, media (Facebook), and new distribution points (Amazon).

To kickstart your review of the marketplace, here are 10 probing questions:

1. How is the category doing relative to the economy?
2. Look at the last five years and explain each of the ups and downs in the category.
3. What is driving category growth? What is holding the category back, the significant open opportunities you can use to your advantage, and the risks to the categories you see in the next few years?
4. What category segments are growing, declining, or emerging?
5. What are the macro trends influencing or changing this category?
6. What is the role of innovation? How fast does it change? Which innovations are transforming the category?
7. Which regional or geographic trends do you see?
8. Who holds the balance of power in the category: brands, suppliers, channels, or consumers?
9. Look at other issues: Operations, inventory, mergers, technology, innovation, investments, global trade.
10. What is the overall value of the category? Any price changes? Major cost changes?

2. The consumer review

In this section, I will show you how to use consumer tracking data, the brand funnel analysis, and how it matches up to the brand love curve.

How to use consumer tracking data

Tracking or household panel data helps you understand what's going on in the marketplace and will match up to what's happening at the store level. As discussed in the strategy section, you are either trying to get more people to use your brand (drive penetration) or try to change the way they use your brand (drive purchase frequency). This tool uncovers the data; then you need to put a story to that data.

A. **Penetration** is the percentage of households who purchased your brand product at least once during a measured period.

B. **Buying rate** or **sales per buyer** is the total amount of product purchased by the average buying household over an entire analysis period, expressed in dollars, units, or equivalent volume.

C. **Purchase frequency** or **trips per buyer** is the number of times the average buying household purchases your product over a time period (usually one year).

D. **Purchase size** or **sales per trip** is the average amount of product purchased on a single shopping trip by your average buyer. It can be calculated in dollars, units, or equivalent volume.

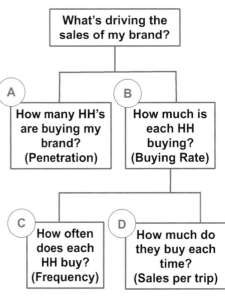

How to analyze your brand using brand funnels

Every brand should understand the details of its brand funnel, the best tool for measuring your brand's underlying health. It is the equivalent to knowing your blood pressure or cholesterol scores. A classic brand funnel should measure awareness, familiarity, consideration, purchase, repeat, and loyalty. At the very least, you should measure awareness, purchase, and repeat. It is not just about understanding the absolute scores on the funnel but rather the ratios that explain how good of a job you are doing in moving consumers from one stage of the funnel to the next.

I will show you how the robustness of your brand's funnel explains where your brand sits on the brand love curve. The broader the funnel, the better connected your brand is with consumers.

Absolute brand funnel scores

A. Using the first chart, with **absolute brand funnel scores**. You can compare your scores to last year, competitors, or category norms.

B. Use **brand funnel ratios**, which is the percentage score for how well your brand can convert consumers from one stage of the funnel to the next. To create ratios, divide absolute score by the score above it on the funnel. For example, take the familiar score of 87% and divide it by the awareness score of 93% to determine a conversion ratio of 94%. This means 94% of aware consumers are familiar.

Brand funnel ratios

C. In the second chart, sort absolute scores and ratios in a horizontal way to allow a comparison. These are the same scores as "A" and "B" in the first chart. The crucial numbers for Gray's Cookies are the **ratios** of 94%, 94%, 77%, 25%, and 12% at the top of the chart. Use a competitor (Devon's) to allow a direct comparison.

D. Find **ratio gaps** by subtracting competitor's ratio scores from your brand's ratio scores. The first ratio gap of -4% (94% - 98%) means Devon's does a 4% better job converting consumers from aware to familiar.

E. As you create ratio gaps, you can see where your ratio is either stronger or weaker than the competitor. Start analyzing the **significant gaps** between the two brands and tell a strategic story to explain each gap. Gray's and Devon's have similar scores at the top part of the funnel, but Gray's starts to show weakness (-23% and -51% gap) as it moves to repeat and loyalty.

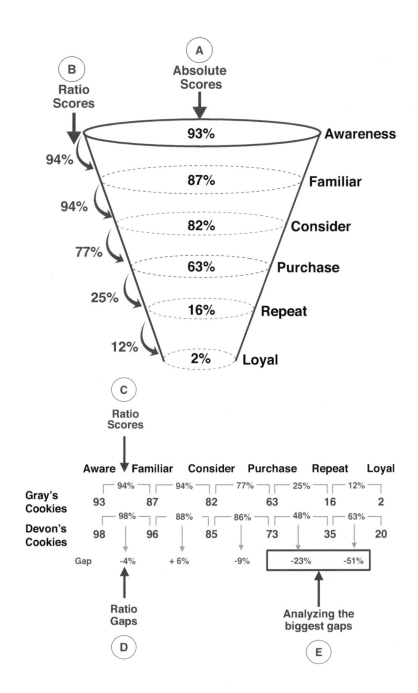

Matching consumer analysis to the brand love curve

You can begin using your consumer tracking, brand funnel, market share, and the voice of the consumer to help explain where your brand sits on the brand love curve.

	Indifferent	**Like It**	**Love It**	**Beloved**
Voice of the consumer	No opinion, low interest, low importance. Do not care and have doubt. Have never bought.	Have a basic idea what brand stands for, but have no connection. See it as ordinary, not different.	See brand as better, High satisfaction, loyalty and frequency. Willing to recommend to their friends.	Outspoken fans who believes everything about the brand (product, experience, service) is better.
Market Indicators	Skinny brand funnel, market share squeeze, low unaided awareness. Low growth and shrinking margins.	Low conversion to sales, high percent bought on deal, low loyalty, strong private label share. Programs have low ROI	Robust brand funnel, healthy tracking scores, market share gains, high share of requirements.	Dominant share, net promoter scores, usage frequency and recommendations. High growth and profits.

Awareness
Consider
Purchase
Repeat
Loyal

- **Indifferent brands** have skinny funnels, starting with inferior awareness scores. Consumers have little to no opinion. Concerning performance, you will see low sales and poor margins. Your brand plan for indifferent brands should increase awareness and consideration to kickstart the funnel.

- The **like it brands** have funnels that are solid at the top but quickly narrow at the purchase stage. Consumers see these brands as ordinary and purchase only on a deal. When they are not advertised or on sale, sales fall off dramatically. These brands need to close potential leaks to build a loyal following behind happy experiences.

- The **love it brands** have a robust funnel but may have a smaller leak at loyal. They have stronger growth and margins. Look for ways to feed the love and turn repeat purchases into a ritual or routine.

- The **beloved brands** have the most robust brand funnels and positive consumer views. These brands should continuously track their funnel and attack any weaknesses before competitors exploit them. Also, it is time to leverage that brand love to influence others.

To kickstart your review of the consumers, here are 10 probing questions:

1. Who are your possible target consumer segments? Are they growing? How do you measure them?
2. Who are the consumers most motivated by what you have to offer?
3. Who is your current target? How have you determined demographics, behavioral or psychographic, geographic, and usage occasion? Generational trends?
4. How is your brand performing against KEY segments? Share, sales, panel or funnel data, tracking scores? What about by channel or geography?
5. What drives consumer choice? What are the primary need states? How do these consumer needs line up to your brand assets? Where can you win with consumers?
6. Map out the path to purchase and use brand funnels to assess your brand's performance in moving through each stage. Are consumers changing at stages? Are you failing at stages?
7. What are the emerging consumer trends? How does your brand match up to potentially exploit them? Where would your competitors win?
8. What are the consumer's ideal brand experiences and unmet needs we can address?
9. What are the consumer's emotional and functional need states? How does the brand perform against them? How are you doing in tracking studies to meet these benefits?
10. What is the consumer's perceptions of your brand and your competitors? Voice of the consumer.

3. The channel review

Gain an understanding of the retail channels and significant customers you sell through. Then look for potential strengths to build upon or gaps to fix, including market share performance, store listings, shelf presence, or merchandising by channel or by customer.

	Tops	Sams	CVS	Target	A&P	Costco	7-11
8 count Choc Chip	●		●				●
16 count Choc Chip	●	●			●	●	
8 count Mint Chip	●		●				●
16 count Mint Chip	●	●			●		
8 count Lemon	●		●			●	
48 count Variety				●		●	

Start with a **distribution gap analysis** to determine where your brand has a presence on the shelf. You can look at this by channel or specific customers, then look at it for the overall brand or go right down to the specific product level.

Use a **"fair share index"** to find gaps. An index takes any measurement share and divides it by your overall market share. For instance, if you were getting 30% of display, yet your market share is 40%, your fair share index would be 0.75 (30% divided by 40%). Wherever your fair share index is below 1.0 represents an opportunity to close that gap.

Start at the macro level by looking at your brand's performance in each of the channels, looking at the fair share index for the overall distribution, then by region, then by customer. This analysis helps to determine where you might dig deeper.

Create customer scorecards for your biggest customers to track how well your brand is performing against that customer's tools:

A. Start with how well that customer is performing by looking at that customer's share of the market and their growth rates.

B. Assess how your brand is performing with the customer, looking at your brand's share with the customer, share point change, and share index back to your overall share?

C. Look at your brand's average pricing with that customer and compare to your average price or the customer's average category price.

D. Look at how well your brand is doing with tools of the customer with both coop ads (flyers) and merchandising indexes (displays) to see if they match up to your share index.

Align with your sales partner to lay out issues, opportunities, and risks to determine where your brand can have the biggest impact.

Customer A	Scores	
Overall Sales Dollars	39	
Share of Category	11%	A
% dollar change	+19.1%	
Your Brand Share	33%	
% change	+3.3 points	B
Share Index	105	
Your brand's avg Price	$6.33	
% change	+3.3%	C
Price Index	125	
Share of Co-Op Ads	33%	
% change	+18%	
Co Op Index	143	
Share of Merch	25%	D
% change	-2%	
March Index	111	

Here are ten probing questions to kickstart your channels review

1. How are each the channels performing? Are there regional differences by channel? Channel shifts?
2. Are there new and emerging channels? Are there channels on the horizon, not yet developed?
3. What are the strengths and weaknesses of each channel?
4. Do you understand the strategies of your retail customers?
5. Do you have the competencies to service your customers?
6. Who are the top 5 customers? What are their main strategies? How does our brand fit into that plan?
7. Who are your primary and secondary customers? Have you segmented and prioritized for growth versus opportunity? How large are they? What are their growth rates?
8. How is each customer performing? How profitable is that customer for your brand?
9. How is your brand doing within each customer? What are your brand's strength and weaknesses?
10. How is the relationship with the customer? Who is the category captain of your key accounts, and why?

4. The competitive review

Brands who think they **"don't have a competitor"** are naive. Assess your competitors' brand positioning to understand how well they are meeting the needs of consumers. Who is their target, and what are their main benefit and reasons to believe? Do they have a brand idea, and how consistently do they deliver that big idea?

Look at your competitor's market share over the past 5-10 years with explanations for the ups and downs, including new launches, distribution changes, significant investments, competitive dynamics, economic challenges, or impact of technology improvements.

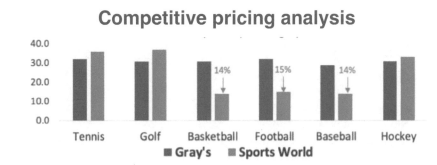

Use any of the tools I have shown to dissect your closest competitors, looking at positioning, innovation pipeline, pricing, distribution, brand tracking, brand funnels, share, consumer perception, and brand strategies.

Pricing

A. First, look at the **average price** and change versus a year ago for each competitor. Match up the data to what your sales partner says about the different prices for each channel.

B. Depending on channel/brand, you should look at the **deal pricing**, percent on deal, and coop ad (flyers). Compare both channels and customers to prior years.

When in a real competitive battle, complete your competitor's brand plan, laying out the vision, analysis, strategies, tactics, and even assumed budget levels. Getting in the shoes of your competitors will help you better understand their mindset, what moves they might make, and how they may attack you in the future. This war game process enables you to build a counterattack in your brand plan.

Here are 10 questions to kickstart your competitor review:

1. Who are your main competitors? How do they position themselves?
2. What are your competitor's use of communication, new products, and go-to-market strategy? How are they executing against each?
3. Describe your competitor's operating model, culture, and organization structure.
4. What are your competitor's strengths, weaknesses, opportunities, threats?
5. How is your competitor doing regarding market share, customer market shares, investment, margins, innovation, culture, share of voice, or any regulatory advantage?
6. Map out the competitor's brand plan: vision, goals, key issues, strategies, and tactics.

7. What is the culture at your competitor and what is the role culture plays in their brand?
8. What is the investment stance and expected growth trajectory of your competitor's brand? How much and where do they invest? What are the marketing and commercial focus? What is their ROI?
9. What are your competitor's brand strengths, brand assets, and reputation?
10. Are there any public materials about the competitor, including strategy and financial results?

5. The brand review

You need to do a complete view of your brand through the lens of consumers, customers, competitors, and employees. Use brand funnel data, market research, program tracking results, pricing analysis, distribution gaps, and financial analysis.

You should use ad tracking data to look at aided and unaided awareness scores, and purchase scores, including the share of last five purchases, uniqueness, and purchase intention.

Tracking	LY Ad	New Ad	Norm
Aided Recall	38	73	62
Unaided Recall	30	48	46
Brand Recognition	10	30	23
Brand Link	.33	.72	.50
Main Message	64	59	60
Uniqueness	38	32	22
Purchase Intent	10	22	9

U&A studies

One excellent starting point for the brand is a Usage and Attitude (U&A) study, which can help uncover issues on your brand. For a major brand, you should do a U&A study each year. Here are the benefits:

- Identify what the consumer may see as your brand's core strength, including your brand's product, promise, experience, and price. Identify the key drivers for both trial and brand loyalty.
- Understand how the consumer thinks, shops, and makes decisions on brands.
- Know why consumers buy specific brands and what makes those brands distinctive, uncovering both the rational and emotional benefits. Identify any perceived gaps in the consumer's mind between your brand promise, consumer expectation, and the overall brand performance.
- Explain how well your brand matches up in the consumer's mind, relative to your competitors.
- Gain an overall view of various consumer segments, looking at lifestyle and demographic dimensions, how they consume media, how they shop, and overall attitudes on key drivers or brand benefits.
- Map out the consumer purchase journey looking at how they become aware, what makes them consider, what type of search they do, the factors behind purchase decision, product satisfaction, what influences repeat purchase, how they build brands into their routines, and what triggers them to become brand fans.

Leaky bucket analysis

I created the leaky bucket analysis tool as a way to uncover problems for your brand. While the brand funnel analysis usually looks at how well you move consumers from one stage to the next, the leaky bucket helps to explain why consumers fall out of the purchase journey.

I have taken the four stages of the brand love curve and created **eight total stages of the consumer purchase journey**, looking at: unaware, noticed, interested, bought, satisfied, repeater, fan, and outspoken. For each stage, map out how the consumer sees the brand and the most significant reason consumers reject the brand. Once you find the leak on your brand, you can build strategies to help **close those leaks**.

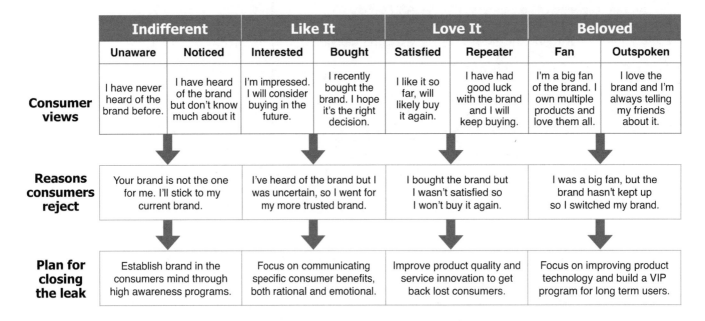

	Indifferent		Like It		Love It		Beloved	
	Unaware	**Noticed**	**Interested**	**Bought**	**Satisfied**	**Repeater**	**Fan**	**Outspoken**
Consumer views	I have never heard of the brand before.	I have heard of the brand but don't know much about it	I'm impressed. I will consider buying in the future.	I recently bought the brand. I hope it's the right decision.	I like it so far, will likely buy it again.	I have had good luck with the brand and I will keep buying.	I'm a big fan of the brand. I own multiple products and love them all.	I love the brand and I'm always telling my friends about it.
Reasons consumers reject	Your brand is not the one for me. I'll stick to my current brand.		I've heard of the brand but I was uncertain, so I went for my more trusted brand.		I bought the brand but I wasn't satisfied so I won't buy it again.		I was a big fan, but the brand hasn't kept up so I switched my brand.	
Plan for closing the leak	Establish brand in the consumers mind through high awareness programs.		Focus on communicating specific consumer benefits, both rational and emotional.		Improve product quality and service innovation to get back lost consumers.		Focus on improving product technology and build a VIP program for long term users.	

10 probing questions to assess your brand's performance:

1. What consumer benefit can you win with, which is ownable, unique, and motivating for consumers?
2. What is your market share? Regionally? By channel? Where is your strength? Where is your gap? What is your biggest gain versus prior periods? What is your biggest gap?
3. How are you performing on key brand tracking data? Penetration? Frequency? Sales per buyer or per trip? What are your brand's scores on the brand funnel?
4. What is driving negative perceptions and causing consumers to leave your brand?
5. How is your communications program tracking data doing? Where could you improve?
6. What are the underlying attitudes about your brand and how it fits in with the consumers' lives? Where do consumers see you in relation to your competitors?
7. What is your culture? Do you have alignment with the brand story and your employees?

8. What is your freshness index of new products and services measuring a consistent exploration, testing, and delivery of product extensions, product improvements, new formats, brand stretching, game-changing technology and blue ocean exploration?
9. Do you have alignment between the brand story that attracts consumers and your employees who deliver the desired consumer experience? Alignment with operations, sales, and innovation?
10. How does your production process, sourcing, forecasting, supply, shipping, servicing, tracking, measurement gives you a competitive advantage?

How to build the ideal analytical slide

When telling your analytical story through a presentation, start every slide with an analytical conclusion statement as your headline, then have 2-3 key analytical support points for your conclusion. Provide a supporting visual or graph to show the thinking underneath the analysis. Finally, you must include an impact recommendation on every slide. Never tell your management a data point without attaching your conclusion of what to do with that data.

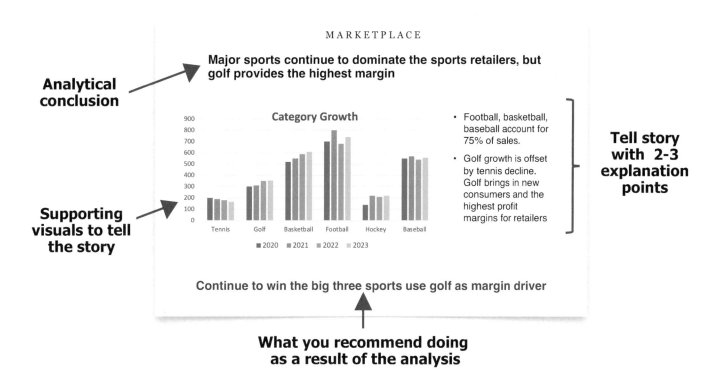

Putting together your business review

This process assumes you will put together a presentation of 20 slides for your management team. Each of the five sections should have 3-5 ideal slides. The conclusion statement at the top of each slide gets carried forward to a summary page for each of the five sections. You then draw out an overall conclusion statement for that section. You will have five conclusion statements, which you bring to the front of your presentation to form an overall summary page. From there, you draw out one major brand challenge you are seeing in the deep dive.

How to build each of the five analytical sections of the business review

A. For each of the five sections of your deep dive business review, use all the data you have dug into to draw out the three hypothetical conclusions. Then build one ideal slide for each conclusion, adding the 2-3 critical support points, and layer in the supporting visual charts. This type of analysis is an iterative process where you have to keep modifying the **conclusion headline** and the support points to ensure they work together.

B. Once you have nailed the conclusion headline for each page, you should build a summary chart for each of the five sections, which takes those three conclusion statements and builds a **section conclusion statement**. The example above shows how to do it for the category, which you can replicate for the consumer, channels, competitors, and the brand.

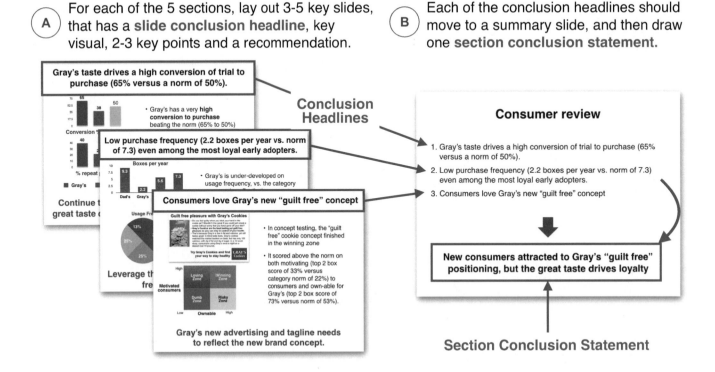

C. For each of the five sections, take each **section conclusion statement**, move them to an overall business review summary slide, and draw one big summary statement for each of the five sections.

D. Use those section conclusion statements to draw out an overall **business review major issue**, which summarizes everything in the analysis.

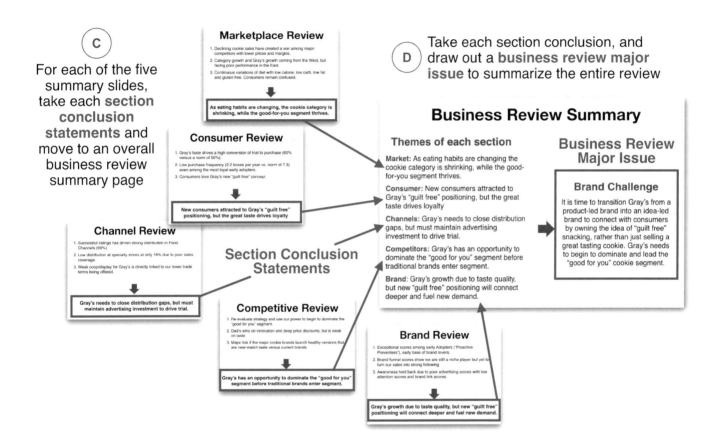

This process allows you to build a 20-slide business review with four slides for each of the five sections and a summary slide up front. You can use the same process to create any other type of document. It forces you to dig deep into all the issues, which helps you organize it in a way you can tell your overall story. You can find our business review presentation template on our website at **beloved-brands.com**

Strategic Thinking & Analytics

Build your brand around your core strength

What is your brand's super power?

Product
Story
Experience
Price

To be loved and successful, brands must know who they are and then stand with pride, conviction, and confidence. What is your brand's super power? What is your brand's secret sauce?

Too many brands try to have a few core strengths cluttering up their brand positioning, so they end up with no real perceived strength that stands out. Our core strength model forces you to select one of four possible options for you to win with: product, brand story, experience, or price.

For many marketers, their immediate response is an urge to pick two or three core strengths, believing the myth that having many strengths makes your brand stronger. A focus will make your brand stronger.

Here is the game I have created to help choose your brand's core strength.

- Using the diagram on the next page, start with four chips. You must place one chip where you believe you have the highest competitive advantage to win.
- Then put two chips at the medium level that backs up and supports the core strength.
- Finally, the game forces one chip to be at the low end, which is almost a throwaway weakness that will not be part of the strategy.

It is a great game to try with your team, as it sets up a great debate among your team members.

The Beloved Brands Core Strength Model

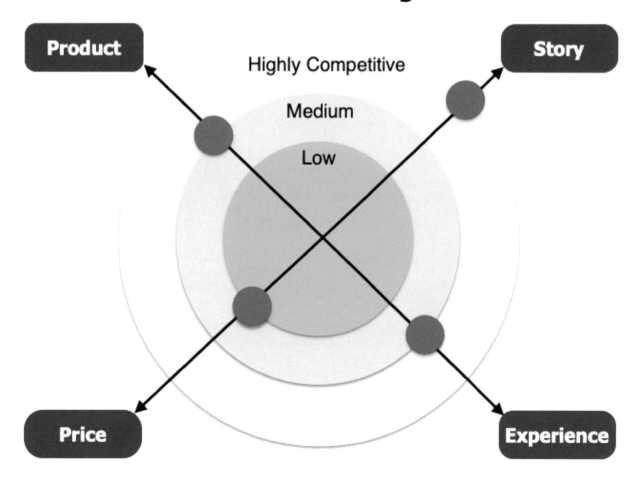

- **Product-led** brands should invest in R&D while communicating the consumer benefits, features, and claims for what makes the brand better.

- **Story-led** brands need to invest in advertising, with the story, idea, or brand purpose communicating what makes the brand different.

- **Consumer Experience-led** brands have to invest in creating a culture with strong operations. Build your brand communications around the idea that, "Our great people make the difference in creating amazing experiences for our consumers."

- **Price-led** brands must invest in operational efficiency with the brand communications explaining how "We are smarter and able to deliver the same quality at a lower cost."

Product-Led Brands

When you are a **Product-led brand**, you must own the "better" position in your category. Make sure your capabilities line up by investing heavily in continuous innovation to maintain category leadership in new technology, superiority claims, and the latest product formats. Use your product capabilities to aggressively defend against any challengers. Leverage product-focused mass communication, directly highlighting the product's superiority and comparing product benefits and features to those of other competitors.

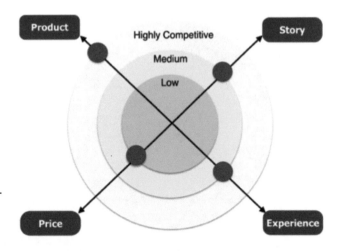

Within your mass communications, you can layer in "how the product is built" into the brand story to reinforce your brand's product point of difference. Use online product reviews sites, bloggers, and expert influencers to reach the trend influencer consumers on all new product innovations.

When selling to consumers, use a rational approach, highlighting technical features, new claims, and the logic behind the purchase decision. One issue to watch out for in product-led brands is the struggle to build and drive an emotional connection with consumers.

As the brand matures, it must find ways to layer a brand idea on top of the product to inspire the consumer to connect on a deeper level. Fantastic product-led brands include Samsung, Tide, YETI, HBO, Rolex, Five Guys, or Ruth's Chris. The product manages to create a high degree of consumer loyalty, even if the brand struggles to project an emotional message.

In a world where the quality of content is subjective, **HBO** stands out as the most consistent delivery of high quality movies and shows. HBO is a machine, producing the industry's highest-quality content for the past few decades, averaging 7.0 on iMDB, which is higher than Disney, Netflix, Hulu, and Amazon.

While **Netflix** entered the market with high quality content, they have recently chosen quantity over quality, and now produce the industry's worst scores. While they produce a lot of highly reviewed shows like Squid Game (8.0) or Stranger Things (8.7), they also pump out Too Hot to Handle (4.7), The Ultimatum (5.4).

Story-Led Brands

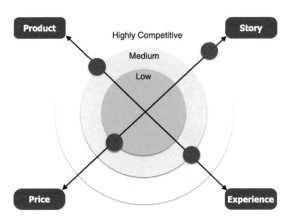

When the **brand story** is your brand's key strength, focus the strategy on ways to be different. Build your capabilities by investing in gathering consumer insights and knowledge, equal to how a product-led brand spends on patents. To tell the brand story, use emotional brand communication that connects the most motivated consumers with the brand idea, lining up everything—brand story, product, and experience—under that brand idea.

Story-led brands should cultivate a community of core "brand lovers" who can then talk about the brand story and influence others within their network. These brands should use a soft sell approach and never bring the price to the forefront, as it can take away from the idea. Some of the more successful story-led brands include Apple, Nike, Virgin, LEGO, Disney, Dove, RedBull and W Hotels – some of the most beloved brands of our times.

Most recently, the **Tesla** brand has borrowed a lot of Apple's core principles. Tesla builds everything around the story of "Tesla will save the planet with innovation." Tesla uses many innovative approaches, including the visionary charm of their leader, Elon Musk, who appears to be the new generation's answer to Steve Jobs. Musk has become a spokesperson for a generation of consumers who want to save the planet. Tesla's environmental activities around the world go far beyond expectations.

A great example of the mystique of the Tesla brand is how quickly it mobilized to help out **Puerto Rico** after a hurricane knocked out the island's power in 2017. Even as various levels of government were arguing over who should do what, Tesla brought 700 solar panels to the Hospital del Niño, where the batteries restored service to 3,000 patients who needed constant care.

In 2016, Tesla topped **Consumer Reports'** Annual Owner Satisfaction Survey at an incredible 91% rating, 5% higher than a Porsche, and 15% higher than Toyota and Honda. The same year, over 400,000 consumers put down $1,000 for a specific Tesla model that did not yet exist. On top of that, these new cars would not roll off the factory lines for another three to four years. Consumers see Tesla as more than just a vehicle, but rather an investment in a movement for the future. Even as Tesla struggles to meet demand, the company keeps adding to its brand story. Most recently, Tesla consumer ratings have fallen. What is the cause, and is it concerning?

Consumer Experience-Led Brands

When the **consumer experience** is your brand's lead strength, the strategy and organization should focus on creating a link between your culture and your brand. Make sure your capabilities line up by investing in your people. They are your product. Use your brand purpose ("Why you do what you do") and brand values to inspire and guide the service behaviors of your people. Then build a culture and organization with the right people who can deliver incredible experiences.

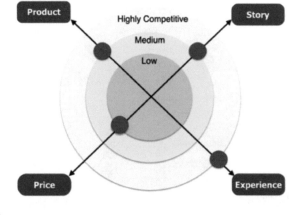

Experience-led brands need to be patient with how fast they build the brand, as the quick mass media approach might not be as fast or efficient as the product-led or idea-led brands. The most effective communication tools for consumer experience-led brands include word of mouth, earned media, social media, online consumer reviews, the voice of key influencers, and consumer testimonials. These brands can make a mistake if they put too much emphasis on price, which can diminish the perceived consumer experience.

Some of the best consumer experience-led brands include Ritz-Carlton, Emirates Airline, Airbnb, T-Mobile, Amazon, Chick-fil-A, Trader Joes, LuluLemon, Zappos, TopGolf, and Starbucks.

Airbnb does a fantastic job of delivering a fabulous consumer experience. They deliver on their brand idea of "Don't just go there. Live there." Airbnb takes all the hard work travelers have been doing, and they put it right in front of the consumer. You can sort by city, even down to the neighborhood, sort by the type of residence, specify a few needs (Wi-Fi, pet-friendly), then enter your price range. With most of the rentals, you can see 15-20 photos to give you an idea of the space. You make your choice, select the dates, provide government ID to confirm your identity and then your offer goes to the owner. Moments later, or when they wake up, they reply saying yes. There is a bit of hunting that goes on, but it adds a thrill to the travel experience. Overall, it is so much easier than everything the traveler, looking to rent a house or flat, has done in the past.

Airbnb has nailed the creation of the brand idea of **"Don't just go there. Live there."** Airbnb's data says 86% of the consumers who use Airbnb pick the platform because they want to live more like a local. That insight of living rather than visiting inspired the brand's latest and largest marketing campaign, "Live There."

Price-Led Brands

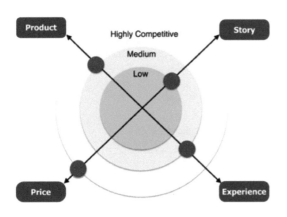

When **price** is your brand's lead strength, you must focus on ways to drive efficiency to ensure the lowest possible cost structure. Make sure your capabilities line up by investing in the fundamentals around production and sourcing to maintain a low-cost competitive advantage. They must use the brand's power to win negotiations. These businesses have to drive cash flow with fast moving items that deliver high turns and high volume to compensate for their lower prices. The winning price-led brands need to own the low price positioning by fiercely attacking any potential competitive challenges.

Regarding advertising, the smartest message explains your secret for how you are smarter than your competitors, and you can offer lower prices. Also, use call-to-action marketing to keep high sales turns.

There is a big difference between low-price and cheap. Price-driven consumers are not always willing to sacrifice product quality. They expect lower prices but still want robust performance standards. However, these price-driven consumers have shown they are willing to accept a lower-quality consumer experience. Since price is such a rational reason to buy, consumers do struggle to love the price-led brands.

Walmart is one of the best price-led brands. No one is more efficient at brick-and-mortar retail. While many department store competitors sell through their inventory in 100 to 125 days, Walmart sells through its inventory in 29 days – one day before they even have to pay for it.

Walmart successfully beat century-old retailers, such as Sears, Kmart, and JC Penney. It also destroyed the "mom and pop" shops of small towns across America. The company's outward sales pitch is price, but efficiency drives its internal culture, and their real secret is to focus on fast-moving items. Walmart uses its brand power to bully suppliers, who give in just to be part of Walmart's high sales volumes.

Now Walmart faces its toughest battle with Amazon, in what some are calling, "Clicks versus Bricks," as online has disrupted traditional retail. While Walmart has struggled to create an emotional bond with consumers, Amazon is one of the most beloved brands on the planet. Amazon uses smart pricing with extraordinary customer service to delight its consumer base. Walmart will be in the most desperate battle of its life.

Case study: How Starbucks rebuilt a consumer experience around coffee

Starbucks is one of the best consumer experience-led brands. While certain consumers believe it is a great coffee, in some blind taste tests, Starbucks coffee has finished middle of the pack. Starbucks builds everything around the consumer experience. The brand views itself as being in the "moments" business.

The brand stresses the importance of the culture with its staff and uses service values to deliver incredible guest experiences. Employees wear their green aprons with pride.

STARBUCKS BECOMES A FALLEN ANGEL

For consumers, Starbucks offers the perfect moment of escape between home and work. To spark pleasant moments, Starbucks offers a unique combination of Italian coffee names, European pastries, relaxed and friendly staff, comfortable leather seats, and indie music. Overall, Starbucks creates a warm atmosphere, all in support of a fabulous experience. The experience the brand creates makes the coffee taste great.

Starbucks had tremendous success in growing its brand in the 1980s and 1990s. By 2003, people viewed Starbucks as one of the most modern beloved brands in the marketplace. Starbucks had earned a very healthy position and began looking for new opportunities to grow beyond coffee. As Starbucks defined the brand as an "escape," it naturally looked for other areas where consumers escaped.

In 2003, Starbucks created its own music recording company, won eight Grammys, launched a movie, and partnered with William Morris to scout for music, books, and films. Starbucks even opened an "entertainment" office in Los Angeles.

Within five years, Starbucks had lost focus on who it was. These new businesses had become a significant distraction; Starbucks' core coffee brand suffered dramatically. Without the inspired leadership on coffee, sales plummeted, and the stock price fell from $37 to $7.83. The company had to cut 18,000 jobs and close 977 stores. The Starbucks brand was in a complete free fall. Would it be yet another trendy brand to fade off into the sunset?

Starbucks desperately needed to refocus. The company exited the entertainment business and returned everything to the coffee ritual. It closed each store location for an entire day to rebuild its capabilities by retraining every barista—a symbol of what is most important to the brand's consumer experience. Starbucks built new food capabilities to support this new focus by investing in sandwiches, snacks, and pastries around the coffee routine to gain more share of requirements and stretch the coffee routine into lunch and dinner. All these efforts rekindled the consumer experience.

Using our five elements of strategic thinking allowed Starbucks to complete its turnaround plan.

1. Set a vision of what you want

- Starbucks wished to become a cherished favorite moment of the day. The question for Starbucks was how to build smartly around the consumer experience to drive significant growth in same-store sales.

2. Invest in building capabilities to deliver the brand strategy

- Starbucks needed to regain its strong bond with consumers, refocus on the consumer experience, and build the brand through its culture-led essence, supported by a phenomenal team of employees. Starbucks wanted to bring this culture to the forefront of the consumer experience.

3. Focused accelerator to propel strategy

- In 2008, Starbucks refocused on shifting the coffee ritual beyond mornings. It wanted to build an all-day gathering place. The company broadened its portfolio around coffee by adding desserts, snacks, and sandwiches. The biggest accelerator to propel this strategy is that Starbucks saw an opportunity in its under-utilized retail locations, which remained relatively empty after 11 a.m. The company wanted the broader portfolio to boost lunch and dinner sales and earn a higher share of the consumer's wallet and higher same-store sales.

4. Breakthrough market impact to create a tipping point

- Starbucks closed every store for a day to refocus on its service, then built a broader portfolio around coffee. The company successfully reconnected with the most loyal Starbucks fans. Starbucks turned the morning coffee routine into an all-day life ritual, allowing Starbucks to focus on becoming a consumer experience brand and a gathering place to savor moments with friends and colleagues.

5. Performance result that pays back

- No longer seen as a destination just for morning coffee but rather an escape at any point in the day, Starbucks saw double-digit growth for five straight years. Meanwhile, the stock price increased 10-fold over that period.

Starbucks brand strategy statement using our A + B + C + D

Let's take this Starbucks' strategy and turn that thinking into a strategy statement using our A + B + C + D method, and then show how it fits into a brand plan. Here are the two main statements.

1. Re-build the consumer experience by re-training the entire staff on service behaviors **(A)** to get lapsed consumers **(B)** to make Starbucks a gathering place for local consumers **(D)** to drive a higher share of requirements. **(D)**

2. Enhance the Starbucks menu **(A)** to get current consumers to buy sandwiches & snacks at lunch **(B)**, to stretch the brand into new time slots **(C)** to gain a higher share of the consumer's wallet with added sales and profit per location. **(D)**

The Starbucks Brand Plan

If you took the strategic thinking model and began to outline a brand plan for Starbucks, these would be the core elements:

- **Vision:** Build a cherished meeting place to gather as a favorite moment in consumers' day.

- **Goals:** Increase same-store sales and earn a higher share of requirements among Starbucks loyalists.

- **Key Issues:**
    1. How do we build an overall consumer experience beyond coffee?
    2. How do we drive significant growth in same-store sales?

- **Strategies:**
    1. Re-build the consumer experience by re-training the entire staff on service behaviors **(A)** to get lapsed consumers **(B)** to make Starbucks a gathering place for local consumers **(C)** to drive a higher share of requirements. **(D)**
    2. Enhance the Starbucks menu **(A)** to get current consumers to buy sandwiches & snacks at lunch **(B)**, to stretch the brand into new time slots **(C)** to gain a higher share of the consumer's wallet with added sales and profit per location. **(D)**

- **Tactics:** 1) Focus staff on creating amazing consumer experiences. 2) Retrain all baristas. Launch exotic, refreshing coffee choices, light lunch menu, increase dessert offerings. 3) Create shareable experiences to motivate brand lovers to influence others. Strategic Thinking & Analytics

How to build a tight bond with your most cherished consumers

"How tightly connected is your consumer to your brand?"

I first came up with the idea of a brand love curve when I ran a marketing department with 15 different consumer brands, which exhibited various degrees of success. Honestly, it was hard for me to keep track of where each brand stood. I did not want to apply a one-size-fits-all strategy to brands with dramatically different needs. I could have used some traditional matrix with market share versus category growth rates or stuck with revenue size versus margin rates.

Every day on the job, I noticed brands that had created a stronger bond with their consumer outperformed brands that lacked such a close connection. I started to refer to the high-performance brands as "beloved" because I could see how emotionally engaged consumers were with the brand.

At the other end of the scale, I referred to the inferior performance brands as "indifferent" because consumers did not care about them. They failed to stand for anything in the consumer's mind; they were not better, different, or cheaper. I could see how these brands were unable to create any connection with their consumers and they faced massive declines.

Everything seemed to work better and easier for beloved brands. New product launches were more impactful because the brand's loyal consumers were automatically curious about what was new. Retailers gave these the beloved brands preferential treatment because they knew their consumers wanted them.

With a beloved brand, retailers knew their consumers would switch stores before they switch brands. Everyone in my organization, from the President to the technician in the lab, cared more about these beloved brands. No one seemed to care about the indifferent brands. Internal brainstorm sessions produced inspiring ideas on beloved brands, yet people would not even show up for brainstorms on indifferent brands.

Our agencies bragged about the work they did on beloved brands. Even my people were more excited to work on these beloved brands, believing a move to the beloved brand was a big career move while being moved to an indifferent brand was a career death sentence.

These beloved brands had better performance results and better consumer tracking scores on advertising. They saw a stronger return on marketing investment, with a better response to marketing programs, higher growth rates, and higher margins. The overall profitability fuelled further investment into beloved brands.

Why does brand love matter?

Brand building starts with cultivating close relationships with consumers. The best brands of today follow a very similar path to the rituals of a personal courtship.

Through the eyes of consumers, brands start as complete strangers, randomly purchased a few times without much thought. They become acquaintances and, when the brand successfully delivers on expectations, they move into something similar to a trusted friendship.

As the consumer sees a consistent experience and trust, they begin to open up, and the romance begins.

The consumer allows their emotions to take over and, without knowing, they start to love the brand. As the brand weaves itself into the best moments of the consumer's life, the consumer becomes an outspoken fan, an advocate, and one of the many brand lovers who cherish their relationship with the brand.

As long as the brand delivers on the excitement of the original promise that attracted the consumer on their first encounter, the brand moves into a position where the consumer sees it as a forever love.

To replicate how brand building matches up with the building of a relationship, I created the brand love curve, which outlines how consumers move through five stages: unknown, indifferent, like it, love it, and onto the beloved brand status.

Our brand love curve steers your consumer strategy

For new brands, they were completely **"unknown"** to consumers. Unless there were genuinely compelling messages, consumers would walk past without even looking. To achieve some success, the priority for these brands is to get noticed within the clutter of the market.

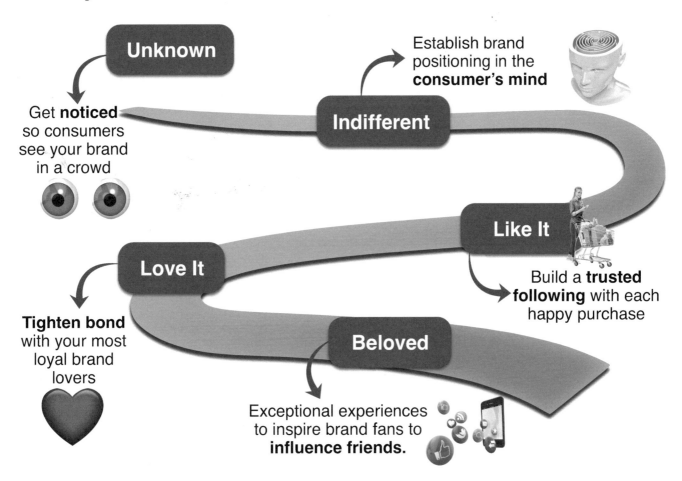

Unknown

Get **noticed** so consumers see your brand in a crowd

Establish brand positioning in the **consumer's mind**

Indifferent

Like It

Love It

Build a **trusted following** with each happy purchase

Tighten bond with your most loyal brand lovers

Beloved

Exceptional experiences to inspire brand fans to **influence friends.**

At the **"indifferent"** stage, consumers feel O.K. about the brand, similar to how they usually feel about commodities, like fruit and vegetables. These brands satisfy the consumer's basic needs. Consumers will only buy the brand when it is on sale, but switch back to their other brand choice when it is not. Make your brand more than just a commodity. Brands need to be better, different, or cheaper. Otherwise, they will not be around for long, and you waste your investment.

Brands that reach the **"like it"** stage experience the first sign of business success. Their consumers see the brand as a logical, functional, and smart choice. However, the lack of any emotional connection leaves the purchase up to chance. Consumers will still switch brands randomly. Brands at the like it stage stress the product performance so much they forget to trigger any emotions.

Brands at the **"love it"** stage start to see more emotionally engaged consumers. The rule of love you must follow: Consumers must love the brand before you can tell consumers you love them. Consumers see the brand as a favorite choice, usually connected to a favorite part of their day. They are loyal and build the brand into a routine. These brands must also find a way to demonstrate their love toward consumers and continue to tighten the bond with their most loyal brand lovers.

The **"beloved brand"** stage is where the brand becomes iconic, with a core base of brand lovers who cherish and defend the brand. These consumers see the brand as a personal choice, a badge they proudly hold in their hand or wear on their feet. At the beloved stage, the brands must create magical experiences that inspire brand lovers to share with their friends.

20 consumer activities

The **brand love curve** should guide strategic and tactical decisions that go into the writing of your annual brand plan. Here are **20 potential brand activities** that match up to where your brand sits on the curve and how to move your brand to the next stage. This tool helps cascade your strategy down to the execution stage where the brand strategy sets up a specific execution strategy of your partner.

Unknown	Indifferent	Like It	Love It	Beloved
Get noticed so consumers will **see brand** in the crowd	Establish brand positioning in the **consumer's mind**	Build a **trusted following** with each happy purchase	**Tighten bond** with your most loyal brand lovers	Experiences that inspire brand fans to **influence others**
1. Set up 2. Launch event 3. Core message 4. Find fans	5. Mind shift 6. Mindshare 7. New news 8. Turnaround	9. Drive penetration 10. Drive usage 11. Build routine 12. Cross-sell	13. Build memories 14. Maintain Love 15. Deeper love 16. Reasons to Love	17. Create magic 18. Leverage Power 19. Attack yourself 20. Use loyalists
Attention	**Mind**	**Purchase**	**Heart**	**Influence**

The game plan for unknown brands

All brands start at the unknown stage. Many new brands struggle to break through to reach consumers or build the distribution due to doubting retailers. They face leadership team conflicts, confusion around the value proposition, inconsistent messages to consumers, and everyone in the organization seems to move in different directions. The risk is that you will be seen as a product—not yet a brand idea.

Too often, companies at this early stage fixate more on selling with desperation to anyone who wants to buy. Sure, the cash flow helps. However, when the consumer sees the brand as a commodity, the product has no real differentiation from competitors. This strategy will make it hard to command a price premium or gain any efficiency. Substantial investment is needed to establish both brand awareness and broad distribution. The unknown brands need to stand out in the crowd.

A three-point game plan for unknown brands:

1. Create a brand idea that expresses your consumer benefit and build everything around that idea, both internally and externally
2. Focus your limited resources against a focused target, positioning, strategies, and activities.
3. Passionately express your brand purpose as a rallying point, both internally and externally.

Action plan for unknown brands:

- **Brand set-up:** Establish capabilities around production, brand promise, advertising, public relations, consumer experience, distribution, and manage the purchase moments.
- **Launch event:** Build hype and desire to gain attention and awareness with consumers to help hit minimum desired sales levels with channels.
- **Build a core message:** Amplify brand idea and niche consumer benefit to a core audience to establish a consumer reputation.
- **Find early lovers:** Find a small base of early adopters to drive trial among those who are already motivated by what you do. Use their energy to turn them into brand fans who can influence others.

The game plan for indifferent brands

Indifferent brands act like commodities. They are usually too product-focused and not yet able to find a way to separate the brand from competitors. These brands suffer from very skinny brand funnels with low awareness at the top of the brand funnel, with low purchase rates, low repeat scores, and low brand loyalty scores.

These brands struggle to gain new users or drive frequency. Without a brand idea or unique positioning, the advertising suffers from poor tracking scores, and the innovation shows little payback. Lower payback makes it hard to justify marketing investment in advertising, innovation, or in-store.

Indifferent brands rely on price promotions to drive volume, resulting in a margin squeeze. They struggle to achieve the economies of scale needed to drive down the variable cost of goods.

They have no power with retailers, so they are unable to get their fair share of shelf space, display, or price promotions. Private label brands threaten their sales levels. The indifferent brands need to establish the brand positioning and, in turn, the reputation in a consumer's mind.

A three-point game plan for indifferent brands:

1. Focus your brand's limited resources on proving your brand has a point of difference in the consumer's mind.
2. Create a brand idea to establish your brand's uniqueness to stand out in the cluttered market.
3. Put more passion, emotion, and risk into your work.

Action plan for indifferent brands:

- **Mind shift:** Drive a new brand positioning or reinforce current positioning to change your reputation.
- **Mindshare:** Draw more attention than competitors by being better or different.
- **New news:** Launch breakthrough innovation to enter the consumer's mind.
- **Turnaround:** Focus energy on gaps or leaks in your brand's execution. Use the fix to shift minds.

The game plan for "like it" brands

Brands at the like it stage have established a degree of success in the market, and they have created a rational brand positioning with consumers.

However, they lack the emotional connection to build a bond with consumers. They make gains during heavy marketing support periods but fall back down during the non-support periods. These brands appear content to hold onto their share and grow at the rate of the category. These brands have awareness but they lose out to competitors as the consumer moves to the purchase stage. As a result, they usually require a higher promotional trade spend to close the sale, which cuts into profit margins.

A vital consumer tracking score to watch is "made the brand seem different," which will help separate your brand from the pack. The brand needs to begin to layer in the emotional benefits and focus on creating a stronger following with each happy purchase.

A three-point game plan for brands at the like it stage:

1. Focus resources to build a more significant following with happy purchases.
2. Leverage the brand idea to start making an emotional connection to build a following.
3. Increase consumer engagement by adding more passion to your brand execution.

Action plan for brands at the like it stage:

- **Drive penetration:** Persuade new consumers to try the brand.
- **Drive usage:** Get happy consumers to use more or use it differently.
- **Build routine:** Get happy consumers to build a routine around the brand so the brand becomes a habit.
- **Cross-sell:** Get happy consumers to use your brand's other products or services.

There are a lot of brands that get stuck at the like it stage, with a high degree of success at this stage. They could be the market leader, own the main functional benefit that consumers are looking for, and become part of a habit for consumers. However, they leave themselves at risk of being replaced by the next superior product. Moreover, they are unable to leverage the emotions to command higher pricing, usage frequency or get loyal consumers to follow into adjacent categories.

The game plan for "love it" brands

Brands at the love it stage start to see a higher emotional connection with a base of brand fans. These brands also start to gain a stronger usage frequency, as the brand becomes a more significant part of the consumer's life routines. With strong consumer tracking results, the brand can leverage more efficient marketing spend. You will notice loyal consumers are highly responsive to advertising and innovation. This thinking makes the marketing spend much more efficient, opening up a pathway to higher profits.

These brands should be able to leverage their power with retailers and influencers. Even in a competitive market, these brands should be able to gain share and widen their leadership stance. With high net promoter scores, they should be able to leverage word-of-mouth or social media recommendations, and positive online brand reviews (Yelp or Trip Advisor) to influence new users.

Brands at the love it stage must look for unique ways to reward consumers and further tighten their bond with their most loyal brand lovers.

A three-point game plan for brands at the love it stage:

1. Tug at the heartstrings to help build a community of brand fans.
2. Shift to the creation of consumer experiences that turn purchases into routines and rituals.
3. Turn the love for your work into a bit of magic for the consumer.

Action plan for brands at the love it stage:

- **Build memories:** Create consumer experiences that link the brand with life moments.
- **Maintain love:** Reinforce the brand strengths with your core base of brand fans.
- **Deeper love:** Match the passion of your consumers to drive consolidation and get these consumers to use your brand across a broader degree of uses.
- **Reasons to love:** Reinforce brand messages to your most loyal users.

The game plan for beloved brands

Brands at the beloved stage are the iconic leaders in their category. These brands have an extremely healthy and robust brand funnel with likely near-perfect brand awareness (over 95%), high conversion to purchase, strong repeat, and very high loyalty scores. These brands have achieved good penetration and purchase frequency scores.

Tracking results show an immediate reaction to new marketing programs with high brand link scores on advertising and high trial on innovation. They have a dominant share position at least within a specific segment.

They have the power to take a dominant stance in the marketplace, to squeeze out smaller brands, and to reduce the influence of other competitors. These brands have strong net promoter scores and have cultivated a community of outspoken brand fans. They can use their power with retailers to gain preferential shelf space and drive traffic. The company should manage the brand as an asset. These brands should work to create magical experiences that will inspire brand fans to talk about them and influence others.

A three-point game plan for brands at the beloved stage:

1. Focus on maintaining the love the brand has created with core brand fans.
2. Consistently challenge and perfect the consumer experience.
3. Broaden the offering and selectively broaden your audience.

Action plan for brands at the beloved stage:

- **Create magic:** Continue to surprise and delight your brand lovers.
- **Leverage power:** Drive growth and profit from your brand's source of power.
- **Attack yourself:** Continue to assess and close leaks to improve before competitors attack.
- **Use loyalists:** Leverage brand lovers to whisper with influence with their network.

Summary of the five major brand strategies help move your brand from one stage of the brand love curve to the next

- For **unknown** brands, the strategic focus should be to stand out so consumers will notice the brand within a crowded brand world, where they see an estimated 5,000 brand messages per day.

- For **indifferent** brands, the strategy must establish the brand in the consumer's mind so they can see a clear point of difference over their current brand choice.

- At the **like it** stage, the strategy is to separate the brand from the pack, creating happy experiences that build a trusted following over time. Only after they trust the brand, they begin to open up.

- At the **love it** stage, the focus shifts tightening the bond with the most loyal brand fans.

- At the **beloved** stage, the strategic challenge is to create outspoken, loyal fans who are willing to whisper to their friends on the brand's behalf.

Case study: Special K moves from indifferent to beloved

In the 1990s Special K just sat there with a small and dying share in cereal. It only had the one flavor with zero innovation. Special K was an indifferent brand, with little consumer opinion, and for those who did buy Special K, they were not exactly the most ardent fans of the brand. Not only was the original flavor somewhat bland, but everything about the brand was bland.

Special K needed to stand for something. Special K built everything around the brand idea of "We inspire and empower women to take control and maintain their healthy body." To separate themselves in the mind of consumers, they launched the Special K Challenge with a straightforward message: "With Special K, just twice a day for two weeks, you can lose 6 pounds or better yet, drop a jean size."

Special K launched the red berries cereal, which was a phenomenal market success. Equally, it taught the brand that healthy could taste great. From there, it built a series of delicious new products across categories such as cereal, snacks, water, and shakes. It built each new product around the brand idea.

The Special K brand gained share in the cereal category and pulled loyal consumers into all the new categories. Sales grew five-fold, and Special K became a beloved brand.

Here are the five elements of smart strategic thinking that allowed Special K to move from indifferent up to a beloved brand.

1. Set a vision of what you want
- Special K wanted to be the healthy food brand that empowers women to take control of their weight and live healthier, happier lives. It needed a brand idea and a way to build everything around that brand idea.

2. Invest resources in solidifying your capabilities to deliver the strategy
- Special K shifted from a product-driven strategy to a story-led brand that helps women maintain their weight, providing low-calorie alternatives across the challenging food temptation moments of the day. It built engaging consumer advertising and delicious tasting innovation behind the brand idea.

3. Focused accelerator to propel strategy
- The brand saw the opportunity to focus on those women who were frustrated by "lose and gain" diet fads. Tired of big promises that set people up to fail, consumers were looking for easy alternatives they could execute within their healthy lifestyle.

4. Leverage a breakthrough market impact
- Special K built everything around the brand idea of helping women "take control of their weight." The red berries launch transformed the brand and gained the consumer's permission to enter new food categories. It built a series of tasty new products across categories of cereal, snacks, water, and shakes.

5. A performance result that pays back

- Special K gained a significant market share of the cereal category, moving to number one in many markets. The brand also took its new loyal consumers into all the other categories, such as cereal bars, protein snacks, shakes, chips, crackers and, most recently, the launch of frozen quiche. Special K now earns five times the sales as a beloved grocery brand.

Special K brand strategy statement using our A + B + C + D approach

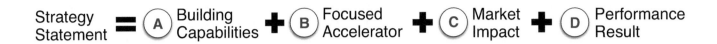

1. Advertise Special K's brand idea of "empowering women" **(A)** focused on prospective consumers who are frustrated by "lose and gain" diet fads **(B)**, to drive trial **(C)** and gain market share. **(D)**

2. Build an innovation plan with low-calorie products across the grocery store **(A)** to get our most loyal Special K brand fans **(B)** to try each new item **(C)** to help successfully enter into new categories. **(D)**

The Special K Brand Plan

If you took the strategic thinking model and began to outline a brand plan for Special K, these would be the core elements:

- **Vision:** Be the delicious and healthy choice food brand across every tempting category of the grocery store.

- **Goals:** Increase share in the cereal category. Successfully enter one new grocery category per year. Drive net promoter score and strengthen usage frequency and loyalty scores.

- **Key Issues:**
  1. How do we build an overall brand story to connect and develop a core base of brand lovers?
  2. How do we take the "empowering women" brand idea into new food categories?

- **Strategies:**
  1. Advertise Special K's brand idea of "empowering women" **(A)** focused on prospective consumers who are frustrated by "lose and gain" diet fads **(B)**, to drive trial **(C)** and gain market share. **(D)**
  2. Build an innovation plan with low-calorie products across the grocery store **(A)** to get our most loyal Special K brand fans **(B)** to try each new item **(C)** to help successfully enter into new categories. **(D)**

- **Tactics:** New master brand advertising to project brand idea. Continue to improve shakes and potato chips product lines. Launch into breakfast snacks. Explore product innovation into pitas and pizzas.

Thank you to Millward Brown for your contributions of the Best Practices for TV Advertising Creative

Strategic Thinking & Analytics

How to win the competitive battle for your consumer's heart

You must decide if you will position your brand to be better, different, or cheaper. Otherwise, you will not be around for very long.

A winning brand position matches what consumers want with what your brand does best, always better than your competitors. I will outline four types of competitive brand strategy situations: the power player, challenger brand, disruptor brand and the craft brand. You must identify and choose one competitive situation, which best fits where you are today, and where you want to go next.

How to find your space in the market to win

To find the competitive space in which your brand can win, on the next page, I introduce a Venn diagram of competitive situations that we will use throughout this chapter. The Venn diagram will resurface again, in the brand positioning chapter. You will see three circles.

The first circle comprises everything your consumer wants or needs. The second circle includes everything your brand does best, including consumer benefits, product features, or proven claims. Finally, the third circle lists what your competitor does best.

Your brand's **winning zone** (in green), is the space that matches up "What consumers want" with "What your brand does best." This space provides you a distinct positioning you can own and defend from attack. Your brand must be able to satisfy the consumer needs better than any other competitor can.

Your brand will not survive by trying to compete in the **losing zone** (in red), which is the space that matches the consumer needs with "What your competitor does best." When you play in this space, your competitor will beat you every time.

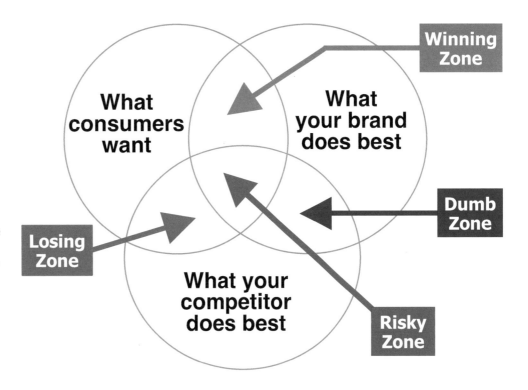

As markets mature, competitors copy each other. It has become harder to be better with a definitive product win. Many brands have to play in the **risky zone** (in grey), which is the space where you and your competitor both meet the consumer's needs in a relative tie.

There are four ways you can **win the risky zone**:

- **Dominate:** Use your brand's power in the market to squeeze out smaller, weaker brands.
- **Gain first-mover advantage:** Be the first to capture that space to earn a reputation you can defend
- **Innovate:** Win with innovation and creativity to make your brand seem unique
- **Captivate:** Build a deeper emotional connection to make your brand seem different

If you only focus on using product features to differentiate your brand, you will fail. As the market matures, competitors copy each other. And that winning green space gets very small. Instead, you can carve out a winning brand positioning space when you focus on the emotional benefits. In our brand positioning chapter, I will show you a logical way to engage with our **Emotional Cheat Sheet** that has 40 emotional benefits.

Sadly, I always have to mention the **dumb zone (in blue)** where two competitors "battle it out" in the space consumers do not care. One competitor says, "We are faster," and the other brand says, "We are just as fast." No one bothered to ask the consumer if they care about speed. Both brands are dumb.

Competitive Situations

Brands rarely experience competitive isolation. Even in a **blue ocean** situation, the euphoria of being alone quickly turns to a **red ocean**, cluttered with the blood from nasty battling competitors. The moment we think we are alone, a competitor is watching and believing they can do it better than we can. When you ignore your competition, believing only the consumer matters, you are on a naive pathway to losing. Competitors can help sharpen our focus and tighten our language on the brand positioning we project to the marketplace.

Regarding **marketing war games**, I will use this Venn diagram to map out four types of competitive brands:

1. Power players
2. Challenger brands
3. Disruptor brands
4. Craft brands.

Power players

Power players lead the way as the share leader or perceived influential leader of the category. These brands command power over all the stakeholders, including consumers, competitors, and retail channels.

Regarding positioning, the power player brands own what they are best at and leverage their power in the market to help them own the position where there is a tie with another competitor.

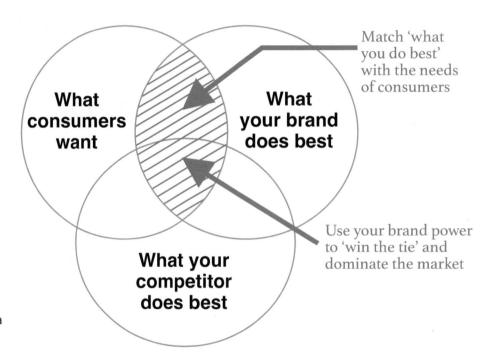

Match 'what you do best' with the needs of consumers

Use your brand power to 'win the tie' and dominate the market

Owning both zones helps expand the brand's presence and power across a bigger market. These brands can also use their exceptional financial situation to invest in innovation to catch up, defend, or stay ahead of competitors.

Power player brands must defend their territory by responding to every aggressive competitor's attacks. They even need to attack themselves by vigilantly watching for internal weaknesses to close any potential leaks before a competitor notices. Power player brands can never become complacent, or they will die.

One of the best contemporary power player brands is **Google**, which has managed to dominate the search engine market. The company's extreme focus and smart execution gained market power and squeezed out Microsoft and Yahoo. Focused on providing knowledge for consumers, Google has continued to expand its services into a bundle of products with e-mail, maps, apps, docs, cloud technology, and cell phones. The combination of Google and Facebook now accounts for over 70% of all digital advertising spending. There have been many failed attempts to knock them off, but each have failed. TikTok is now making the latest challenger.

Challenger brands

Challenger brands must change the playing field by amplifying what your brand does best while simultaneously repositioning the power player brand you want to take down.

While your first instinct would be to attack the power player's weakness, the smarter move is to reposition one of the power player's well-known strengths into a perceived weakness. This strategy helps move the power player brand outside of what consumers want.

When you attack a power player brand, be ready for the leader's potential defensive moves and anticipate a response with full force, as the power player brand has more

What consumers want

What your brand does best

What your competitor does best

Amplify what your brand does best to those frustrated by the power player

Reposition the power player competitor into the dumb zone by turning their strength into a weakness, to disconnect them from what consumers want

significant resources than you. Be highly confident that your attack will make a positive impact before you begin to enter into a war. The worst situation is to start a war, you cannot win, as it will drain your brand's limited resources, only to end up with the same market share after the war.

Since the power player leader tries to be everything to everyone, you can narrow your attack to slice off those consumers who are frustrated with the leading brand. Tap into their frustration to help kickstart a migration of consumers away from the leader. If you can gain these lost consumers, you can quickly change share positions.

One of the best examples of a challenger brand that made significant gains is the **Pepsi Challenge** from the 1970s. It was a direct offensive attack on Coke. In blind taste tests, Pepsi was the preferred brand. Pepsi is a much sweeter taste, so in a quick hit, it was the chosen brand. Coke is an acquired and memorable taste. The blind taste test took away the Coke brand name and the emotional feelings of that brand. At the same time, Pepsi amplified its strength as the "new generation" and positioned the brand as the solution to consumers ready to reject the "old taste" of Coke. This approach was so powerful it was even a contributing factor to the launch of a sweeter "New Coke."

Disruptor brands

Disruptor brands move into a blue ocean space, alone. They use a new product, distribution channel, target market, or price point. They are so different that they appear to be the only brand that can satisfy the consumer's changing needs.

When successful, the disruptor brand repositions the major players, making them appear unattached to consumers.

While everyone wants a game-changer, it is a high-risk, high-reward competitive situation. The trick is you have to be "so different" to catch the consumer's attention and mindshare. Being profoundly different increases the risk you may fail. Also, your success may invite other entrants to follow. At that point, you become the new power player of the new segment. You have to continue attacking the major players while defending against new entrants who attack your brand.

Uber, Netflix, and Airbnb are contemporary brands that effectively use modern technology to create such a unique offering that they cast major category-leading brands or entire industries as outdated and outside what consumers want. Uber disrupted the taxi market, Netflix is revolutionizing the way we watch TV, and Airbnb has had a dramatic impact on hotels. These brands have a smarter ordering system, better service levels, and significantly lower prices.

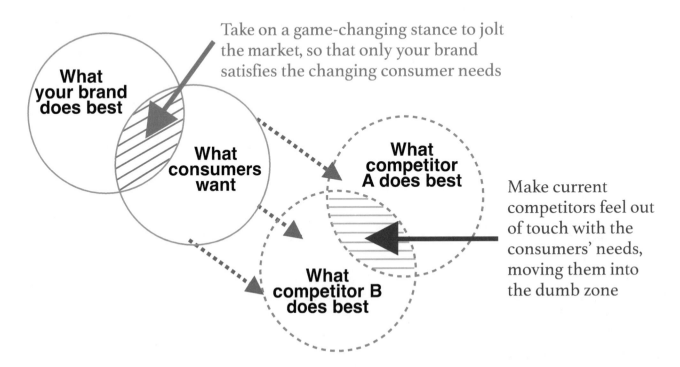

Craft brands

Craft brands must win a small space in the marketplace that offers something unique to a highly engaged target. These brands succeed when they are far enough away from major competitors that the leaders ignore them because craft brands stay hidden away.

Craft brands build themselves behind a micro-benefit, including gluten-free, low fat, locally grown, organic or ethically sourced. These craft brands take an antagonistic approach to the rest of the category, portraying every other brand in the category as old-school, overly corporate, unethical, flawed in the manufacturing or the use of ingredients. Many times, these brands take a very aggressive marketing stance, calling out the other brands as unethical or stupid. Craft brands believe it is better to be loved by the few than liked or tolerated by many.

Craft brands own a small space with a highly engaged target, far enough away from major competitors.

Avoid directly competing with market leaders.

A fantastic of example a craft brand is **Five Guys Burgers**, which uses fresh, high-quality beef and a commitment not to begin cooking your burger until you order it. The portions are more substantial than typical fast food, and they charge super-premium prices. Five Guys have gone in the opposite direction to most fast food restaurants, whose meals seem frozen and microwaved. Five Guys expanded rapidly with word-of-mouth helping the brand earn a reputation as "the best burger." Now that Five Guys has become a global brand, McDonald's has to figure out an adequate competitive response.

Another excellent example of a craft brand is **Dollar Shave**, which launched as an online subscription model for razor blades. Dollar Shave uses smart sourcing and a direct-to-consumer distribution model. This efficient model eliminates costs and allows the brand to sell razors at a fraction of the cost you pay for Gillette. For consumers, the price of razor blades has gotten out of control, no matter how much innovation the leaders try to portray. Dollar Shave's advertising openly mocked Gillette, yet it started in such a small niche, so Gillette ignored them. While year one sales were only $30 million, without a competitive response from Gillette, Dollar Shave continued to grow year-by-year, until Unilever recently purchased the brand for $1 billion.

The consumer adoption curve

In every category, a consumer adoption curve maps out how various types of consumers adopt innovation and new products. The curve divides consumers into trend influencers, early adopters, early mass, and the late mass audience.

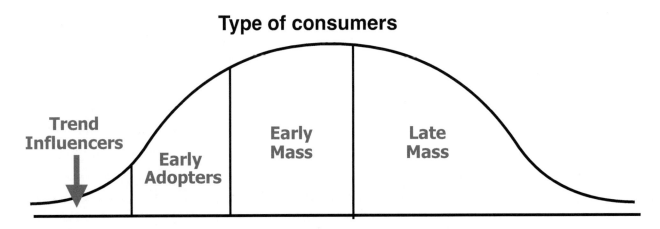

The **trend influencer consumers** are at the beginning of the curve, representing 2-3% of the consumers. They investigate every innovation in the categories they are interested in, right on the edge of what is new. They keep in touch with leading experts, love genuine leapfrog innovation, and despise the "death by incrementalism" approach of the safer and more prominent brands. They like to see themselves as experts, and they are always willing to share that knowledge with friends.

The **early adopter group** represents 10-15% of consumers who play the bridge role between the trend influencers and the mass market. They try to keep up and enjoy being the first within their network to try the latest and greatest innovation. They loudly influence the masses of anything new and proven. They have an instinctual judgment in which products will succeed and use their influence to validate a new product poised to take off.

From there, the mass market consumers represent 80% of the market, divided equally between **early and late mass type consumers**. The early mass consumers are willing to eventually take on new products when the products feel safe to use. The late mass consumers are usually resistant to change, and they feel comfortable staying with out-of-date products.

We each fit into one of these types of consumers, dependent on the category. You might be an early adopter of technology, but the early mass in fashion, late mass in music and yet a trend influencer in the best restaurants around the city. With our social network, we are starting to know who are the trend influencers or early adopters within a particular product category. When we buy something outside our area of expertise, we openly reach out to them for advice.

Brands must evolve their strategy as they move from the craft brand to the power player brand

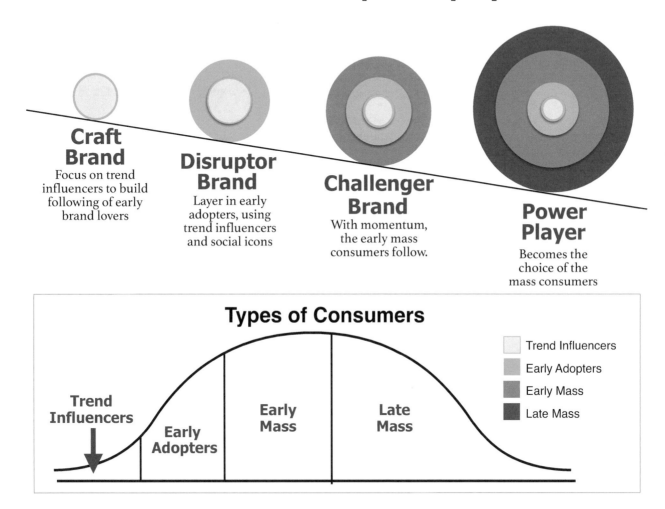

Craft Brand
Focus on trend influencers to build following of early brand lovers

Disruptor Brand
Layer in early adopters, using trend influencers and social icons

Challenger Brand
With momentum, the early mass consumers follow.

Power Player
Becomes the choice of the mass consumers

Types of Consumers

Trend Influencers

Early Adopters

Early Mass

Late Mass

Trend Influencers
Early Adopters
Early Mass
Late Mass

Many brands start in someone's garage or over a kitchen table at midnight

Start-ups should deploy a **craft brand strategy**. To stand out, be utterly different to a core group of trend influencers who are frustrated with major competitors. Be willing to take a "high risk/high reward" strategy. It is O.K. if your brand alienates those who are not yet ready to take on something new. Playing it too safe will lead to your destruction. Do not worry about the mass audience, and avoid trying to be too big, too fast.

As your brand grows, you can transition to a **disruptor brand strategy**. Utilize your core audience of trend influencers to gain a core base of early adopters. While a craft brand attracts the attention of trend influencers, the disruptor brand must dial up its aggressive stance and call out the major brands. Use your significant point of difference to pull consumers away from the category-leading brands to make them seem detached from the needs of the consumer.

As your brand continues to grow, you can use your increased resources and power to take on a **challenger brand strategy** against the leader. You can use the influence of the trend influencers and early adopters to attract the early mass audience. With a significant consumer base, more brand power, and increased financial resources, your brand must gain hard-fought proximity, allowing you to go head-to-head with the power player leader. The challenger brand should turn the leader's strength into a weakness, pushing it out of what consumers want, while creating a new consumer problem for which your brand becomes the solution.

At the **power player stage**, the strategy shifts to maintaining your leadership position. You should take on a defensive strategy, to attack in response to any player who threatens your brand. While the trend influencers and early adopters played an essential role in making the brand a household name, you have to be comfortable that your earliest brand fans will eventually leave your brand and look for what is next. They may even call you a "sell-out." Stay focused on the mass audience.

How Apple evolved from the innovative craft brand to a power player

Apple started as a classic **craft brand** in the 1970s and 1980s, positioning their Macintosh as the computer for the "rest of us." The brand stayed niche with a "making computers simpler" message against IBM personal computers. It focused on a niche consumer who favored the intuitive and artistic side of personal computers, as opposed to IBM's business computers.

Apple evolved in 2001 to a **disruptor brand strategy**, when iTunes completely disrupted the music industry. iTunes gave consumers the ability to have 10,000 songs in their pocket, buying one song at a time with perfect digital quality. They made CDs feel disconnected from consumers and a thing of the past.

In 2006, Apple used its market power and substantial resources to deploy a **challenger strategy**, with the "I'm a Mac" TV ads to go head-to-head with Microsoft. Apple repositioned every one the potential Microsoft strengths into a frustration point for consumers. The ads set up Mac as the only solution for consumers.

Since 2012, Apple has become a **power player brand**, with stock prices continuing to climb beyond their wildest dreams. It is now a brand for the masses. The company attacks itself internally to stay at the top. Apple takes a fast-follower stance on technology, which frustrates those who loved Mac in the early days. While Apple's early brand lovers from the 1980s may be disappointed with the Apple of today, the brand must now play to the mass audience and let the true influential innovators, who once loved them, find someone else to love. In 2016, Apple's most substantial growth came from the 55+ age segment, a clear sign that the brand is for everyone. How long can Apple stay on top before someone starts to disrupt or challenge them?

Cluttered brands

I did say there are only four types of competitive brands. That is true. However, some brands are uncompetitive. I call these brands the **"cluttered brands."** They get stuck in the cluttered mess of the market, without a defined target market or a defined point of difference. Consumers cannot describe them and, even worse, the brands cannot express themselves.

These brands lack a loyal base of consumers and are unable to generate any positive growth or price premiums. They end up as an indifferent commodity, disconnected from consumer

What consumers want

What your brand does best

What your competitor does best

Cluttered brands just sit in the market, with no defined positioning, no target market, and no insights. These brands end up in the dumb zone, disconnected from what consumers want.

needs. Without sales growth or profits, they struggle to invest back into their brand, which further accelerates the path of decay. You do not want to find yourself in the cluttered brand space.

Examples of cluttered brands are **General Motors, Burger King, Gap Clothing,** and **Sears**, all of whom lack any clear brand positioning. The only way to break this vicious downward spiral is to start over and follow the strategy of the craft brand. Try to own a small niche and build around a unique brand positioning to a smaller motivated target.

Examples of brands who reinvented themselves and chose a specific niche include Old Spice, which went from your grandfather's aftershave to the fresh new product for young males. Also, LG used the launch of high-end laundry and premium TVs, to escape the negative image associated with its GoldStar brand.

Competitive strategy attack choices

As you engage in competitive strategy, you must decide how **aggressive** you are willing to be, whether you wish to attack to gain share or defend to slow down any losses.

The other dimension is the **focus of your attack**, whether you will build up the strengths of your brand or diminish the strengths of your competitor. That leaves your brand with four strategic attack options:

		Diminish strengths of competitor	Build up strengths of your own brand
Aggressiveness	Attack to gain share	**Weaken competitor**	**Full assault**
	Defend to slow losses	**Slow down competitor**	**Maintain strong core**

Focus of attack

1. **Full assault:** You recognize an opportunity in the market where your strengths are considered superior to your competitor, and you see an opportunity to gain share. Focus on playing up your competitive advantage – whether you use your brand positioning, product innovation, or distribution channels – to enhance the purchase moment or the overall consumer experience.

2. **Maintain strong core:** When you recognize attempts by an aggressive competitor, retreat and maintain your core audience by playing up the accepted strengths of your brand. This strategy can retain share against an aggressive competitor (or at least slow down the losses).

3. **Weaken competitor:** When you recognize a dramatic weakness in your competitor, this opens up the opportunity to gain share by attacking your rival.

4. **Slow down competitor:** When you recognize you are at a competitive disadvantage, attacking back on an element of your competitor can buy you time, so you can regroup behind the scenes to close the competitive gap. While you may lose share in the short term, once you have fixed that gap, you can look to rebuild your share by going back after any consumers you may have lost.

Case Study: Strategic thinking behind Apple's recovery

In 1996, the Apple brand bordered on bankruptcy. It was just another computer company without any real point of difference. Years of overlooked opportunities, flip-flop strategies, and a mind-boggling disregard for market realities caught up with the company. The Windows 95 launch by Microsoft had severely eroded Mac's technology edge. Apple was rapidly becoming a minor player in the computer business with shrinking market shares, price cuts, and declining profits.

Apple looked like it would not survive, as it was a poorly run organization through the early 1990s. Executives made terrible decisions with inconsistent strategies and, most importantly, there was no brand idea for what Apple should be. After Steve Jobs came to Apple in 1997, he shifted the focus to rebuilding Apple around the brand idea of "Apple makes technology so simple that everyone can be part of the future." He took a consumer-first approach in a market dominated by an obsession with gadgets, bits, and bytes.

Five elements of smart strategic thinking for Apple's turnaround plan:

1. Set a vision of what you want
- Apple's vision is to make it easy to get everyone to be part of technology in the future. The main issue was how to create Apple fans then mobilize them to spread the word to the masses.

2. Invest resources in solidifying your capabilities to deliver the strategy
- Apple invested and aligned everything behind a brand idea defined as "Apple makes technology so simple; everyone can be part of the future." They use this brand idea at every touchpoint, including the brand positioning, communication, innovation, purchase moment, and experience.

3. Focused accelerator to propel strategy
- For decades, Apple consistently focused on empathizing with—and taking advantage of—the consumer's frustration with technology. In the 1980s, Apple attacked IBM personal computers as being too complicated. In 2005, Apple used "I'm a Mac, and I'm a PC" advertising to attack Microsoft. Each time, Apple used its "consumer-first" mentality to transform leading-edge technology into accessible consumer technology.

4. Leverage a breakthrough market impact
- Apple takes a fast-follower stance taking current technology and make it simple to use. Every Apple platform, including desktops, laptops, phones, watches, tablets, and music delivers "simplicity." Apple deploys high profile launch hype to use vocal advocates to spread the word.

5. Performance result that pays back
- Apple created a consumer bond with their brand fans to enter new categories. Apple is now the most beloved consumer-driven brand, with premium prices, stronger market share, sales, and profits. Apple has used brand love to help drive a remarkable 40x revenue growth over ten years, skyrocketing from $5.7 billion in 2005 to $240 billion in 2015. This rapid growth helps cover the high costs of advertising and R&D, giving Apple very healthy operating margins, up over 35%. All this strategic effort has increased Apple's market capitalization approaches $1 trillion.

Apple strategic statements sing our A + B + C + D method

1. Advertising **(A)** to competitive users who are frustrated by the flaws of PCs **(B)** to inform them of how much simpler Macs are and get them to seek more information **(C)** to use increase penetration to gain share. **(D)**

2. Launch iTunes **(A)** aimed at competitive music consumers with a disruptive stance against the music industry **(B)** to inform consumers of iTunes superiority to CD's **(C)** to gain trial and entry into music industry. **(D)**

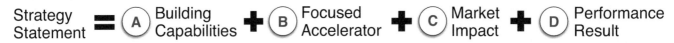

Strategy Statement **=** (A) Building Capabilities **+** (B) Focused Accelerator **+** (C) Market Impact **+** (D) Performance Result

The Apple Brand Plan

- **Vision:** Apple wants everyone in the world to be part of the future.

- **Goals:** Continue aggressive sales growth, geographic expansion into China, launch new consumer-friendly technology each year.

- **Key issues:**
  1. How do we convey Mac's superior user experience versus the traditional PC?
  2. How do we enter the music industry and increase the availability of online music to support our iPod?

- **Strategies:**
  1. Advertising **(A)** to competitive users who are frustrated by the flaws of PCs **(B)** to inform them of how much simpler Macs are and get them to seek more information **(C)** to use increase penetration to gain share. **(D)**
  2. Launch iTunes **(A)** aimed at competitive music consumers with a disruptive stance against the music industry **(B)** to inform consumers of iTunes superiority to CD's **(C)** to gain trial and entry into music industry. **(D)**

- **Tactics:** TV advertising to highlight new features and challenge competitors. Launch innovation each year including phones, tablets, online music, watches, and personal computers. Launch specific products for China. Increase retail space around the world. Build out the e-commerce program.

Strategic Thinking & Analytics

How to address your brand situation before you make your next move

Before moving towards a plan, you must fully understand the situation you face. Each year, conduct a deep-dive business review to assess the health of your branded business. A smart brand strategy is a smart business strategy. You are running a live business, with a need to drive sales, manage costs, and produce profits. Without addressing the competitive and consumer factors you face, all your great strategic thinking will come collapsing down around you.

I will outline four distinct situations your brand could face:

- Fuel the momentum
- Fix it
- Realignment
- Start-up

Apply the right strategy and leadership to the right situation you face

When business results are healthy, fuel your momentum by staying on course and attacking small weaknesses. When things are going well, everyone within your organization will resist a change plan. When the external results are abysmal, your management team will look for opportunities to turn around those results quickly. They will be impatient. Manage the short-term and long-term fix it plans at the same time. When different silos operate entirely autonomously within your organization, it causes unnecessary conflict and confusion that holds your brand back from maximizing its full potential. Build a realignment plan to get everyone moving in the same direction. Whether you are in an entrepreneurial start-up or entering into a new business from within a corporation, follow the plan for a start-up.

Fuel the momentum

Many marketers are notorious for wanting to make their mark. When they come into a brand situation, they see a long list of flaws left by the previous leader. They think it is time to do things right and change the way everyone operates. However, if you put a change plan in place when everything is going well, you will face significant resistance.

When brands have a strong market share position, steady sales growth, strong profitability, strong underlying brand health measures, and they align the team on the direction for the future, the brand leader should keep the momentum going. It is harder than you think.

Fuel the momentum plan:

- **Assessment indicators:** Steady sales growth, profitability, strong share position, and no looming competitive threat.
- **Strategy:** Continue to fuel growth drivers, close any small gaps, and stay vigilant of looming threats to the current growth rates.
- **Leadership style to engage:** Motivational leadership style that keeps everyone inspired, aligned, and focused.

Your role as the leader should be to continue to fuel the growth drivers while resisting the temptation to make wholesale changes. Use the time to learn the success factors while looking at future scenarios that could threaten the current momentum.

You can attack what you see as smaller weaknesses and gaps that you feel will add to the overall growth rate. Use a motivational leadership style that keeps everyone inspired, aligned, and focused.

Fix it

When a brand faces poor external results with a decline in sales, shrinking market share, and lower profit margins due to lower prices or rising costs, the brand leader needs to create a turnaround plan that will fix it. From my experience, you will need both a short-term and long-term fix. The quick fix helps address the hemorrhaging results that are impacting the bottom line of the company.

However, most fix it situations have a more in-depth cause, hidden beneath the surface level. You will need a change management leadership style that challenges everyone and everything. You will need a new plan, which includes a new vision filled with new ideas. Explore the need for different people to join the team. Losing can be contagious to the culture of a team. You will need to create a new attitude.

Fix it plan:

- **Assessment indicators:** Poor external results, declining sales, shrinking profitability, falling share position, and losing competitive battles.
- **Strategy:** Quick wins stop declines. Dig in deep to find underlying causes. Need long-term fixes for communication, innovation, selling and in-store
- **Leadership style to engage:** Use a transformational change management style to challenge everything and everyone.

The quick fix can buy you time with management to implement what you see as the longer-term fix it plan. Any immediate wins also give the team a much-needed boost of motivation.

Dig deep into a full business review to understand the underlying causes happening in the market. Evaluate changing consumers needs, new competitors, changes in the retail landscape, and changes in technology. Close leaks using a brand funnel analysis. Go through every investment decision. Cut all spending that fails to drive results and reinvest in the new plan. Invest only in programs that give you an early breakthrough win and payback. Once you have the plan in place, make sure you have the right talent in place to make it happen.

The quick fix plan

- Find early, and obvious potential wins to stop the hemorrhaging.
- Emphasize results to fuel a performance-driven culture.
- Use all early wins to boost team motivation.
- Celebrate every victory, big or small.
- Eliminate wasteful spend, low margin or resource draining projects

The long-term fix

- Conduct a deep-dive business review of the market, consumers, competitors, channels, and the brand. Focus on the top three issues emerging from the review.
- Invest in a new brand plan with a brand idea supported by a unique brand positioning.
- Make focused investment decisions, and take smart risks to fix the brand communication, product innovation, purchase moment, and the consumer experience.

Realignment

A brand itself needs a consistent delivery of the brand promise. Issues arise when the brand promise shows up inconsistently across the advertising, in-store, new products, the overall consumer experience. It creates a confused and cluttered mess in the marketplace. You do not want the team behind the scenes of the brand moving in different directions.

When different functions operate in silos, you see the marketing and sales team each delivering their distinct brand messages, and the product development team invents products in a lab without any direction from brand or input from consumers. The consumer experience team lacks cohesion and consistency, and consumers begin to notice a confused brand.

When I consult on a situation that looks splintered, I ask various leaders to describe the brand in seven seconds. The answers I get suggest a confused team. I hear:

- It depends on who you ask.
- It's complicated.
- I've never thought about it.
- I can't.

Realignment plan:

- **Assessment indicators:** Internal silos among functions behind the brand. Conflict over action plans. Confused messages.
- **Strategy:** Realign the team by employing a cross-functional team to build a new brand positioning, an organizing brand idea, and a brand plan to get everyone on the same page. Build a shared vision, purpose, values, strategies, and execution.
- **Leadership style to engage:** Participative leadership style to bring everyone together to listen to all points of view and unify them under a shared plan.

In situations like this, bring an energetic and focused leadership style to keep the team aligned. Use a highly participative leadership style to bring everyone together, to listen to all points of view and unite the team under a shared plan. Everyone on the team must move in the same direction to the same brand plan. A high-functioning team must agree on the following:

- Target market
- Main consumer benefit
- An organizing brand idea
- Articulation of the brand idea for each function
- Brand vision
- Brand purpose and values
- Shared goals
- Key issues
- Strategies
- Execution plans and activities you will invest in

Each functional team should then complete their plan to ensure it aligns with the overall brand plan. Each team needs clear marching orders, firm decisions, goals, budgets, and timelines.

Start-up

Start-up situations are either about the launch of a new brand in the market or the launch of a current brand in a new category. At this stage, you move quickly from blank slate to a new brand idea, a new brand plan, and a new team.

The first mistake many start-ups make is believing a product alone is good enough. Even at the start-up stage, you need a brand idea to help organize everything. Consumers are more likely to buy into an idea than a product.

The second mistake is to sell to anyone and even adjust your product or service to fit every different type of consumer who wants to buy. While you might feel desperate for revenue early on, you need to stay focused on your target and brand positioning. The goal for your brand is to build a reputation you can own. If you try to be everything to anyone, you will end up as nothing to everyone.

Start-up plan:

- **Assessment indicators:** New product, yet to launch in the market or a new segment of the market.
- **Strategy:** Blowfish marketing plan, with a focused target market, a targeted main message, focused strategy and focused executions. Make the brand appear bigger than it is to those who matter the most.
- **Leadership style to engage:** Entrepreneurs need a participative and transactional style to roll up the sleeves and get the necessary tasks done.

Build a "blowfish" brand plan.

A blowfish can make itself appear bigger than it is.

The idea of a blowfish brand plan is to make focused decisions and investments, so the brand appears bigger than it is, especially to those consumers or influencers who matter the most.

For instance, when you focus and invest in a tight target market, those consumers will begin to think the brand is bigger than it is. On the other hand, resist the temptation of going after a broad target market too early, or you will stretch your dollars so thin no one will even notice you. Go after a niche consumer benefit, so your brand can eventually own a trusted reputation in narrow competitive space.

Resist the temptation to try to be everywhere at once, as it spreads your resources so thin you will have a small presence anywhere. When you focus, your brand can start to dominate a focused distribution channel or media channel.

Focus! Focus! Focus!

Build the right team that fits the people to the strategy, not the strategy to the people. Build out the team's capabilities by acquiring the skills, behaviors, relationships, and capacity to fit the needs of the brand plan and execution. As start-up brands are continually learning, keep in mind that it is okay to maneuver and adjust your strategies – but do not change your overall vision.

Case Study: Taylor Swift uses social media to continue the momentum and connect with her fans as "friends"

Taylor Swift uses her 120 million followers to connect with fans as "friends" and build a beloved brand. She has a vision, direction, and the final say of her brand portrayal. Let's use our smart strategic thinking model to explain her brilliance in how she has fuelled a decade momentum, while everyone other superstar falls.

Elements of strategic thinking to explain Taylor Swift's momentum

1. Set a vision of what you want

- Every pop star wants #1 songs and sold-out concerts for as long as possible. Taylor also wants to portray herself as an average small-town girl living a big city celebrity life.

2. Invest resources in solidifying your capabilities

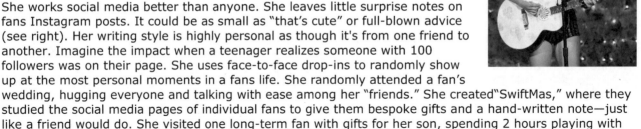

- Taylor's most loyal fans are young women, 13-27; who are discovering life. She treats her fans as "new friends along for the ride." She uses social media to show she's doing ordinary things in her crazy world. She uses face-to-face events to shock a few fans, making those fans watching feel closer to Taylor.

3. Focused accelerator to propel strategy

- She works social media better than anyone. She leaves little surprise notes on fans Instagram posts. It could be as small as "that's cute" or full-blown advice (see right). Her writing style is highly personal as though it's from one friend to another. Imagine the impact when a teenager realizes someone with 100 followers was on their page. She uses face-to-face drop-ins to randomly show up at the most personal moments in a fans life. She randomly attended a fan's wedding, hugging everyone and talking with ease among her "friends." She created "SwiftMas," where they studied the social media pages of individual fans to give them bespoke gifts and a hand-written note—just like a friend would do. She visited one long-term fan with gifts for her son, spending 2 hours playing with her son, as though she were a good friend.

4. Leverage a breakthrough market impact

- With each program, Taylor comes off as open, authentic, and genuine, who loves connecting with her fans. In a cluttered world of social media, her perfect image remains the "normal girl doing normal things anyone might do." Her image has allowed her to overcome any natural pain points a celebrity goes through. She's had many bad personal relationships. What would a normal girl do when she breaks up? Write a song about what a jerk each guy was. She took on Apple over low royalty payments; Apple backed down, and then Taylor did an Apple TV ad. She pulls off everything with a relative ease.

5. Performance result that pays back

- Taylor is beloved by her fans, keeping her momentum going for over a decade. With sold-out concerts, #1 hits, and many Grammy awards. Her fans (friends) think they know her. Maintaining a considerable following makes it easy to create hype around albums or concert tours.

Taylor Swift strategic statements using our A + B + C + D method

1. Create intimate experiences through social media **(A)** to her 140M followers **(B)** by engaging her most loyal brand lovers **(C)** to keep the bond tight to maintain high album sales and concert revenue. **(D)**

2. Build deeper and more meaningful songwriting **(A)** by appealing to her most loyal fans who grew up alongside Taylor **(B)** to reposition her as a mature "indie artist" **(C)** to keep her music sales strong. **(D)**

Strategy Statement **=** (A) Building Capabilities **+** (B) Focused Accelerator **+** (C) Market Impact **+** (D) Performance Result

The Taylor Swift brand plan

- **Vision:** Recording superstar, who is a small-town girl living the big-city celebrity life.

- **Goals:** #1 songs, concert sales, social media followers, video views.

- **Key issues:**

   1. How do we stay connected with our most cherished fans, who see themselves as friends of Taylor?

   2. How do we continue Taylor's star power momentum, as Taylor's core base of fans moves into their 20s and 30s?

- **Strategies:**

   1. Create intimate experiences through social media **(A)** to her 140M followers **(B)** by engaging her most loyal brand lovers **(C)** to keep the bond tight to maintain high album sales and concert revenue. **(D)**

   2. Build deeper and more meaningful songwriting **(A)** by appealing to her most loyal fans who grew up alongside Taylor **(B)** to reposition her as a mature "indie artist" **(C)** to keep her music sales strong. **(D)**

- **Tactics:** Maintain strong following, engage with fans directly on social media, create surprise and delight events, use quick videos to show Taylor's behind-the-scenes life (small-town girl living a big-city celebrity life), stand up on key issues such as bullying and the rights of artists.

> ## Comment Taylor left on a fan's Instagram post:
>
> **Taylor Swift:** Hannah. Eyes, eyes yes. Wow!!! You have the prettiest, wildest, most child-like eyes. (Composes herself!) Okay. About this guy. I think we grow up thinking the only love that counts as true love is the kinda that lasts forever or is fully realized. When you have a broken heart, the first thing a stranger will ask is 'how long were you two together?' As if your pain can be determined by how long you were with someone. Or if you were with them at all. I don't think that's how it works. I think unrequited love is just as valid as any other kind. It's just as crushing and just as thrilling.

Brand Positioning

How to define the ideal target market to build your brand around

Most marketers think of the type of consumers they want to attract. Why not change your thinking and go after those consumers who are already motivated by what your brand offers? So instead of asking, "Who do we want?" you should be saying, "Who wants us?"

I use **seven fundamental questions** to define and build a profile of your ideal consumer target:

1. What is the description of the consumer target?
2. What are the consumer's main needs?
3. Who is the consumer's enemy who torments them every day?
4. What are the insights we know about the consumer?
5. What does the consumer think now?
6. How does the consumer buy?
7. What do we want consumers to see, think, do, feel or whisper to their friends?

Who is your consumer target?

One of the biggest mistakes I see marketers make is picking too broad of a target market. A tight target market decides who is in the target and who is not in the target.

There is a myth that a bigger target will make the brand bigger, so the scared marketer targets "everyone." There seems to be an irrational fear of leaving someone out. Spreading your brand's limited resources across an entire population is completely cost-prohibitive. While targeting everyone "just in case" might feel safe at first, it is riskier because you spread your resources so broadly you never see the full impact you want to see. This fear of missing out (FOMO) gives your brand a lower return on investment and eventually will drain your brand's limited resources. Please focus.

Every time I go to the airport, I see the shoeshine person looking down at people's feet, qualifying potential customers based on whether they are wearing leather shoes. It reminds me of how simple it is to target those consumers who are the most motivated by what you do. Sure, they could be missing out on the very few people who have leather shoes in their suitcase. However, using a focused approach to profile consumers is a smart way to maximize your return on effort. If shoeshiners can narrow the focus of their target to people wearing leather shoes, why is it so difficult for you to narrow down your target to those who care the most about what your brand does?

A good target market not only decides who is in your target but who is NOT in your target.

Instead of going after who you want, go after those who want you

If you have a golf ball that goes longer than any other golf ball, go after those golfers who already hit it long and want to hit it even longer. If you have a new recipe for chicken noodle soup, go after those who love chicken noodle soup. And if you are selling a mortgage, go after those consumers who want to buy a house. Damn, that sounds simple. Then why do I see golf marketers go after people who hate golf, soup marketers go after those who don't give a damn about soup and banks trying to sell mortgages to everyone.

To illustrate this point of focus, I look at three types of potential target markets:

- **Selling target:** This is pretty much everyone, as you sell to anyone who comes in the door and wants to buy, regardless if they fit your ideal target. However, "everyone" should never be a marketing target. You are spreading your resources so thin your message will miss out on really capturing those consumers most likely to respond, which provides an efficient payback.

- **Marketing target:** You should focus your limited resources on those consumers who have the highest likelihood of responding positively to your brand positioning, advertising, and new product innovation. A tighter target market provides the fastest and highest return on investment.

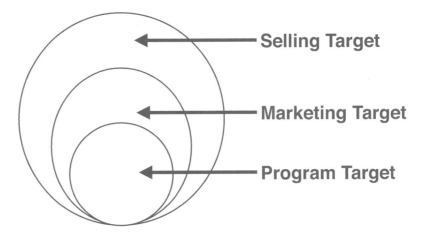

- **Program target:** When working on a specific campaign, narrow the target even further. Focus on people you want to stimulate to see if you can get them to see, think, feel or do things that will benefit your brand. A specific program target is smart when launching a new product, or aligning with a promotional time of year (including back-to-school or Christmas).

The case of the crazy bank that targeted everyone

I worked with a bank that told me its target market for a first-time mortgage (home loan) was adults aged 18-65, new customers, current customers, and employees. Sarcastically, I said, "You have forgotten about tourists and prisoners." As I pressed to help them to narrow their consumer target, they pushed back saying they did not want to alienate anyone just in case. I cringed at the word "alienate" and the idea of "just in case."

Sure, the odd 64-year-old might be tired of renting for the past 40 years, but they would not be offended having a 32-year-old in the ad. You have to realize that people know when they are a natural outlier, and they aren't offended when they are. The age target that would be most motivated by a first-time mortgage ad would be someone who is in their late twenties or early thirties.

I improved the target definition, even more, by adding, "They are looking to buy a house." This thinking is equal to the shoeshine person looking for someone wearing leather shoes. No one buys their first house on impulse, and no one ever wanted a mortgage without buying a house. Consumers usually spend 6-12 months looking for a house. It sounds obvious, but why was it lost on the bank?

Think about the difference the focused target makes on the marketing programs. Instead of randomly advertising to everyone on mass media, your brand should focus your limited resources on the consumer who is most open to your message and where they are most willing to listen. Advertise on real estate websites during their lunch hour when they take a break to search the web for new housing options. Use billboards outside new housing developments and use radio ads on Saturday afternoons to capture them while they drive around looking at new homes.

Who is most likely to try your brand or love your brand in the future?

There are various ways to divide up the market to identify the most motivated possible audience. Here are three main ways to segment the market:

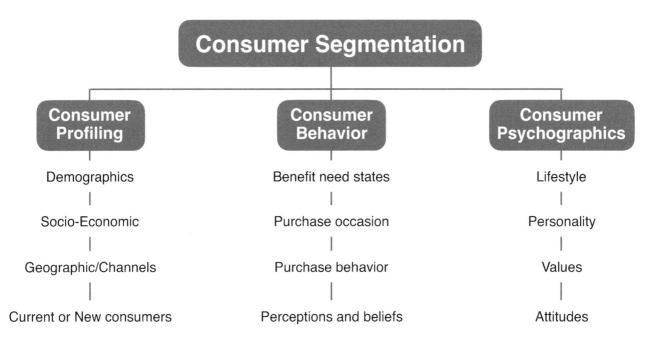

1. **Consumer profiling:** Using demographics is one of the easiest ways to segment. While some resist demographics, you will eventually have to put someone in the ad and likely buy media using age. Then add in socioeconomic and geographic elements, and how they shop. Choose to focus on either current customers or new customers, but never both at the same time. Trying to drive penetration and usage at the same time will drain your resources. These are two dramatically different targets needing two different messages, two types of media, and potentially two different types of product offerings.

2. **Consumer behavior:** Divide the market based on consumer need states, purchase occasions, life stages, or life moments. You can also divide the market based on purchase behavior, perceptions, or beliefs.

3. **Consumer psychographics:** Psychographics look at commonly shared behaviors, such as the consumer's shared lifestyle, personality, values or attitudes.

Segmentation forces you to focus. Please do not spend tons of money on a segmentation study and then try to figure out how to go after each segment with a completely different brand message. I have seen marketers do this, and it is borderline crazy. That is not the right way to use these studies. A brand can only ever have one reputation. While this shows 12 different ways you can segment, a good starting point is to use a combination of 3 or 4 segmentation elements to narrow down your target. The choice depends on the category.

What are your consumer's needs?

If you can make consumers buy, you will never have to sell. The best brands do not go after consumers; they get consumers to crave their brand and come after them. The process I will take you through involves matching up what your consumers want and need with what your brand does best.

Possible functional needs

To help get you started, I have mapped out twelve functional need states to help you understand the potential spaces your brand can play in.

Possible emotional needs

I have also mapped out twelve emotional need states your brand can play in. These need states mean something different for each category of brands, but it should be a good starting point for you to brainstorm where you can add specific words that fit your brand situation.

Who is your consumer's enemy?

While products solve small problems, the best brands beat down the enemies that torment their consumers every day. Put yourself in the shoes of your consumer and find their most significant frustration pain point they feel no one is even noticing or addressing.

Explore our our Consumer Enemy Cheatsheet

Our consumer enemy cheatsheet pinpoints the negative side of the consumer's emotional needs. If consumers are feeling stupid, a brand can offer simplicity and education. To combat feelings of pessimism, a brand can inspire hope. When consumers feel uneasy, a brand can guarantee safety. Consumers feeling trapped will gravitate to a brand offering opportunity. Those feeling overlooked cherish personalized experiences.

Uninformed   Incompetent
Feeling stupid
Uncertain   Unknown

Unmotivated
Sense of pessimism Failure
Unsuccessful   Uninspired

Unsettled   Uptight
Physically   **Feel uneasy**
Will Power
Mentally   Uncertain

Restricted
Limited **Feel trapped**
No choice   Confined

Invisible   Unpopular
Hurt **Getting** Self-esteem
overlooked
Unacknowledged

Outsider
Judged **Feel** Unhappy
Rejected
REJECTED.   Unappreciated

Powerless   Scared
Out of Hectic
control Busy
Stressed   Anxiety

Questioning
Goes Confusion
against Lost
beliefs
Ethics   Standards

Imposter   Unworthy
Not myself **Doubts of**
insecurity
Shy
Lack of confidence

Distanced   Alienated
Isolation and exclusion
Rejected   Rejected   Lonely

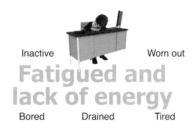

Inactive   Worn out
Fatigued and lack of energy
Bored   Drained   Tired

Shame   Flustered
Humiliated or embarrassed
Mortified   Accomplish

The Starbucks mom

Put yourself in the shoes of the Starbucks consumer. As a 38-year-old mom of two, she rises at 6:15 a.m. to ready the family for the day. By 7:45 a.m., she's dropped the kids off at daycare and school, then dashes to work. Driving a van, I ferry them to soccer, dance, tutoring, and hockey. Embraced by hugs at the end of the day, I fall into bed after tucking them in, spent. I need a break.

Who is the enemy of the Starbucks mom? A hectic life they can't escape

The Starbucks brand fights her enemy, with a 15-minute moment of escape between work and home. Starbucks has no children's playground, just lovely leather seats. No loud screams, just soft acoustic music. The cool 21-year-old college student not only knows her name but her favorite drink. Starbucks becomes that moment in the day when they can finally escape all the deadlines, and realities of life.

 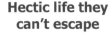

 Problem	Enemy
Not enough time in life	Hectic life they can't escape
Grass stains on kids clothes	Judgment of mother-in-law
Safety concerns	Fearing mindless other drivers

Your consumer's enemy

If you want to understand your consumer's pain points, think of how you would project their enemy and express how your brand fights that enemy on their behalf. Shifting from solving a rational consumer problem to beating down an emotional consumer enemy is a great starting point to reach into the emotional need states of your consumer. For Tide, while grass stains are a problem, the judgment of a mother-in-law is far worse. Yes, drivers care about overall safety, their bigger concern is mindless other drivers that scares them into buying a Volvo.

Moment of accelerated needs

At certain moments in our consumer's life, their physical and emotional needs will accelerate, creating openness for consideration of specific products or services. Brands win by capturing consumers right at these moments when their motivation is very high, and their knowledge remains low.

What are the moments your consumer is most open and willing to engage with a brand?

- Consumers would have a heightened need to quit smoking when they have a first child, a significant health scare, or a 40th birthday.

Rare Earth Expeditions Company	Adventure Travel	Mid-life crisis escape Bucket list boomer Trying to find yourself Tough day at work
GRAY'S QuitFix	Quit Smoking	First child Major health scare New Year's Eve 40th or 50th birthday

- College students are most open to changing food habits when they go to college and see what peers eat.
- When consumers get married, they will decide what essential household brands to use.
- Between 50 and 55, vitamin consumption goes up 8-fold. Something must have accelerated their needs.

Consumer insights

Consumer insights are little secrets hidden beneath the surface, which explain the underlying behaviors, motivations, pain points, and emotions of your consumers. Your consumers may not even be able to explain the insight until you play it back to them. You want consumers to say, "Yeah, that's exactly how I feel." Brands must think of consumer insights as a potential competitive advantage, equal in importance to intellectual property.

Avoid relying too heavily on facts and data alone without any context or story. Too many marketers think that data, trends, and facts are insights. Here is a data point: "People in Brazil brush their teeth four times per day, compared to 1.7 times per day for North Americans." Do you think that is an insight? Some people do. But when you think of how little you know about this data point, you realize you need to go deeper into the context to gain an understanding.

Consumer Insights are little secrets hidden beneath the surface, that explain the underlying behaviors, motivations, pain points and emotions of your consumers.

You must start to ask more questions, by asking who, what, when, where, or asking how and even why, that's when we begin to turn the fact into an insight.

Stereotypes and clichés are dangerous. I once heard someone say, "Women over 50 are stuck in their ways, and not willing to change their routines." That is not a valid statement for many categories. Here are two examples of women over 50 making dramatic changes: a) Women take 8x more vitamins at 55, compared to 50 and b) The fastest growth for the Apple brand has been women over 50. Be careful you don't stereotype; especially when you are not in the target market, you are going after.

Common knowledge offers no competitive advantage. I hear insights all the time that are not unique secrets. For instance, "Golfers wish there was a way they could hit the ball longer and straighter" offers no competitive advantage. Everyone in the golf industry knows this. Dig deeper.

Watch out that you don't use insights just related to your product rather than about the consumer's LIFE! Too many marketers use insights like, "Whenever I get hungry, I love eating my Gray's chicken nuggets." This type of statement is too blatant to be an insight, yet people put stuff like this all the time.

How to find smart ownable insights that will engage and move consumers

Go deep to understand and explain trends lying beneath the data. Think like a therapist: Listen, observe, collect, challenge, and carefully draw conclusions you can play back to the consumer for assurance. Use the voice of the consumer, social media, to listen and use our emotional cheat sheet to draw conclusions.

Hunt through the data to draw hypothetical insights. The dictionary definition of the word insight is "seeing below the surface." Sort through every data point, including market share information, panel data, testing and tracking results, brand funnel, customer sales, etc. With each data point, keep digging until you see a data break that needs explaining. Ask yourself, "So what does that mean for the consumer?" over and over until you see the "Why it matters" come to life and explain the cause of the consumer's behavior.

Make sure it fits with your consumer's life. Try to map out a day-in-the-life, weekly life or even the life stages your consumers goes through to understand their insights and pain points. Take a holistic view of the consumer, to ensure you figure out where your brand fits in with their life. Ask questions that force you to go deeper, avoiding clichés that keep you stuck at the surface level and stop you from getting to the sincere, rich, and meaningful consumer insights.

> While PRODUCTS solve small problems we didn't know we had...
>
> ...BRANDS beat down the enemies that torment us every day.

Find something that is an inspiring connection to engage and move consumers. We need to find that magic secret, going deep below to show the consumer we get them. Insights enable brands to connect with their consumers on a deeper emotional level, showing 'we get you.'

When you do it right, smart consumer insights **get consumers to stop and listen** to your brand's promise or brand story, engage in the latest innovation and believe the consumer experiences fits perfect with their life. With a comedian, I laugh at jokes that tell me exactly what I am already thinking. It connects with me because I thought I was the only one felt that way. That's an insight!!!

| **Random Data** | **Sort Data** | **Arrange Data** | **Data-Driven Insight** |

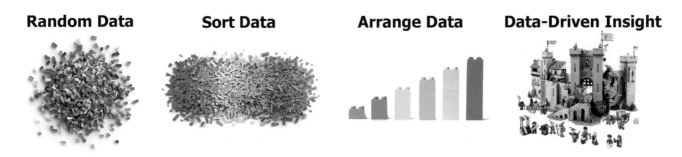

The 360-degree mining for consumer insights

Building a complete picture of your consumer by looking at multiple sources is an excellent methodology to find consumer insights. Start with market data, and then add your observations, the voice of the consumer, emotional need states, and life moments:

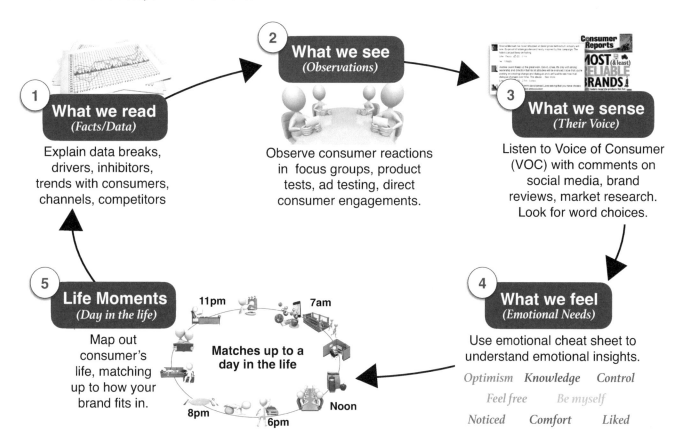

1. **What we can read:** Use available data such as market share results, tracking studies, or category trends. Look for underlying explanations of the data breaks, drivers, inhibitors, as well as new trends among consumers, channels, and competitors. Tell the story beneath the data.
2. **What we see:** Observations of consumer reactions, coming from focus groups, product tests, advertising testing, and direct consumer engagements to add to the insights. Watch how consumers respond.
3. **What we sense:** Listen to the voice of the consumer (VOC), assessing consumer comments on social media, brand reviews, and market research. Listen for specific word choices, tone, and phrases the consumer's use.

4. **What we feel:** Use observations and listening to match the emotional need states with how the use of your brand makes them feel.
5. **Day-in-the-life moments:** Map out the consumer's life with explanations of underlying behaviors, motivations, pain points, and emotions at any moment of the day or week. Conclude how parts of their life could impact their path to purchase.

Once you have completed all five areas of the 360-degree mining process, get in the consumer's shoes, observe, listen, and understand how they think, act, feel, and behave. Be empathetic to their fears, motivations, frustrations, and desires. Learn their language and use their voice. Learn the secrets that only they know, even if they cannot explain. Insights are a great way to demonstrate "We know you" because the number one reason consumers buy a brand simply that "It is a brand for me."

Case study: Consumer insights for healthy eating

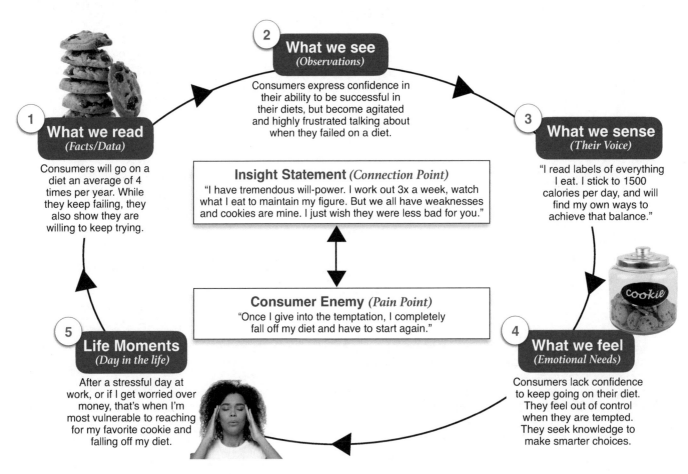

Bringing the insights for eating healthier

When I worked in the healthy foods category, it forced me to listen, observe, and go deeper.

- The **starting data point** was, "Consumers will go on a diet an average of 4 times per year. While they keep failing, they also show they are willing to keep trying." It speaks to how hard diets can be, and how many times it takes to achieve success. It shows opportunity for good tasting, healthy food options.

- Adding **observations** from focus groups, I could see how people started off highly confident about their choices. When the conversation shifted to failures, they become very agitated and showed their guilt.

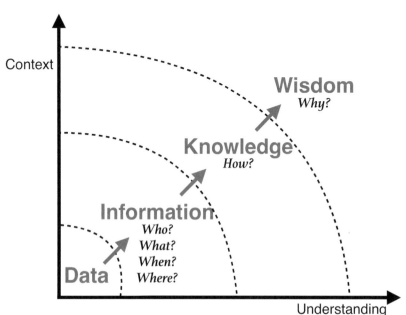

- When I **listened** further, I heard them say, "I read labels of everything I eat. I stick to 1500 calories per day, and will find my own ways to achieve that balance." This demonstrated the potential to use honest communication to provide knowledge to match their need for control.

- Using the **emotional need states**, I gravitated to the consumer's need for optimism or confidence to succeed, how they feel out of control whenever they go on a diet, and how they feel not themselves.

- Observing how quitting food temptations **fits into their lives**, I could see how they turn to unhealthy food choices to deal with stressful moments at work, money issues, or relationship issues. The unhealthy food is an escape, but causes longer term issues.

Consumer insight (connection point):
- "I have tremendous will-power. I work out 3x a week, watch what I eat to maintain my figure. But we all have weaknesses and cookies are mine. I just wish they were less bad for you."

Consumer enemy (pain point):
- "Once I give into the temptation, I completely fall off my diet and have to start again."

How to write meaningful consumer insights

Force yourself to get in the shoes of your consumer and use their voice. Every consumer insight should start with the word "I" to get into the shoes of your consumer. I like to put the consumer insight into quotes to force yourself to use their voice.

To kickstart your brainstorming, find the consumer voice with our simple tool, "I feel _____ whenever I _____" with a human truth in the first blank, and a moment in your consumer's life in the second blank.

Do you know your consumer better than your competition knows your consumer?

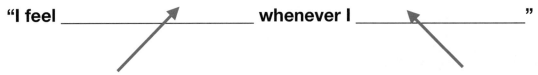

"I feel _____ whenever I _____"

A human truth based on one of:
- underlying behaviors
- motivations/inspirations
- values or beliefs
- pain points
- emotions

A moment in the target's life
- A monumental moment in their life
- Moment of strength or weakness
- Part of the day, week, year
- Celebration moment (Birthday)

Examples of consumer insights

Guilty and disappointed in myself   *Cheat with a cookie. I just wish they were less bad for you*

"I feel _____ whenever I _____"

Brands should think of consumer insights like you do intellectual property. Your knowledge of your consumer is a competitive advantage. The deeper the love a brand can build with your most cherished consumers, the more powerful and profitable that brand will be, going far beyond what the product alone could ever deliver. There is only one source of revenue; not the products you sell, but the consumers who buy them.

Consumer insights must show up at every consumer touchpoint

Knowing the secrets of your consumers can be a potent asset for your brand. The best brand communication should be like whispering an inside-joke that only you and your friend get. When the consumer insight connects, it makes consumers stop and say, "Hmmm. That's exactly how I feel. I thought I was the only one who felt like that." When portrayed with the brand's message, whether through packaging, advertising or at the purchase moment, the consumer will think the brand is made just for them.

Completing the target profile

Taking all this work, here is the consumer target profile for the Gray's Cookies brand. The remaining questions will come from your strategic brand plan.

Target	Pro-Active Preventer Cookie Lovers
Target Description	• Suburban working women, 35-40, who are willing to do whatever it takes to stay healthy. They run, workout and eat right. For many, food can be a bit of a stress-reliever and escape.
Accelerated needs	• 40th birthday, going on vacation, spring coming, new year's resolution, tighter clothing.
Their enemy	• Guilt, failure, out of control diet, temptation.
Insights that tell their story	• "I have tremendous will-power. I work out 3x a week, watch what I eat to maintain my figure. But we all have weaknesses and cookies are mine. I just wish they were less bad for you" • "I read labels of everything I eat. I stick to 1500 calories per day, and will find my own ways to achieve that balance."
What do they think now?	• I have only recently heard of Gray's Cookies. I've tried them a few times and did like them. I wouldn't say I use them all the time.
How are they buying?	• Most have been influenced by friends who have tried. Those who are buying, still do so less frequently than their normal favorite cookies. The household has yet to adopt the product. The mom uses it when she's trying to diet.
We want them to think/feel/do	• **See:** Get noticed so consumers are aware of Gray's, see it on shelf, see actual product. • **Think:** Gray's might be a healthy alternative to my favorite cookies. • **Do:** Try Grays to see if they like the great taste. • **Feel:** Feel more in control with Gray's as part of their routine, and feel less guilt. • **Whisper:** Tell their friends they love Gray's, and share the success they are having.

The consumer profile is part of our brand positioning template that is available for purchase on our website at **beloved-brands.com**

How to define your brand positioning to help your brand win

Build your brand positioning around your core strength: product, story, consumer experience, or price.

If you do not define your brand, then you run the risk of the possibility that your competitors will define your brand. And you might not like it.

I will show you the homework you must do to figure out a winning brand positioning statement. The tools are designed to help decide who your brand will serve and what you will stand for as a brand. In the last chapter, you narrowed the target to those consumers who are most capable of loving what your brand does best.

In this chapter, I will show you how to find the ideal balance between the functional and emotional benefits, to find which ones are simple, interesting, motivating, and ownable for your brand.

Where to play and where to win

Where to Win

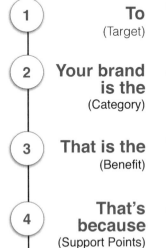

As you create your brand positioning statement, look for the ideal **space to play** and **space your brand can win.**

As I showed in the competitive brand strategy, I will use that same Venn diagram to map out everything your consumers want or need, what your brand does best and what your competitor does best.

The first step is always to find **where to play**, which matches up what your consumers want with what your brand does best. This tool forces you to focus on meeting the consumer's needs.

Next, you layer in what your competition does best, to narrow the space **where your brand can win**. Your brand might be fast, but if your competitor is even faster, then you will lose out if you try to play in that space.

Elements of the brand positioning statement

Four elements make up a brand positioning statement, including who you serve, where you play, where will you win and why consumers should believe you. These are the consumer target, marketplace definition, the consumer benefit, and support points.

1. Who is your **consumer target**? What slice of the population is the most motivated by what your brand offers? Do not just think about who you want, but rather who wants your brand.

2. Where will you play? What is the **competitive set** that defines the space in the market where your brand competes? Positioning is always relative to the other brands your brand competes against.

1   **To** (Target)

2   **Your brand is the** (Category)

3   **That is the** (Benefit)

4   **That's because** (Support Points)

- **Who is in the consumer target?** What slice of the population is the most motivated to buy what you do?

- **Where do you play?** What is the frame of reference that helps to define the space in the marketplace that you compete in?

- **Where do you win?** What promise will you make to the consumer target, thinking about main benefit (rational/emotional)

- **Why should they believe us?** What support points help to back up the main benefit?

3. Where will you win? What is the main **consumer benefit** promise you will make to the consumer target to make your brand stand out as interesting, simple, unique, motivating, and ownable? Do not talk about what you do (features); instead, talk about what the consumer gets (functional benefits), and how the consumer feels (emotional benefits).

4. Why should they believe us? Understand what **support points** and features you need to back up your main promise. These support points should close any possible doubts, questions, or concerns the consumer has after hearing your main promise.

Before you randomly write out a brand positioning statement based on your intuition, I will force you to think deeper to help focus your decisions on the best possible space for your brand to win and own.

The consumer benefits ladder

The consumer benefits ladder helps turn your brand's features into consumer benefits. Stop talking about what your brand does and start talking about what your consumer gets. The four steps to building a consumer benefits ladder:

1. Leverage all available research to define your **ideal consumer target** profile with need states, consumer insights, and the consumer enemy.

2. Brainstorm all possible brand **features**. Focus on those features you believe give your brand a competitive advantage.

3. Move up to the **functional benefits** by putting yourself in the shoes of the consumer. For each feature on your list, ask, "So, what do I get from that?" Challenge yourself to come up with better benefits by asking the question up until you move into a richer zone.

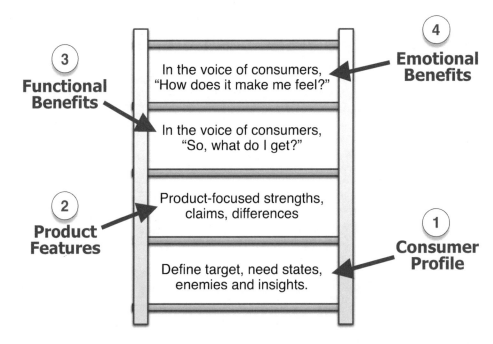

4. Then move up to the **emotional benefits**. Look at each functional benefit and ask, "So, how does that make me feel?" As you did in step 3, keep asking the question until you see a more in-depth emotional space you can win with and own.

Functional benefits cheatsheet

To help brand leaders, I have taken **twelve functional benefit zones** and expanded the list to over 50 potential functional benefits your brand can build around. Our functional benefits zones include helping consumers stay connected, making them smarter, saving money, simplifying life, helping them be healthier, helping their family, providing sensory appeal, helping their experience come to life, working better, enhancing their professional standing, driving business results, and helping execute. As you look through the list, gravitate to 2-3 of the functional benefit zones you think will fit the needs of your consumers and where your brand can do it better than competitors. Start with the words on the cheatsheet below, then layer in your creative language based on specific category words or specific consumer words and phrases they use.

In touch • On trend • Technology • Influencers • Social • **Stay Connected** • Friends / Family

Touch/Feel • Taste / Smell • Reputation • **Sensory Appeal** • Style • Subconscious • Visual identity

Rituals • Occasion • Service • **Experience comes to life** • Proactive • Variety • Responsiveness

Helping hand • **Makes you smarter** • Solutions • Updates • Learning • Advice • Skills

Track Success • Process Costs • Adds Value • **Saves you money** • Product Costs • Invest for future • Reduces time

Comfort • Moments • Education • **Helps your family** • Better Home • Life Stages

Safer • Performance • Lasts Longer • **Works better for you** • Faster • How it is made • Powerful

Reduces • Restores • Soothes • **Helps you be healthier** • Mental Health • Weight / Exercise • Prevents

Integrated • Keeps you organized • Efficient • **Simplifies your life** • Easier to use • Saves time • Hassle Free

Research • Proof Points • New methods • **Enhances professional standing** • Expert opinions • Added services

Higher Sales • Engagement • **Drives business results** • Better service • Higher profit • Fits Strategy • Delivers to end user

Brand Message • **Helps you execute** • Sales Message • Awareness • Perform better • Client experience • New products

Emotional benefits cheatsheet

From my experience, marketers are better at finding the ideal rational benefits compared with how they work at finding the ideal emotional benefits for their brands. As a brand, you want to own one emotional space in the consumer's heart as much as you own a rational space in the consumer's mind. When I push brand managers to get emotional, they struggle and opt for what they view as obvious emotions, even if they do not fit with their brand. I swear every brand manager thinks their brand should be the trusted, reliable, and likable. Use our cheat sheet to dig deeper on emotions. Our emotional cheat sheet has **twelve emotional consumer benefit zones**, which include curiosity for knowledge, control, comfortable, self-assured, sense of optimism, fit with values, feel liked, freedom, get noticed, sense of belonging, revitalized, and pride.

Informed   Competent
Curiosity for knowledge
Wisdom   Smarter

Motivated
Sense of optimism Special
Successful   Inspired

Relaxed
Nurtured   Compassion
Feel comfortable
Easy-going

Exhilarating
Excited **Feel free**
Alive
Intriguing

Cool   Trendy
Get noticed
Popular   Playful

Intimate
Friendly
Happy **Feel liked**
Like-able

Respect   Safe
Stay in control
Trust   Reliable

Honest   Beliefs
Fits with values
Purpose   Standards

Fulfilled
Feel myself **Self assured**
Confidence   Gratitude

Depend on   Affiliation
Sense of belonging
Association   Loyal

Active   Youthful
Feeling Revitalized
Anti-aging   Energized

Overcome   Honor
Sense of pride
Leadership   Accomplish

Consumer Benefits Ladder for Gray's Cookies

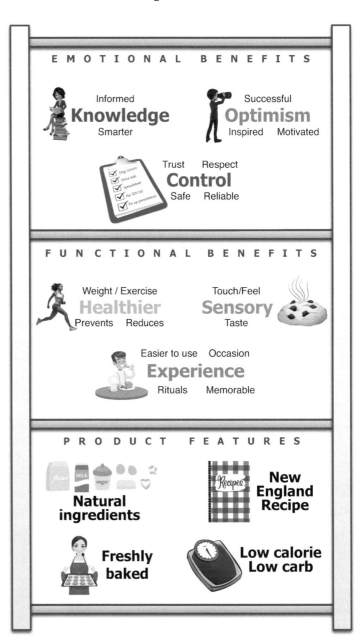

Consumers
Feel

EMOTIONAL BENEFITS

Informed
Knowledge
Smarter

Successful
Optimism
Inspired   Motivated

Trust   Respect
Control
Safe   Reliable

Consumers
Get

FUNCTIONAL BENEFITS

Weight / Exercise
Healthier
Prevents   Reduces

Touch/Feel
Sensory
Taste

Easier to use   Occasion
Experience
Rituals   Memorable

What you
Do

PRODUCT FEATURES

Natural ingredients

New England Recipe

Freshly baked

Low calorie Low carb

Build benefit statements using your benefit clusters

Start by looking at the two cheat sheets and narrow down to potential clusters of the functional and emotional benefits. Match what consumers want and what your brand does best. Take three of the zones from each cheat sheet and add a few support words per zone to create a cluster.

For each cluster, use the words to inspire a brainstorm of specific benefit statements that fit your brand, using the specific brand, consumer or category words. For our Gray's Cookies, I have chosen to build around functional clusters, such as healthy, sensory and experiences, and emotional clusters such as control, knowledge, and optimism. And, here are the best benefit statements from our brainstorm.

Benefit statement brainstorm

Emotional Clusters

Trust   Respect
Control
Safe   Reliable

Informed
Knowledge
Smarter

Inspired   Motivated
Optimism
Successful

- I feel in control of my weight and health
- I feel safer in snacking on this cookie
- I feel less guilt about an indulgence
- I like to know how many calories I eat each day
- I feel more confident in my diet and myself
- I feel knowledgeable about what I'm putting in my body.
- I will feel more motivated to be successful with this cookie
- I feel comfortable that I get more choices
- I will feel inspired to lose weight

- -

Functional Clusters

Weight / Exercise
Healthier
Prevents   Reduces

Touch/Feel
Sensory
Taste

Rituals   Occasion
Experience
Easy to use   Memorable

- I get a low calorie low fat treat.
- I get a cookie made of all natural ingredients.
- I get a great tasting cookie, as good as my current cookie
- I can replace my current favorite cookie with this one
- I get a low calorie snack to make my diet easier
- I can eat this when I'm hungry
- I will be healthier and lose weight
- I can use 5 pounds in 2 weeks.
- I will be able to reduce my daily calorie intake
- I will get the same great taste, just lower calories and fat
- I can get the same sensation I get from eating a cookie

Find the winning statements

Looking at the positioning Venn diagram we have been using, I have created a 2x2 grid to help sort through the potential benefits to find the winners, according to which are most motivating to consumers and most ownable for your brand.

You will see the same four zones from the Venn diagram are now on the consumer benefits sort grid, including the winning, losing, risky, and dumb zone.

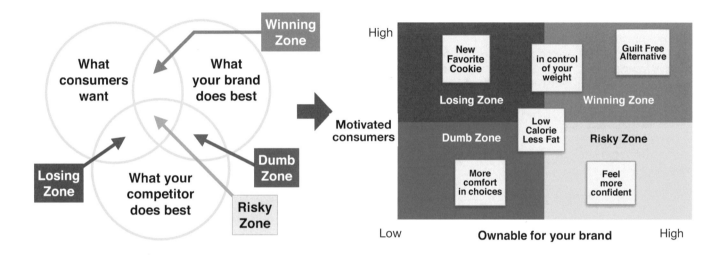

With Gray's Cookies, you can see the "guilt-free" consumer benefit is highly motivating and highly ownable for the brand, landing in the winning zone.

On the other hand, the consumer benefit of "new favorite cookie" is highly motivating but already owned by the major power players, so it falls into the losing zone. They can do it better than Gray's.

The "feel more confident" benefit falls into the risky zone, and might need re-phrasing to be more motivating for consumers. Finally, the benefit of "more comfort in choices" is neither motivating nor ownable, so it falls into the dumb zone.

Our brand positioning presentation template is available on our website at **beloved-brands.com**

Support points

I took one logic class at university, and the only thing I learned was "premise-premise conclusion." It was an easy class, but a life-long lesson that has stuck with me. Here is a classic logical argument statement:

- All fish live in water (premise)
- Tuna are fish (premise)
- Therefore, tuna live in the water (conclusion).

This example fits with my brand positioning statement model, as the main consumer benefit is the conclusion with a need for two support points as the premises. If pure logic teaches us that two premise points are good enough to draw out any conclusion, then you only need two "reasons to believe" (RTB).

Brands that build concepts with a laundry list of RTBs are not doing their job in making focused decisions on what support points are required. With consumers seeing 5,000 brand messages per day, having a long list of support points risks making their brand communications a cluttered mess. Claims can be a useful tool in helping to support your RTB, yet the RTB should never be the conclusion.

Brainstorming support using four types of claims:

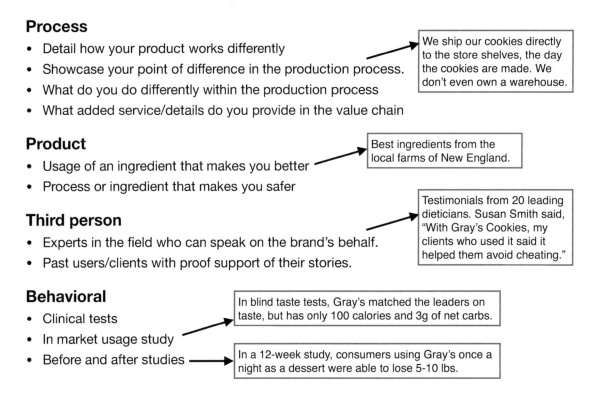

Process

- Detail how your product works differently
- Showcase your point of difference in the production process.
- What do you do differently within the production process
- What added service/details do you provide in the value chain

> We ship our cookies directly to the store shelves, the day the cookies are made. We don't even own a warehouse.

Product

- Usage of an ingredient that makes you better
- Process or ingredient that makes you safer

> Best ingredients from the local farms of New England.

Third person

- Experts in the field who can speak on the brand's behalf.
- Past users/clients with proof support of their stories.

> Testimonials from 20 leading dieticians. Susan Smith said, "With Gray's Cookies, my clients who used it said it helped them avoid cheating."

Behavioral

- Clinical tests
- In market usage study
- Before and after studies

> In blind taste tests, Gray's matched the leaders on taste, but has only 100 calories and 3g of net carbs.

> In a 12-week study, consumers using Gray's once a night as a dessert were able to lose 5-10 lbs.

Using the brand thesaurus to improve your writing

Once you have selected your functional and emotional clusters, you can create a brand thesaurus of key words that define the brand. Using our Gray's Cookies brand example, we can see the difference between the support points we come up with and then rewritten to layer the key words into to the phrase.

Brand Thesaurus

 Informed **Knowledge** Smarter

 Successful **Optimism** Inspired Motivated

 Weight / Exercise **Healthier** Prevents Reduces

 Touch/Feel **Sensory** Taste

 Trust Respect **Control** Safe Reliable

 Easier to use Occasion **Experience** Rituals Memorable

 **Natural ingredients**

 New England Recipe

 Freshly baked

 **Low calorie Low carb**

Hand this brand thesaurus to everyone who works on the brand to keep everyone aligned to the brand positioning. You will see smarter social media posts, in-store signage, and customer presentations.

Support Point		Support Point + Keywords
In blind taste tests, Gray's matched the leaders on taste, but has only 100 calories and 3g of net carbs.		Make the **informed** choice with the **knowledge** that in blind taste tests, Gray's matches the leaders on taste, but with only 100 calories and 3g of net carbs, you can **experience** a **healthier** life.
In a 12-week study, consumers using Gray's once a night as a dessert lost 5-10 pounds.	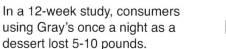	Take **control** over what goes in your body by making **smarter** choices. Studies show people who use Gray's once a night as a dessert had a extra **motivation** to lose 5-10 pounds.

The brand positioning statement

Taking all the homework, here are some thoughts on bringing the brand positioning statement together:

1. **Who is your consumer target?** Keep your target definition focused. Never go after two target markets at the same time. Bring the target to life with need states, consumer insights, and a consumer enemy.

2. **Where will you play?** Define the space you play in, measuring it against those brands you compete with.

3. **Where will you win?** Narrow your benefit down to one thing. Never try to stand for too many things at once—whether too many functional benefits or too many emotional benefits. You cannot be all things to all people. Make sure you talk benefits, not features. The ideal space must be unique and motivating to the consumers while being ownable for your brand.

4. **Why should they believe us?** The role of support points is to resolve any potential doubts the consumer might have when they see your main benefit. Ensure these support points are not just random claims or features that you want to jam into your brand message. They should support and fit with the main benefit.

Here is the final brand positioning statement for Gray's Cookies:

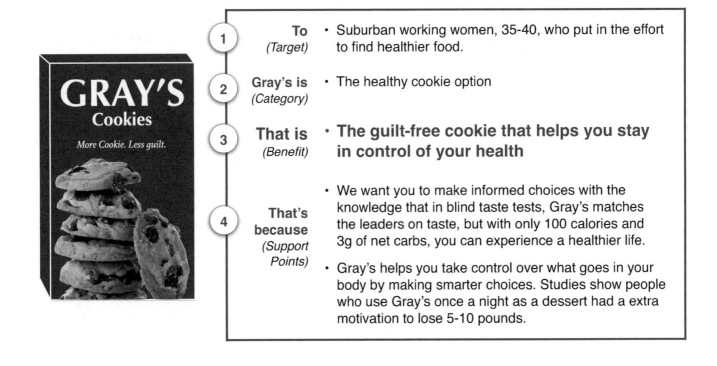

1	**To** *(Target)*	• Suburban working women, 35-40, who put in the effort to find healthier food.
2	**Gray's is** *(Category)*	• The healthy cookie option
3	**That is** *(Benefit)*	• **The guilt-free cookie that helps you stay in control of your health**
4	**That's because** *(Support Points)*	• We want you to make informed choices with the knowledge that in blind taste tests, Gray's matches the leaders on taste, but with only 100 calories and 3g of net carbs, you can experience a healthier life. • Gray's helps you take control over what goes in your body by making smarter choices. Studies show people who use Gray's once a night as a dessert had a extra motivation to lose 5-10 pounds.

GRAY'S
Cookies

More Cookie. Less guilt.

Our process works for a beer brand focused on imagery

1	**To** (Target)	• Bay Area young professionals, who take pride in their work, yet love to connect with friends. No matter where they were born, they feel lucky to call the bay area as their home.
2	**Gray's is** (Category)	• The premium craft beer
3	**That is** (Benefit)	• **The bay area secret that reminds you that you live in the most beautiful place in the world**
4	**That's because** (Support Points)	• **Gray's is only sold in northern California.** Trust me, we've turned down plenty of offers to go national. Even Southern California is too far way, and would take us away from our roots. Getting bigger could wreck everything we've created. • **Every ingredient we use comes from a 2 hour drive from where we live.** With the richness of the farmland around us in northern California, we don't need to go anywhere else.

It also works for a modern electric vehicle brand

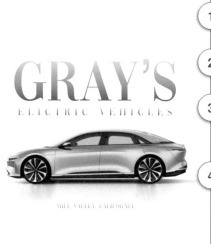

1	**To** (Target)	• Consumers who understand how their purchase choices impact our use of the planet. They believe we need collective action to make a difference.
2	**Gray's is** (Category)	• The electric vehicle
3	**That is** (Benefit)	• **Designed to make a difference to our environment, backed by a shockingly high performance**
4	**That's because** (Support Points)	• We use simple battery software structure to drive exceptionally high speed performance in our cars. And our stylish designs will stand out beyond the mainstream cars choices. • Our engines are designed like technology, sending high speed signals to drive performance. We invest in smarter technology as we move into the future.

Here's an example for a consumer healthcare brand

1	**To** *(Target)*	• Proactive preventers, 35-55, who put in the extra effort to keep their mouth healthier
2	**Gray's is** *(Category)*	• The antiseptic mouthwash
3	**That** *(Benefit)*	• **Gives you the confidence of a cleaner healthier mouth so you can prevent plaque and gingivitis.**
4	**That's because** *(Support Points)*	• When you add Gray's to your brushing routing, you can trust Gray's to get into the hard-to-reach places in your mouth and use its power to confidently kill the germs that could damage your teeth and gums. • Take control of your mouth by adding Gray's to your brushing routine, and you will see a 34% reduction in gingivitis compared to brushing alone.

Here's an example for a sporting goods retailer

1	**To** *(Target)*	• Aspiring athletes who love to play, compete, and win in sports. They are dedicated, motivated, and committed to improving their skills and achieving their goals in sports.
2	**Gray's is** *(Category)*	• The sporting goods retailer
3	**Whose** *(Benefit)*	• **team of experienced athletes will help you find the sports equipment that you need to play, compete, and win.**
4	**That's because** *(Support Points)*	• Our staff members, who are competitive athletes in the sports they cover, will inspire you to discover the best-made equipment that can elevate your performance. • Gray's fitting centers will save you time and set you up with the best sports equipment so you feel highly motivated to overcome any obstacle on the path to achieving your goals.

Brand Positioning

How to create a brand idea you can build everything around

Organize everything you do around a brand idea

With today's consumers being bombarded with 5,000 brand messages a day, the first seven seconds a consumer engages with a brand is a make-or-break moment. The brand must captivate the consumer's mind quickly, or the consumer will move on. The brand must be able to entice consumers to want to find out more, then motivate consumers to see, think, feel, or act in positive ways that benefit the brand. I will show you how to develop a brand idea that serves as your brand's seven-second sales pitch. It is essential for every brand.

What is a brand idea?

To me, the brand idea simplifies everything, not just for the consumer but for everyone working on the brand. The dictionary definition of the word "idea" means a thought, opinion, belief, or mental impression. A brand idea must be all those things. A brand must get consumers to agree on the brand reputation and get employees who work behind the scenes of the brand to agree and deliver. Let's assume they are the same thing. What we are creating is the most significant, most prominent, and yet most succinct definition of the brand. To become a successful and beloved brand, you need a brand idea that is interesting, simple, unique, inspiring, motivating, and ownable.

The brand idea apparatus

In Psychology 101, they teach the three constructs of human personality as the ego, the id, and the superego. In our brand idea apparatus, I see three separate constructs that must all work together similarly:

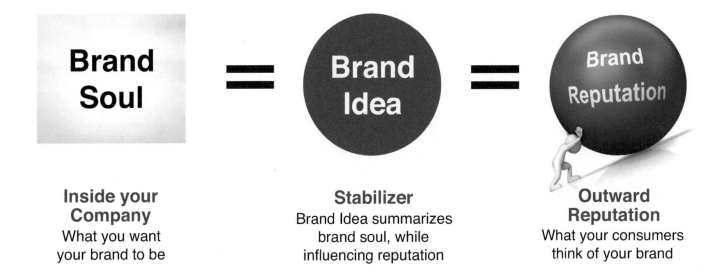

Brand Soul	=	**Brand Idea**	=	**Brand Reputation**
Inside your Company		**Stabilizer**		**Outward Reputation**
What you want your brand to be		Brand Idea summarizes brand soul, while influencing reputation		What your consumers think of your brand

1. The brand soul is a collection of the inner purpose, motivations, and values, which explains, **"What you want your brand to be."** The complexity and mess of a large organization that is filled with silos lead to conflicting opinions and motivations, making it challenging to gain alignment around one brand soul.

2. The brand reputation is the outside view of the brand, which explains, **"What consumers think of you."** Consumers own your brand's reputation in their minds. The complexity of the marketplace has conflicting messages from competitors, expert influencers, and retailers cluttering the opinion of your brand.

3. As the ego of the human mind works to regulate the id and superego, the brand idea works as the **stabilizer** between the inner motivations of those behind the brand and the outward reputation, which is a constantly changing view of the brand. As a stabilizer role, the brand idea must adjust to the actual reputation yet send signals to steer the consumer's mind towards the desired reputation, which helps to express the brand soul.

A brand is in equilibrium when the soul, reputation, and brand idea are equal

The brand idea must represent your brand soul

The brand soul defines the moral fiber for why everyone who works on the brand "wakes up each day to deliver greatness on behalf of the brand." The brand soul must be an inspiration to align the team behind a common purpose, cause, or excitement for why they do what they do. Just like the soul of a human, every brand brings a unique combination of unexplainable assets, culture, motivations, and beliefs. Support your brand purpose with a set of values and beliefs, deeply held in the heart of everyone who works behind the scenes of the brand.

Brand Soul

From the outside eye, the complexity of an organization can appear to be a complete mess. Many organizations are filled with silos of conflicts that get in the way of what the brand stands for with varying opinions on where the brand should go next. Everyone in your organization must be able to describe the brand in the same way, whether they're the most remote sales rep, the technician in the lab, the ad agency, or the CEO.

When a brand is in trouble, the first thing I ask is, "Describe the brand in seven seconds for me." When I start to hear conflicting answers or confusion, I know the team lacks alignment. If you cannot consistently describe your brand within the walls of your organization, how could you ever expect consumers to hold a consistent reputation in their minds?

When the brand does something in conflict with the brand soul, a healthy organization should resist and possibly even reject that action as outside of the cultural norms and beliefs of the brand. To accept something that goes against the brand's soul would put the culture at risk.

I have met brand leaders who would sooner fail than give up on their principles and beliefs. They say, "I don't want to sell out just to be successful." I respect their conviction because they understand themselves. A brand should be extremely personal to trigger the passion of everyone who works on the brand.

The brand idea must manage your brand reputation

The brand reputation lives within the minds of your consumers, out in the crazy, unstructured, unorganized, and cluttered real world. While a brand tries to project itself out to the market, a brand reputation meanders and adjusts to the constant changes and complexities of the marketplace.

There are constant challenges to the brand reputation, including continually changing consumer need states, conflicting voices from competitors, key influencers, or retailer partners.

The role of the brand idea works in the middle, between the brand and the consumer, acting as a stabilizer between the internal passion at the heart of the brand soul and the outward opinions of the brand reputation.

A slogan is not a brand idea

While a brand idea must be short and pithy, please do not mix it up with an advertising tagline. While I love the "Just do it" campaign for Nike, it is an advertising slogan, not a strategic brand idea.

A slogan is not a robust enough idea to help guide the R&D team to design the next Nike shoe. It will not focus HR on who to hire for Nike's retail store and it will not help create the ideal consumer experience. The strategic brand idea for Nike should be, "Nike pushes your athletic boundaries beyond what you think is possible."

Slogan

Brand Idea

At Nike, we push your athletic boundaries to inspire you to go beyond what you thought was possible.

A slogan should never drive your brand strategy. A brand idea should drive your slogan.

Examples of brand ideas

Here are **four examples** of brand ideas that get your brand down to the seven-second brand pitch. Apple is all about simplicity while Red Bull owns extreme adventures to thrive on the edge. The Starbucks brand builds moments of escape around the coffee routine. And Tesla is all about engineered for the future.

We make technology so simple, so that everyone can be part of the future.

Perfect fuel for any extreme adventure so you thrive on the edge of life

A personal moment of escape from a hectic life, between work and home.

Electric vehicle that is engineered for our future with shockingly high performance and stylish designs

What is your one word to describe your brand?

There is power in narrowing your focus down to a one-word brand pitch. Once you figure out that one word, you will never do anything that jeopardizes or goes against that one word.

Every time Apple gets complicated, they fail. Starbucks must always create comfort. No matter how tempting the opportunity, Red Bull and Tesla can never engage in anything that is boring or considered standard.

Brand idea checklist

The brand idea must be **interesting** enough to engage and entice consumers on a first encounter to want to know more. Keep it **simple** enough to gain entry into the consumer's mind. Your idea must be **easily layered** to organize everything you do to match up with the five consumer touchpoints, including the brand promise, brand story, innovation, purchase moment, and consumer experience.

Brand idea checklist

✓ Interesting enough to entice consumers on a first encounter
✓ Simple enough to gain entry into the consumer's mind
✓ Unique enough to build a reputation
✓ Able to motivate consumers to think, feel, and act
✓ inspiring employees to deliver the brand promise
✓ Easily layered to organize everything you do
✓ Ownable, so no other competitor can infringe on your space
✓ Confidently build your brand reputation over time

Your idea must be **unique** enough to build a reputation so consumers will perceive the brand as better, different, or cheaper. Your idea must be able to **motivate** consumers to think, feel, and act in ways that benefit your brand.

The idea must represent the inner brand soul of everyone who works on the brand, **inspiring** employees to deliver the brand promise and amazing experiences.

Finally, the brand idea must be **ownable** so no other competitor can infringe on your space, and you can confidently build your brand **reputation** over time.

The brand idea blueprint

I created a brand idea blueprint, which has five areas that surround the brand idea.

On the internal brand soul side, describe the products and services, as well as the cultural inspiration, which is the internal rallying cry to everyone who works on the brand. On the external brand reputation side, define the ideal consumer reputation and the reputation among necessary influencers or partners. The brand role acts as a bridge between the internal and external sides.

- **Products and services:** What is the focused point of difference your products or services can win on because they meet the consumer's needs and separate your brand from competitors?

- **Consumer reputation:** What is the desired reputation of your brand, which attracts, excites, engages, and motivates consumers to think, feel, and purchase your brand?

- **Cultural inspiration:** What is the internal rallying cry that reflects your brand's purpose, values, and motivations, and will inspire, challenge, and guide your culture?

- **Influencer reputation:** Who are the key influencers and potential partners who impact the brand? What is their view of the brand, which would make them recommend or partner with your brand?

- **Brand role (archetype):** What is the link between the internal soul and the external reputation?

Using archetypes to determine the brand role

Borrowing from the world of psychology, where they use personality archetypes to describe people, we can use brand archetypes to help you figure out the role of your brand, which adds to your brand idea. When a brand offers spiritual, freedom or knowledge, they fit with the explorer, sage, or innocent archetypes. Brands delivering stability, structure, and control fit with the ruler, creator, or caregiver. Brands that take risks create an impact or reach for achievement; they fit with the hero, rebel, or magician. Then, brands that focus on belonging or connections, they may look to the everyman, lover, or jester.

- **Creator:** The artist and dreamers, who are imaginative, expressive, and innovative. They believe they can see a better future.
- **Ruler:** The industry leader, who are confident, responsible, and authoritative. They promise power, control, and stability to their consumers.
- **Caregiver:** The helping hand, who is selfless, empathetic and nurturing. They offer protection, safety, and support.
- **Everyman:** The approachable brand who is down-to-earth, dependable, and honest. They offer a sense of belonging and comfort.
- **Jester:** The carefree brand who is joyful, carefree, and unusual. They give consumers permission to have fun and be happy.
- **Lover:** The idealistic dreamer who is passionate, magnetic and committed. They exude passion and create desire with their consumers.

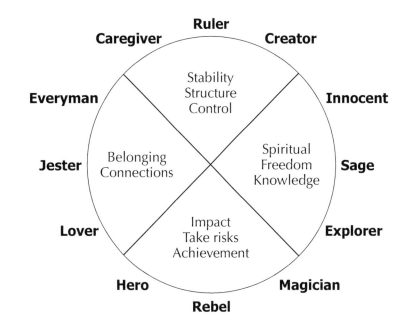

- **Innocent:** The romantic dreamer brands, who are optimistic, wholesome, and pure. They want a safer and more beautiful world.
- **Sage:** Trusted advisor and teacher, which is wise, articulate, and open-minded. They promise wisdom, wanting to help their followers.
- **Explorer:** The self-discovery , which is worldly, independent, and purpose-driven. They promise freedom, innovation, and experiences.
- **Magician:** The visionary brand which is unrelenting, driven, and charismatic. They offer transformative knowledge and new experiences.
- **Rebel:** The anti-establishment brand, which is unconventional, defiant, and free-spirited. You offer the promise of a disruptive revolution.
- **Hero:** The winner brand, which is determined, skillful, and selfless. They fight off the enemy with the promise of triumph and success.

How to find your brand idea

Step 1: Keywords brainstorm for each of the five areas

With a cross-functional team working on the brand, start with a brainstorm of keywords for each of the five areas around the brand idea. Expose the team to the work you have done on the brand positioning statement, including details on the target profile, consumer benefits ladder work, and the consumer benefits sort. Ask participants to bring their knowledge, wisdom, and opinions from where they sit within the organization.

The first step is generating 15-20 words that describe each of the five areas.

Step 2: Turn keywords into key phrases for each of the five areas

Next, get the team to vote to narrow down the list to the best 3-5 words for each section. You will begin to see specific themes and keywords. Take those selected words and build phrases to summarize each section.

Step 1: Keywords brainstorm

Products and services
Low calorie, tasty, delicious, light tasting, low fat, low carb, controls hunger, rich flavors, creamy filling.

Consumer reputation
New, Innovative, Moms, Fresh, Different, surprisingly tasty, Low Calorie, the Diet Cookie, unknown, sugar free.

Cultural inspiration
Delicious, soft, creamy, be as good as a regular cookie, never settle on taste, healthy, low carb, sugar is evil, natural

Influencer reputation
Optimistic, excited, diet, carbs, inspiring, stay in control, knowledgeable, fitness, low calorie, sugar free, all natural.

Brand role
Enabling, supportive, knowledgeable, helping hand, controls hunger, helps indulge, pleasure

Step 2: Turn keywords into key phrases

Products and services
A delicious, low-carb, cookie that helps controls hunger.

Consumer reputation
The fresh face in the cookie aisle, known equally for health and great taste.

Cultural inspiration
Healthy doesn't have to taste bad. We will never settle for OK.

Influencer reputation
Dietitians see Grays as a healthy snack, for a low-carb diet.

Brand role
Gray's is the helping hand that allows people to control their cravings and maintain their weight.

Step 3: Summarize it all to create a brand idea

Once you have phrases for all five areas, the team should feel inspired to use their creative energy to come up with the brand idea. Find a summary statement that captures everything around the circle. Try to get a few different options for the brand idea you can test with both consumers and employees.

Brand idea example for Gray's Cookie

Products and services
A delicious, low-carb, cookie that helps controls hunger.

Consumer reputation
Fresh face in the cookie aisle, known equally for health and great taste.

The best tasting yet guilt free pleasure so you can stay in control of your weight

Cultural inspiration
Healthy doesn't have to taste bad. We will never settle for OK.

Influencer reputation
Dieticians see Grays as a healthy snack, for a low-carb diet.

Brand role
Gray's is the helping hand that allows people to control their cravings and maintain their weight.

Brand idea example for a beer brand

Products and services
Our world class brew master fully admits that he focuses more on quality than quantity. His uncompromising standard ensures only our best beers are shared with you.

Consumer reputation
It's been the drink of choice for locals since the 1980s. It's part of every major celebration and get together.

The bay area secret that has become part of every celebration

Cultural inspiration
We salute the rich farmland of northern California, sourcing all our ingredients within a 2 hour drive of where we live.

Influencer reputation
When someone moves to San Fran they are introduced to Gray's, and welcomed to the place they now call home.

Brand role
The idealistic dreamer who grew up here. We are passionate, magnetic and committed to the bay area.

How to write a brand concept

With all the homework you have done on the brand positioning and brand idea, you have everything you need to write a brand concept. Write your concept in as realistic a manner as possible, narrowing it down to one main benefit and two support points. It should be realistic enough to fit on your package, new product innovation, advertising copy, or your sales message. Too many brand leaders try to write concepts that include everything, with a long list of claims and reasons to believe. There is no value in writing a concept just to pass a test, and then find yourself unable to execute the concept in the market.

The ideal brand concept

Main headline should capture the brand Idea

Use consumer insights or enemy to captivate consumers

Use support visual to summarize concept

The promise statement brings main consumer benefit to life

Support points with two reasons to believe

Motivating call-to-action, to help prompt purchase intent

Guilt free pleasure with Gray's Cookies

Do you feel guilty when you stick your hand in the cookie jar? Wouldn't it be great if you could just sneak a cookie without worry that you have gone off your diet?

Gray's Cookies are the best tasting yet guilt free pleasure so you can stay in control of your health.

That's because Gray's is low in fat and calories, yet still tastes great. In blind taste tests, Gray's cookies matched the market leaders on taste, but has only 100 calories, with 2g of fat and 3g of sugar. In a 12-week study, consumers using Gray's once a night as a dessert lost 10 pounds.

Try Gray's Cookies and find your way to stay healthy

GRAY'S Cookies

- **Headline:** The main headline should capture the brand idea. The headline is the first thing consumers will see, and it will influence how they engage with the rest of the concept.

- **Insights:** Start every concept with a consumer insight (connection point) or consumer enemy (pain point) to captivate the consumer enough to make them stop and think, "That's exactly how I feel." Your consumers feel more engaged with your concept. The enemy or insight must also set up the brand promise.

- **Promise:** The promise statement must bring the main consumer benefit to life with a balance of emotional and functional benefits. For Gray's, I combined the "great taste" functional benefit and "stay in control" emotional benefit into a main brand promise statement.

- **Support points:** The support points should close off any gaps that consumers may have after reading the main benefit. An emotional benefit may require functional support to cover off any lingering doubt.

- **Call-to-action:** Complete the concept with a motivating call-to-action to prompt the consumer's purchase intent, which is a significant part of concept testing. Adding a supporting visual is recommended.

You can use our concept process to test new product ideas

At the early stages of your innovation process, I recommend turning the best ideas into product concepts that you can use to get feedback from consumers. Below, you can see two different innovations. The first is for a simple new format for a 2-pack, while the second idea for a brand stretch into launching Gray's ice cream. Both use the same concept elements—idea, insight, benefit, support, call to action and a visual.

Different Format

New guilt-free Gray's Cookies on the go

Do you feel guilty when you are stuck at work without something healthy? Wouldn't it be great if you could just sneak a cookie without worry of going off your diet?

Gray's 2 pack cookies allow you the best tasting yet guilt free pleasure anywhere, anytime.

That's because Gray's is low in fat and calories, yet still tastes great. In blind taste tests, Gray's cookies matched the market leaders on taste, but has only 100 calories, with 2g of fat and 3g of sugar. In a 12-week study, consumers using Gray's once a night as a dessert lost 10 pounds.

Try Gray's 2-pack cookies and find your way to stay healthy

Brand Stretching

New guilt-free ice cream from Gray's

Do you feel guilty when you grab some ice cream after dinner? Wouldn't it be great if you could just relax with ice cream without worry that you have gone off your diet?

Gray's Protein Ice Cream is the best tasting yet guilt free pleasure so you can stay in control of your health.

That's because Gray's is low in fat and calories, yet still tastes great. In blind taste tests, Gray's protein ice cream matched the market leaders on taste, but has only 100 calories, with 2g of fat and 3g of sugar. In a 12-week study, consumers using Gray's once a night as a dessert lost 10 pounds.

Try Gray's Ice Cream and find your way to stay healthy

Use your brand idea to organize everything you do

The brand idea should steer everyone who works behind the scenes of the brand.

Brand leaders must manage the consistent delivery of the brand idea over every consumer touchpoint. Whether people are in management, customer service, sales, HR, operations, or an outside agency, everyone should be looking to the brand idea to guide and focus their decisions.

With old-school marketing, the brand would advertise on TV to drive awareness and interest, use bright, bold packaging in store with reinforced messages to close the sale. If the product satisfied consumers' needs, they would repeat and build the brand into their day-to-day routines.

Today's market is a cluttered mess. The consumer is bombarded with brand messages all day, and inundated with more information from influencers, friends, experts, critics, and competitors. While the internet makes shopping easier, consumers must now filter out tons of information daily. Moreover, the consumer's shopping patterns have gone from a simple, linear purchase pattern into complex, cluttered chaos.

There are **five main touchpoints** that reach consumers, including the brand promise, brand story, innovation, purchase moment, and consumer experience. Regardless of the order, they reach the consumer; if the brand does not deliver a consistent message, the consumer will be confused and likely shut out that brand. While brands cannot control what order each touchpoint reaches the consumer, they can undoubtedly align each of those touchpoints under the brand idea.

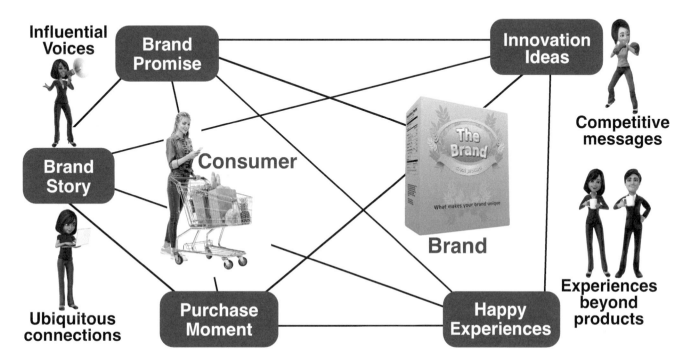

How the brand idea stretches across the five consumer touchpoints

- **Brand promise:** Use the brand idea to inspire a simple brand promise that separates your brand from competitors, and projects your brand as better, different, or cheaper, based on your brand positioning.

- **Brand story:** The brand story must come to life to motivate consumers to think, feel, or act while establishing the ideal brand's reputation to be held in the minds and hearts of the consumer. The brand story should align all brand communications across all media options.

- **Innovation:** Build a fundamentally sound product, staying at the forefront of trends and technology to deliver innovation. Steer the product development teams to ensure they remain true to the brand idea.

- **Purchase moment:** The brand idea must move consumers along the purchase journey to the final purchase decision. The brand idea helps steer the sales team and sets up retail channels to close the sale.

- **Consumer experience:** Turn usage into a consumer experience that becomes a ritual and favorite part of the consumer's day. The brand idea guides everyone who works on the brand to deliver great experiences.

Example of the brand idea map for Gray's Cookies

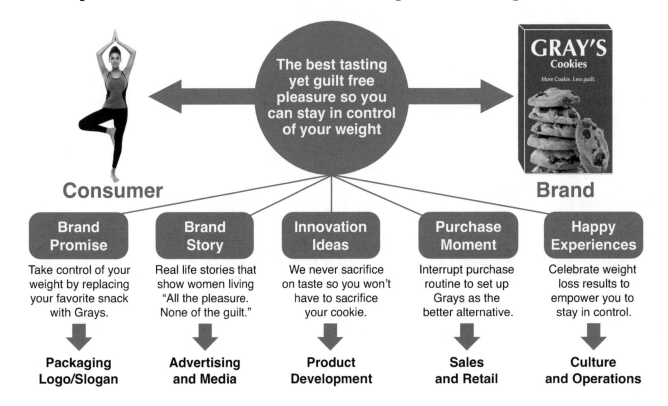

The best tasting yet guilt free pleasure so you can stay in control of your weight

Consumer

Brand

GRAY'S Cookies — *More Cookie. Less guilt.*

Brand Promise	Brand Story	Innovation Ideas	Purchase Moment	Happy Experiences
Take control of your weight by replacing your favorite snack with Grays.	Real life stories that show women living "All the pleasure. None of the guilt."	We never sacrifice on taste so you won't have to sacrifice your cookie.	Interrupt purchase routine to set up Grays as the better alternative.	Celebrate weight loss results to empower you to stay in control.
Packaging Logo/Slogan	Advertising and Media	Product Development	Sales and Retail	Culture and Operations

Marketing your brand to employees inside your own company

The best brands consistently deliver. When you build your brand idea, I recommend you use a cross-functional team, including salespeople, R&D, human resources, finance, and operations.

Use your internal brand communications tools to drive a shared definition of the brand idea, as well as getting everyone to articulate how their role delivers that brand idea. Give the external and internal brand story equal importance to the consumer experience you create for your brand. Everyone who works on the brand should use the brand idea as inspiration, and to guide decisions and activities across every function of your organization. It is the people within the brand organization who will deliver the brand idea to the consumer. Everyone needs a shared understanding of and talking points for the brand.

When you work on a brand that leads to the customer experience, your operations people will be responsible for the face-to-face delivery of your brand to the consumer. Develop a list of service values, behaviors, and processes to deliver the brand idea throughout your organization.

Case study: Impeccable service separates Ritz-Carlton

Ritz-Carlton does a lot of things right to earn the high prices they can charge for the best locations, beautiful rooms, excellent beds, and incredible meals. In reality, every luxury hotel has beautiful, luxurious things to offer. Ritz-Carlton focuses its attention on delivering impeccable service standards to separate the brand from other hotels. What Ritz-Carlton has done so well is operationalize it so that culture and brand are one.

One idea Ritz-Carlton talks about is meeting the "unexpressed" needs of guests. As marketers, even with mounds of research, we still struggle to figure out what our consumers want.

However, Ritz-Carlton has created a culture where bartenders, bellhops, and front-desk clerks instinctively meet these "unexpressed needs." Employees carry around notepads and record the expressed and unexpressed needs of every guest, then they use their instincts to try to surprise and delight these guests.

Employees are fully empowered to create unique, memorable and personal experiences for guests. Unique means doing something that helps to separate Ritz-Carlton from other hotels. To be memorable, the staff to do something that truly stands out. Moreover, personal is defined as people doing things for other people. Is that not what marketers should be doing? So what is getting in your way?

Ritz-Carlton bakes service values right into its culture. The Ritz-Carlton phrase used with its staff is "Keep your radar on and your antenna up" so everyone can look for the unexpressed needs of their guests. These could be small wins that delight consumers in a big way to treat every guest as unique and special. Like any hotel, things do go wrong.

When a problem does arise, the staff is encouraged to quickly brainstorm and use everyone's input to turn a problem into a potential "wow" moment for their guests. Every staff member is empowered to deliver high service levels; each employee is allowed to spend up to $2,000 to solve a customer issue, right on the spot. They do not even need permission from a manager.

Here is a fantastic story that makes its way around the Ritz-Carlton world. A guest who had just left the hotel called to say that their three-year-old son had forgotten his stuffed giraffe in their room. The parents said their boy could not stop crying. The only thing these distraught parents could think of to tell their son is that the giraffe was staying on vacation a little longer. So the staff found the giraffe and overnighted it to the boy. Most luxury hotels would have done that. That was not enough for Ritz-Carlton. Knowing the story the mom had told their son about staying on a bit longer, the staff also included a photo album of the giraffe's extended stay, including sitting by the pool, getting a massage in the spa with cucumbers on his eyes, and working out on the treadmill. Imagine how the parents felt and the signal it sends to them about what to think of the Ritz-Carlton staff. This type of "wow" story has become legendary within Ritz-Carlton and is often told within the Ritz-Carlton pre-shift meetings around the world to inspire staff to deliver.

Using your brand idea to build a brand credo document

Having spent time at Johnson & Johnson, I was lucky to see how their credo document has become an essential part of the culture of the organization. Not only does it permeate throughout the company, but you will also likely hear it quoted in meetings daily. It is a beautifully written document and ahead of its time.

GRAY'S Cookies

Our Brand Credo

At Gray's Cookies, we help people make healthy food choices, so they can stop feeling guilty about having a cookie.

Turn brand idea into an inspiring promise statement

We believe healthy can taste great. We believe our Gray's Cookies can have the taste, popularity and cravings of any cookie you have ever had. Yet, it is perfect for the modern world, as it is made to be low in fat and low in calories.

Use brand's point of difference to outline expectations

We do our homework on health, with great tasting cookies backed by science. We use blind taste tests to show Gray's matches the market leaders on taste. At Gray's Cookies, we the best tasting food starts with all natural ingredients. Our kitchens need to work tirelessly to ensure our cookies taste incredible, so they become our consumer's favorite snacks.

Connect with the people who work on brand by tapping into their personal motivation with your purpose, values and core beliefs

Healthy can taste great

You should have all the material you need to create a brand credo document.

- Start with your **brand idea** and turn it into an inspiring **promise statement**, which explains to your people how they can positively impact your customers.
- Use your brand's core point of difference to outline the **expectations** of how everyone can support and deliver the point of difference. A great exercise is to get every department to articulate its role in delivering the brand idea.
- Connect with your people by tapping into the **personal motivation** for what they can do to support your brand purpose, brand values, and core beliefs. Make it very personal.

Translate your brand idea into a brand story

You can extrapolate all the work you have done so far into a brand story, which explains, "who you are."

- Turn your brand idea into an inspiring promise statement you will deliver.
- Match brand purpose to consumer insights showing why it matters. This thinking makes it highly personal, explains the story behind why you do what you do. This part of the story will connect with consumers.
- Use your brand's core belief to connect with consumers and demonstrate what you do to support that belief.
- Talk about what makes your brand different and what claims you have to support your difference.
- Outline the ways you want to connect with your consumer and the promise you will make to them.

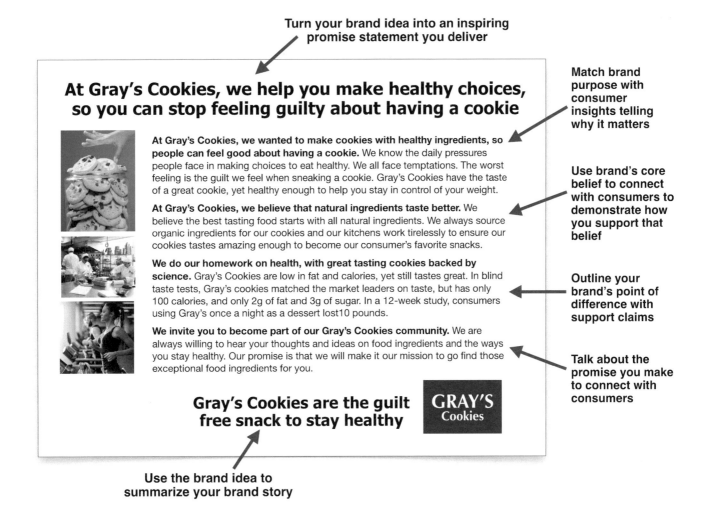

Turn your brand idea into an inspiring promise statement you deliver

At Gray's Cookies, we help you make healthy choices, so you can stop feeling guilty about having a cookie

Match brand purpose with consumer insights telling why it matters

At Gray's Cookies, we wanted to make cookies with healthy ingredients, so people can feel good about having a cookie. We know the daily pressures people face in making choices to eat healthy. We all face temptations. The worst feeling is the guilt we feel when sneaking a cookie. Gray's Cookies have the taste of a great cookie, yet healthy enough to help you stay in control of your weight.

At Gray's Cookies, we believe that natural ingredients taste better. We believe the best tasting food starts with all natural ingredients. We always source organic ingredients for our cookies and our kitchens work tirelessly to ensure our cookies tastes amazing enough to become our consumer's favorite snacks.

Use brand's core belief to connect with consumers to demonstrate how you support that belief

We do our homework on health, with great tasting cookies backed by science. Gray's Cookies are low in fat and calories, yet still tastes great. In blind taste tests, Gray's cookies matched the market leaders on taste, but has only 100 calories, and only 2g of fat and 3g of sugar. In a 12-week study, consumers using Gray's once a night as a dessert lost10 pounds.

Outline your brand's point of difference with support claims

We invite you to become part of our Gray's Cookies community. We are always willing to hear your thoughts and ideas on food ingredients and the ways you stay healthy. Our promise is that we will make it our mission to go find those exceptional food ingredients for you.

Talk about the promise you make to connect with consumers

Gray's Cookies are the guilt free snack to stay healthy

GRAY'S Cookies

Use the brand idea to summarize your brand story

Summarizing the brand with a Brand Key model

The Brand Key model allows marketers to lay out all elements of their brand on one page, including the target, competition, functional benefits, emotional benefits, values, brand idea, discriminator and RTB support points.

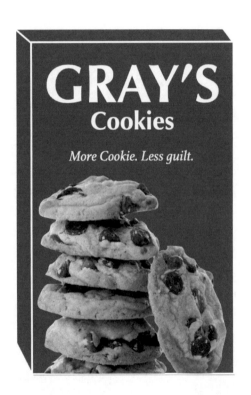

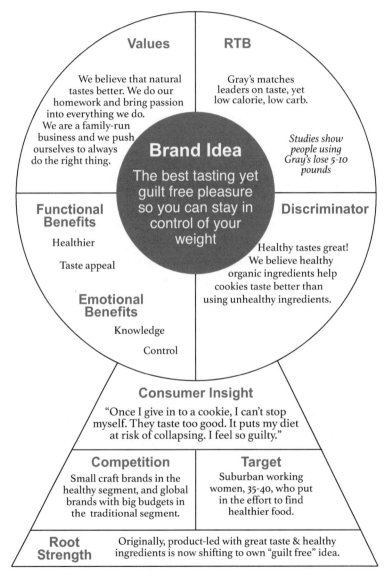

Values

We believe that natural tastes better. We do our homework and bring passion into everything we do. We are a family-run business and we push ourselves to always do the right thing.

RTB

Gray's matches leaders on taste, yet low calorie, low carb.

Studies show people using Gray's lose 5-10 pounds

Brand Idea
The best tasting yet guilt free pleasure so you can stay in control of your weight

Functional Benefits

Healthier

Taste appeal

Discriminator

Healthy tastes great! We believe healthy organic ingredients help cookies taste better than using unhealthy ingredients.

Emotional Benefits

Knowledge

Control

Consumer Insight

"Once I give in to a cookie, I can't stop myself. They taste too good. It puts my diet at risk of collapsing. I feel so guilty."

Competition

Small craft brands in the healthy segment, and global brands with big budgets in the traditional segment.

Target

Suburban working women, 35-40, who put in the effort to find healthier food.

Root Strength

Originally, product-led with great taste & healthy ingredients is now shifting to own "guilt free" idea.

The hub-and-spoke brand management system

Brand management was built on a hub-and-spoke system, with the brand manager expected to sit right in the middle of the organization, helping drive everything and everyone around the brand. However, it is the brand idea that lies at the center with everyone connected to the brand expected to understand and deliver the idea.

Our brand positioning presentation template

Looking at all the brand positioning tools we have introduced throughout our book, below is an ideal process for how to lay out the slides to create your ideal presentation, whether to sell-in your positioning ideas to management, or setup for your brand book. Our brand positioning templates are available to purchase at **beloved-brands.com**

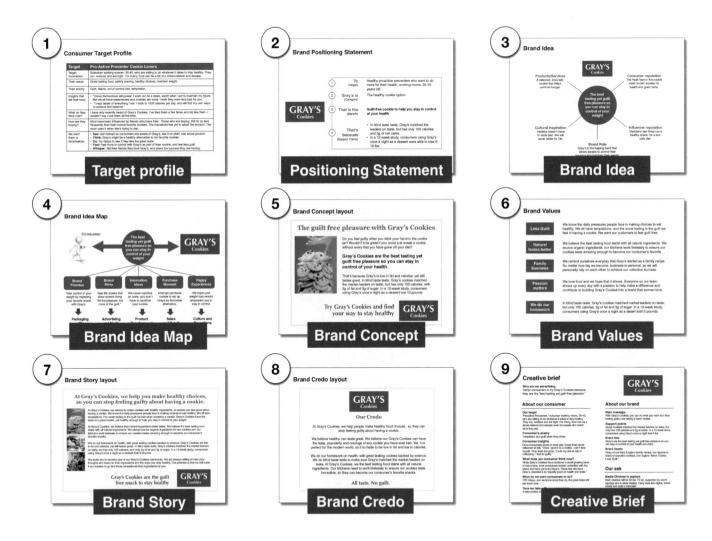

Case study: How Apple builds everything behind the "simplicity" brand idea

The brand idea for Apple is "making technology so simple that everyone can be part of the future." Apple takes a consumer-first mentality, as they transform leading technology advancements into "consumer-accessible" technology, helping fuel the perception among the mass audience that Apple is an innovative leader.

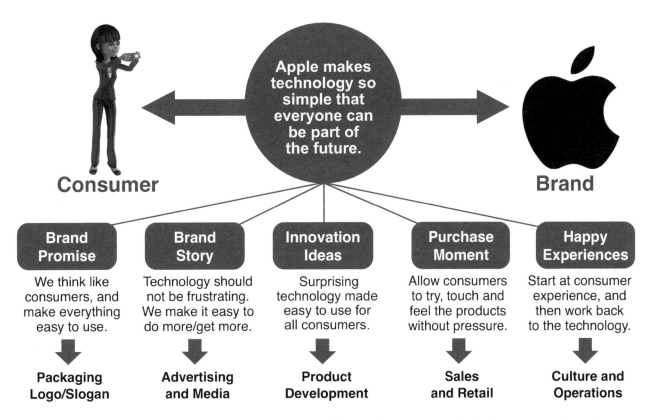

Apple has done a great job in taking that brand idea and stretching it across their brand story through advertising, and their innovation plan (as they have entered many new technology categories). Apple has also used their brand idea to guide how they manage the purchase moment (to make sure their retail outlets are easy for consumers), and how they create happy experiences for consumers.

When they don't nail the ideal consumer experience, they go out of their way to help out. They also have a genius bar and on-site lessons, which help increase the knowledge of consumers.

Apple's advertising has delivered "simplicity" since the 1970s

Apple's advertising has been relatively consistent for over 40 years and incredibly connected with consumers. The early print ads of the 1970s talked about how we designed the computer, so you don't have to worry about the details.

The "1984" TV ads for the Mackintosh launch spoke about the freedom from machines. Although the message was a little ahead of its time, it fit with simplicity.

The brilliance of the side-by-side "Mac versus PC" TV ads epitomized the brand idea by making the PC seem overly complicated and frustrating while setting up the Mac as the simple alternative.

Apple builds product innovation around simplicity

Apple has taken many failed technology ideas like online music, tablets, or mp3 players, and turned them into consumer-friendly platforms such as iTunes, iPads, and iPods. With each new product, Apple uses launch hype to generate excitement to spark the enthusiasm of the early adopters who spread the word. Also, Apple has successfully taken its cherished brand fans into new categories.

Apple makes it simple to purchase Apple products including its own retail store experience

Apple uses simplicity to manage the purchase moment through its retail stores, making sure the experience is simple and straightforward. All staff carry a credit card machine and complete the transaction very quickly. No lines or cash registers. Simplicity shines through the store layout, with the genius bar for one-on-one tech questions and support and the training area to teach classes. The brand also puts every Apple product on display to allow consumers to take them for a test drive.

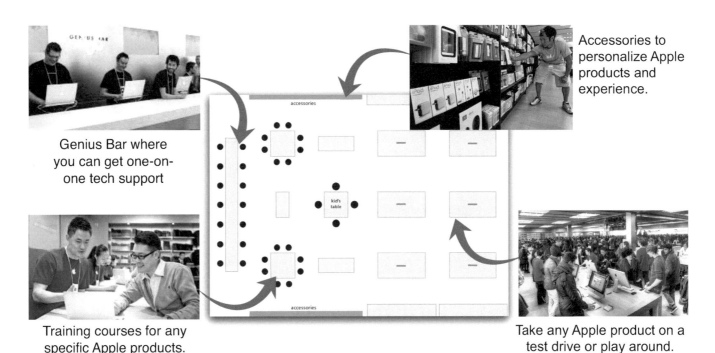

Accessories to personalize Apple products and experience.

Genius Bar where you can get one-on-one tech support

Training courses for any specific Apple products.

Take any Apple product on a test drive or play around.

Even when Apple products are in other stores, the brand has used its power with that retailer to create a distinct store-within-a-store concept, which replicates a similar look and experience from Apple's own retail locations.

Apple obsesses about the consumer experience

As Steve Jobs famously said, "You have to start with the customer experience and work backward to the technology." Apple even believes opening your Apple products should be like unwrapping a gift.

The brand wants the consumer to be able to use any Apple product right away rather than spending hours loading software or setting up your machine. Regarding product integration, Apple products work together, and they work the same way, which makes it very simple for consumers when they move from one Apple product to another.

Works straight out of the box. No setup needed.

Fully integrated Apple Care Support.

Integration helps Apple products work together and work the same.

Apple allows everyone (from kids to seniors) to experience computers.

Apple must attack the viruses to their brand idea

While the brand idea guides everyone to deliver, it should also expose when you do not deliver. Every time Apple fails to deliver simplicity, it eats away at that brand reputation, like a virus attacking their brand idea.

For instance, when there are way too many damn dongles for the Macs, when Apple was caught slowing down the battery on the iPhones to encourage people to trade up to newer model iPhones, as it has become insanely difficult to book timely appointments with their Genius Bar, or when Apple removed the headphone jacks on their phones to force consumers to wireless Beats headphones, you are frustrating those consumers who bought into Apple because of the idea of simplicity.

To stay as beloved, Apple must attack these viruses and fix everything that gets in the way of delivering simplicity, or they risk damaging their relationship with their most cherished consumers.

Brand Plans

How to build a brand plan everyone can follow

Brand Plan Process

Have you ever noticed people who say, "We need to get everyone on the same page" rarely have anything written down on one page? The same people who use the term "fewer bigger bets" are fans of little projects that deplete resources.

People say they are good decision-makers, yet struggle when faced with two distinct choices, so they creatively find a way to justify doing both options.

A brand plan is an opportunity to make decisions on how to allocate your brand's limited resources to the smartest ideas that will drive the highest return. Think of the plan as a decision-making tool to align your team with the best financial investment choices and the best decisions on how to deploy your people. The plan should then align and focus everyone who works on the brand, including the leader who writes the plan.

In this chapter, I will show you how to get your **annual brand plan** and your **five-year brand strategy roadmap** down to one page each!

Our brand plan presentation template is available for purchase on our website at **beloved-brands.com**

Start with the five questions worksheet

While it is easy to get writer's block, it can be worse when you sit at your computer staring at a blank screen with the word "Vision" staring back at you. Here are **five simple questions** to help you kickstart your first thoughts about your brand plan and decide on the big picture elements of your plan before fine-tuning and perfecting the writing. (JWT planning guide, by Stephen King)

1. Where could we be?

2. Where are we?

3. Why are we here?

4. How can we get there?

5. What do we need to do?

Your written answers will start to reveal a rough draft outline of your brand vision, analysis, key issues, strategies, and some thinking on your execution and measurement, which form the entirety of your brand plan.

When you start your brand plan, the worst thing you can do is open up a PowerPoint document and begin to type away on a blank page. You will get writer's block, or you will assemble a complete mess. Remember back to when you wrote a term paper in college. The essay was always easier to write and a much better end product when you took the time to write out a rough draft outline before you started the final document.

To start your rough outline, force yourself to write out **three bullet points** for each of the five simple questions. Make it challenging to narrow down your list to the top three points, as the extra effort now will help focus your mind on the most significant points.

Brand plan rough draft

1 **Where could we be?**
- Make Gray's a $100 Million brand by 2030.
- Be the first 'healthy cookie' to generate the craving, popularity and sales of a mainstream cookie.
- Become the dominant leader of the healthy cookie segment that is twice what it is today.

2 **Where are we?**
- Small group of early adopters have fuelled Gray's early success, creating an early loyal base of brand fans.
- Current leader of the "good for you" cookie segment, mostly against small, sleepy niche brands.
- Quite a few gaps to fix, poor performance in mass/drugs channels, no e-commerce option, usage frequency is low.

3 **Explain why we are here?**
- We have not figured out the priority choice for growth: find new users or fix the low usage frequency among loyalists.
- Low awareness and non-food distribution is holding us back from gaining share and becoming a mass brand.
- Facing a high risk of competitive launches from Nabisco or Pepperidge Farms.

4 **How can we get to your major goal?**
- Focus investment on driving awareness and trial with new category consumers to increase size of the healthy segment.
- Continue to invest in innovation that helps build a strong base of loyal, outspoken, passionate fans for Gray's
- Build a defence plan against new entrants to defend with consumers, brand reputation, and at store level.

5 **What tasks/activities do we need to do?**
- New TV ads and sampling to drive trial of the new Gray's Cookies using our "Guilt free choice" brand positioning.
- Build innovation pipeline with improved taste, wider range of flavors, convenience pack, and explore direct to consumer.
- Broader distribution using new listings, planogram recommendations and in-store specialty store merchandising team

It is very easy to get lost in the planning process. Many brand leaders will spend a few weeks writing a plan. As you solicit conflicting input from across the organization, it will add a layer of confusion to the plan you must sort through. It is easy to get lost in a mess.

I recommend you **start with the five questions** then keep coming back to this document a few times throughout the process to make sure you stay on track. These five questions keep you grounded and focused throughout the planning process. Also, as I will mention later, the flow of the plan mirrors the complexity of an orchestra, so it is important to use these five questions to see the entire plan simultaneously to ensure you keep everything flowing together.

The 5-year brand strategic roadmap

The first one-page format is for your **long-range brand plan**. Every brand should have a five-year plan to lay out the big picture elements, including brand vision, purpose, and values. It then layers in the brand idea to guide everyone on how to deliver a consistent brand across the five consumer touchpoints. The key issues lay out which obstacles lie in the way of achieving your vision and the strategies then answer those key issue questions. Keep tactics within the long-range plan as broad guideposts rather than specific programs with detailed execution.

Brand Strategy Roadmap

Vision: Be the first 'healthy cookie' to generate the craving, popularity and sales of a mainstream cookie. $100Million by 2030.

Purpose: We want to help people re-discover the lost secret that the most amazing tasting food is made of natural ingredients.

Values: Consumer first, great taste, healthy, natural ingredients, fast-to-market, family owned.

Brand Idea: Grays are the best tasting yet guilt free pleasure so you can stay in control				
Promise	**Brand Story**	**Innovation**	**Purchase Moment**	**Experience**
Take control of your weight by replacing your favorite snack with Grays.	Real life stories that show women living "All the pleasure, but none of the guilt."	We never sacrifice on taste, you won't have to sacrifice your cookie.	Interrupt purchase routine to set up Grays as the better alternative.	We hope your weight loss results empowers you to stay in control.

Goals: $100 Million brand by 2030, become a mainstream brand, increase usage, longer term penetration gains.

Issues:
1. How do we tighten the bond with our most loyal brand lovers?
2. How do we balance driving penetration and usage frequency?
3. How will we defend Gray's leadership position in the Healthy Cookie segment?
4. How do we leverage "guilt free" idea across new food categories

Strategies	Build community of Brand Lovers	Become alternative to mainstream cookies	Leader of healthy cookie segment	Explore entering new food categories
Tactics	• Social Media to connect brand lovers • Surprise and delight program to most loyal • Geographic expansion	• Drive penetration using advertising & nutritionist PR • Continue to attract new users to Gray's • New flavor launches	• Dominate every store shelf • Attack competitive entries • Leverage influence of brand lovers	• Build "guilt free" idea • Innovation focused on new segments • Early trial with brand lovers

The annual brand plan

As you transition to the annual brand plan, the vision stays the same, but the key issues and strategies become more specific to line up to the particular current situation.

Brand Plan

Brand Vision: Be first 'healthy cookie' to generate craving, popularity and sales of a mainstream cookie. $100 Million by 2030.

Analysis	Issues and Strategies	Execution Plans
P&L forecast • Sales　$30,385 • Gross Margin　$17,148 • GM %　56% • Marketing Budget　$8,850 • Contribution Margin　$6,949 • CM%　23% **Drivers** • Taste drives high conversion of Trial to Purchase • Strong Listings in Food Channels • Exceptional brand health scores among Early Adopters. Highly Beloved Brand among niche. **Inhibitors** • Low familiar yet to turn our sales into loyalty • Awareness held back due to weak Creative. • Low distribution at specialty stores. Poor coverage. • Low Purchase Frequency among most loyal. **Risks** • Launch of Mainstream cookie brands (Pepperidge Farms and Nabisco). • De-listing 2 weakest skus weakened our in-store presence • Legal challenge to taste claims **Opportunities** • R&D has 5 new flavors in development. • Sales Broker gains at Specialty Stores • Use social media to convert loyal following.	**Key Issues** 1. What's the priority choice for growth: find new users or drive usage frequency among loyalists? 2. Where should the investment/resources focus and deployment be to drive our awareness and share needs for Gray's? 3. How will we defend Gray's against the proposed Q1 2014 'healthy cookie' launches from Pepperidge Farms and Nabisco? **Strategies** 1. Continue to attract new users to Gray's 2. Focus investment on driving awareness and trial with new consumers and building a presence at retail. 3. Build defence plan against new entrants to defends with consumers and at store level. **Goals** • Increase penetration from 10% to 12%, specifically up from 15% to 20% with the core target. Monitor usage frequency among the most loyal to ensure it stays steady. • Increase awareness from 33% to 42%, specifically up from 45% to 50% within the core target. Drive trial from 15% to 20%. Close distribution from 62% to 72%. • Hold dollar share during competitive launches. Grow 11% post launch gaining up to 1.2% share. Target zero losses at shelf.	**Advertising** • Drive awareness and trial of Gray's. Target "Proactive Preventers", suburban working women, 35-40. Main Message of *"guilt-free snacking, so you can stay in control of your health."* Media uses 30/15-second TV, specialty health magazines, health event signage, digital, and social media. **Sampling** • Drive trial with in-store sampling at grocery, Costco, health food stores and event sampling at fitness, yoga, women's networking, new moms. **Distribution** • Support Q4 retail blitz with message focused on holding shelf space during the competitive launches. Q2 specialty blitz to grow distribution at key specialty stores. **Innovation** • Launch two new flavours in Q4, improved taste for 2025, convenience pack for 2026. Explore popup cookie shoppe for 2027. **Competitive Defence Plan** • Pre-launch sales blitz to close distribution gaps. At launch, TV advertising, heavy merchandising, locking up key ad dates, BOGO. print, coupons, in-store sampling. • Sales story focuses on *"any new healthy cookies should displace under-performing and declining unhealthy cookies."*

• **Analysis:** The analysis section lays out the summary from the deep-dive business review with an overview of the top three points, which envelop what is driving your brand's growth, what is inhibiting your brand's growth, which threats could hurt your brand and what opportunities your brand faces.

- **Key issues and strategies:** The key issues and strategies section focuses on the top three issues getting in the way of achieving your vision, which you should put in question format. Moreover, the strategic solutions are the answers that match up to each of those questions. Set goals to measure your brand's performance against each strategy.
- **Execution section:** The execution section maps out the specific plans for each of the chosen execution areas that aligns with the most essential consumer touchpoints.

I first came up with this **"brand plan-on a page"** format when I led a team with 15 brands. It helped me see the big picture quickly, rather than having to hunt through a big thick binder. Also, the sales team appreciated the ability to see the entire plan on one page quickly. Most salespeople also had 15 brands to manage with each of their customers. Everyone who works on the brand should receive the one-page plan and keep it close by to steer their day-to-day decisions.

Strategic timeline for your brand

As you map out the various elements of your brand plan, use these timelines as a guide. The vision, purpose, and values should have a lasting power of 5-10 years.

The key issues you face and the strategies you will invest in will have a 3-5 year time horizon. You can write detailed strategies for the upcoming year to ensure they are dealing with the situation you are facing now.

The marketing execution should have a shorter window. The communications plans should map out the investment over the next year, while new product innovation can take a 12-36 view. For Go-to-Market execution through retailers, direct sales, or e-commerce, use a quarterly focus to ensure you take advantage of the live marketplace. The shorter window keeps you flexible on pricing, merchandising, and promotions.

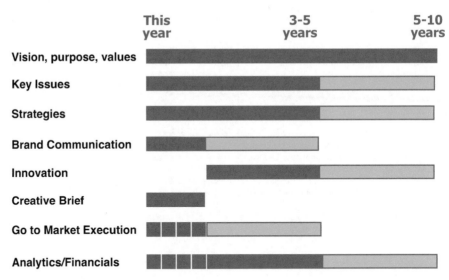

In terms of analytics and financials, you need to look at the long and short-term. I like to include a 5-10 year financial number as part of the vision. Dig in on a deep-dive business review at least once a year, and then use a condensed review as a monthly report that keeps the brand on track to delivering the plan.

Brand vision

A well-written brand vision should be the ultimate end-in-mind achievement, which answers, **"Where could we be?"** Think about significant accomplishments that would make you feel completely fulfilled. Put a stake in the ground to describe an ideal state for your future. Every smart brand plan must start with a brand vision statement. When I see brand teams who struggle, they usually lack a brand vision.

Some organizations get so fixated on achieving short-term goals; they chase every tactic in front of them just to make their numbers. Your vision should steer your entire brand plan. Choose the language and phrases within your vision that will inspire, lead, and steer your team.

> **"If you don't know where you are going, you might not get there."**
>
> — Yogi Berra

Examples of best-in-class brand vision statements

Princess Margaret Hospital
To conquer cancer in our lifetime.

Ferrari
Italian excellence that makes the world dream

Dove
A world where beauty is a source of confidence, not anxiety.

Disney
Make people happy

John F. Kennedy
"I believe that this nation should commit itself to achieving a goal, before this decade is out, of landing a man on the moon and returning him safely to earth."

Volvo
Nobody should die or be seriously injured in a Volvo.

Honda
Be the company that society wants to exist

Patagonia
Be in business to save our home planet

Ikea
Create a better everyday life for the many people.

Amazon
Be the world's most customer-centric company.

Waze
Help people work together to improve the quality of everyone's daily driving.

WWF
To reconcile the needs of human beings and the needs of others that share the Earth.

General Electric
Become #1 or #2 in every market we serve and revolutionize this company to have the speed and agility of a small enterprise.

Use these statements to inspire you as you write your own vision statement. Maybe you will see something that feels familiar to what is in your mind or at least a structure for how you would write your own vision statement.

Your vision should scare you a little and excite you a lot. You should wonder if you can achieve it and then think of how it would feel if you did. While we do not always accomplish every vision, we rarely achieve more than we thought was possible. Once you establish your vision, it sets up the key issues of your plan, including obstacles in the way of achieving your vision, which then sets up the strategies for how to reach the vision. A brand plan has to flow like an orchestra, with each element directly related to the others.

Imagine the perfect picture

To be a visionary, you must be able to visualize your future. You should be able to imagine the perfect picture of your brand in the future, to helps answer, "Where could we be?" Imagine it is five or ten years from now. You wake up in the most fantastic mood.

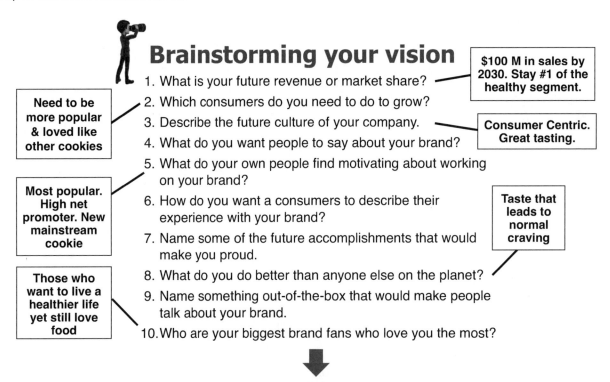

Brainstorming your vision

$100 M in sales by 2030. Stay #1 of the healthy segment.

Need to be more popular & loved like other cookies

1. What is your future revenue or market share?
2. Which consumers do you need to do to grow?
3. Describe the future culture of your company.
4. What do you want people to say about your brand?

Consumer Centric. Great tasting.

Most popular. High net promoter. New mainstream cookie

5. What do your own people find motivating about working on your brand?
6. How do you want a consumers to describe their experience with your brand?
7. Name some of the future accomplishments that would make you proud.

Taste that leads to normal craving

Those who want to live a healthier life yet still love food

8. What do you do better than anyone else on the planet?
9. Name something out-of-the-box that would make people talk about your brand.
10. Who are your biggest brand fans who love you the most?

Brand Vision:

To be the first, 'healthy cookie' to generate the craving, popularity, and sales of a mainstream cookie. Make Gray's a $100 Million by 2030.

Think about where you are in your personal life and your business life. Start to imagine an ideal state of what you want. Visualize a perfect future of what has you in such a good mood and write down the most important things you want to achieve. Here are ten questions to get you thinking about your brand vision

1. What is your future revenue or market share?
2. What consumers do you need to do to grow?
3. Describe the future culture of your company.
4. What do you want people to say about your brand?
5. What do your own people find motivating about working on your brand?
6. How do you want a consumers to describe their experience with your brand?
7. Name some of the future accomplishments that would make you proud.
8. What do you do better than anyone else on the planet?
9. Name something out-of-the-box that would make people talk about your brand.
10. Who are your biggest brand fans who love you the most?

Checklist for what makes a vision great:

✓ Your vision should last **5-10 years**.
✓ It should help you imagine the **ideal** picture of "where could we be."
✓ Describe your **dream**, describing what you see, feel, hear, think, say, and wish for your brand.
✓ It should be **emotional** to motivate all employees and partners to rally behind it.
✓ It must be **easy** to understand, in plain words, which may already be a familiar phrase within the company.
✓ A great vision is a balance between **aspiration** (stretch) and **reality** (achievement).
✓ Consider adding a **financial** (sales or profit) or share **leadership position** (#1) number.

Cautions and caveats when writing your brand vision statements:

1. A vision should not be a positioning statement.
2. Make sure you have not already achieved it.
3. Do not make strategic statements. It is not the "how."
4. Try to be single-minded. Keep tightening it. Do not include everything!
5. Focus on how to build a purpose-driven beloved brand

How to build a purpose-driven beloved brand

Finding your brand purpose answers the big question of **"Why does your brand exist?"** It should force you to explore the underlying personal and honest motivation for why you do what you do. Advertising your brand purpose has risks. We still recommend focusing on consumer benefits. The best brand purpose is the one you never have to tell your consumers, because it oozes naturally out of the culture and they feel its impact.

Ikigai (生き甲斐) is a Japanese concept that means "a reason for being." It is an intersection of what you are good at, what you love, what the world needs, and what you can be paid for. Brand purpose can be a powerful way to connect with both employees and consumers, helping define your brand soul. While our Venn diagram looks somewhat crazy at first, trust me, it works as an excellent tool for building your brand's purpose.

Brand purpose model

Our Venn diagram has four significant factors:

1. Does it fit with what **consumers** need?
2. Does it fit the **core values** of your team?
3. Does it deliver **passion** in loving what you do?
4. Can you build a beloved **business?**

Your brand purpose will come to life at the intersection that meets the consumer needs, fulfills your passion, stands behind your values, and yet still builds a successful branded business.

While the Venn diagram creates the purpose with the intersection of all four circles, you can find your own brand purpose by defining each combination of circles, one at a time, which expresses the four pillars that will deliver your brand purpose

A. Build a tight emotional bond with your most cherished consumers

- Combines consumer needs **(1)** with loving what you do **(2)**. All the passion you put into your work should focus on becoming a favorite brand of your consumers. You should love what you do and love what it does for your consumers. How your consumers react should drive your inner motivations.

B. Build your branded business around a unique, ownable, and motivating brand idea

- Combines consumer needs **(1)** with building a successful branded business **(4)**. Build a brand idea to organize everything you do to deliver a consistent brand that will move consumers through their customer journey and become a beloved, high-growth, powerful, and profitable branded business. How tight you build a bond should drive your business success.

C. Inspire a values-driven culture to provide happy consumer experiences

- Combines living the values of the team **(3)** with creating a successful branded business **(4)**. Your people are the "difference-makers" in delivering an incredible brand. They create a brand worthy of being loved to drive higher prices, lower costs, enter new markets, and create new uses. Link your people to driving the power and profits of your brand.

D. Inspirational work makes it a favorite place to work

- Combines loving what you do **(2)** with the values of the team **(3)**. Your values provide the backbone of your company, a set of beliefs and motivations linked with how people want to work. The values encourage your people to demonstrate their passion and create a culture where your people will never settle for OK when greatness is attainable. Allow people to put their personal passion into the brand; they can share in the pride of the team when the brand is successful.

Example of brand purpose for Gray's Cookies

Use the four pillars to build up the brand purpose. The final purpose statement is, *"Our purpose is to give people a cookie they will never feel guilty about eating. We believe that healthy can taste great."*

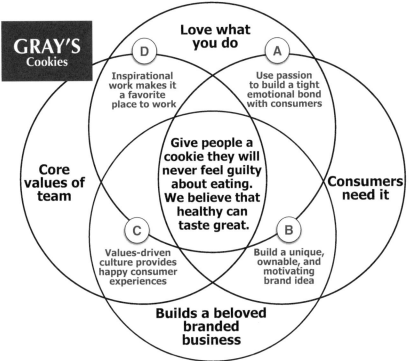

The pillars of purpose

A **Use passion to build a tight emotional bond with consumers**

Gray's are the first 'healthy cookie' to generate the craving, popularity and sales of a mainstream cookie.

B **Build a unique, ownable, and motivating brand idea**

Gray's are the best tasting yet guilt free pleasure so you can stay in control of your health.

C **Values-driven culture provides happy consumer experiences**

Gray's values are consumer first, great taste, healthy, natural ingredients, fast-to-market, and family owned.

D **Inspirational work becomes a favorite place to work**

At Gray's we give our people the confidence to shock our brand lovers with surprising new tastes every year.

Brand values

Brand values form the backbone of your organization. They may come from your **background**, how you grew up, rules you identify with or how you see your priorities in life. Your **beliefs** come from your experience, helping explain why and how you choose to do business, how you treat your people, and how you conduct yourself as a leader and as a person in the community. These beliefs should be personal, ethical, or rooted in frustration for how you see things happening in the world.

Your **inspirations** should excite the team members who work behind the scenes of the brand. Inspirations should stimulate your people to go beyond the norms of effort or passion.

Situation analysis

Before you plan where to go next, you need to understand, **"Where are we?"** A deep-dive business review should take a 360-degree view to dig into the issues related to the marketplace, consumers, competitors, channels, and the brand. Later in the book, I will go deeper into how to conduct a deep-dive business review.

For the brand plan, provide a summary of the factors driving the brand's growth, the factors inhibiting the brand's growth, the untapped opportunities, and the potential threats you see.

The **drivers** are the factors of strength or inertia, which are currently accelerating your brand's growth. These are brand assets, successful programs, favorable consumer, technology, and channel trends. Drivers also include new products, successful advertising, and performance in retail channels.

The **inhibitors** are the factors of weaknesses or friction that slow down your brand's growth. These are the "Achilles heel" of the brand, which could include unfavorable consumer trends, changes in the way people shop, competitive pressures, and even gaps compared to your competitors.

The **opportunities** are specific untapped areas in the market that could fuel future brand growth. They include unfulfilled consumer needs, new technologies on the horizon, regulation changes, competitive openings, new distribution channels, or the removal of trade barriers.

The **threats** are identifiable activities that could impact your brand's growth in the future. These include significant competitive activity, competitive technology gains, changing consumer dynamics, unfavorable distribution changes, or future potential trade barriers, which would impact your brand's growth.

While you brainstorm a long list, **narrow your focus** to the top three points for each of the four areas. As you move from the analysis to the issues, ensure you find a way to continue or enhance the drivers, while you minimize or reverse the inhibitors. You also want to build specific plans to take advantage of the opportunities and reduce or eliminate the most severe threats.

Drivers	Inhibitors
• Taste drives a high conversion of trial to purchase (65% vs. norm of 50%). • Strong listings has driven strong distribution in food channels (95%) • Exceptional brand health scores among early adopters ("Proactive Preventers") making it a highly beloved brand among the niche.	• Awareness among mainstream target (20%) held back due to weak advertising scores. Low attention scores and brand link scores. • Low distribution at specialty stores at only 16%. Poor sales coverage. • Low purchase frequency (2.2 boxes/yr vs. 7.3 norm) even among most loyal early adopters.
Opportunities	Threats
• R&D has 5 new flavors in development. Could launch Peanut Butter in Q4 of 2013 (top 15% in test), Chocolate Chips in Q2 of 2014 (top 50%) • Sales broker could specifically target specialty stores, which are in high growth (+15%/year) • Explore social media to convert strong loyal following into more mainstream mass appeal	• Mainstream cookie brands could enter the 'health' segment through R&D or acquisition. Rumors that Pepperidge Farms will launch in Q1. • De-listing of our 2 weakest skus because of POS thresholds, could weaken our in-store presence. • Legal Challenge to "tastes as good as your favorite cookie".

Strategies

The strategies in the brand plan answer, **"How can we get there?"** Each strategy must provide a clear, definitive answer to each of your key issues. When I was in business school, I had a marketing professor who would say 15 times per class, "It is all about choices. It is all about choices."

The brand plan is a great tool to force you to make **tough decisions**, as you apply your brand's limited resources of dollars, time, people, and partnerships against an unlimited number of choices. It is easy to get distracted by more and more options.

Frame your brand's key issue in question format.

How to do we build out our line up to drive purchase frequency with our loyal brand fans?

The answer to that question becomes your strategy

Build a new products pipeline **(A)** that meet the changing flavors needs of our loyal consumers (B) to delight and tighten their bond with Gray's **(C)** to drive usage frequency and higher share **(D)**.

However, brand leaders must use the brand plan process to limit their choices down to those that move your brand along the pathway towards your stated brand vision. Choose the strategic options that provide the highest return on effort (ROE) or the highest return on investment (ROI).

We showed how to come up with the right key issue questions in Chapter 2 as we used our Strategic ThinkBox to look at your brand's core strength, consumer bond, competitive dynamic and business situation. Once you have the best key issue questions, now is the time to answer them with our strategy statements.

Start with Strategy Statements

As a reminder, you should start off by writing your strategic objective statement using the four components of the **a + b + c + d model** outlined in Chapter 2 on strategic thinking:

Brand Strategy = (A) **Building Capabilities** + (B) Focused Accelerator + (C) **Market Impact** + (D) **Performance Result**

A. **Build capabilities to deliver the vision:** The investment in a capabilities to deliver the strategy including building the brand promise, brand story, purchase moment, product innovation and consumer experience. These crystal clear marching orders to the team leave no room for doubt, confusion, or hesitation. In the example above, Gray's will invest in the purchase moment by *"Build a new products pipeline"*

B. **Focused opportunity:** The breakthrough point where the brand will exert pressure to create a market impact. In the example, the identified opportunity to take advantage of is the *"that meet the changing flavors needs of our loyal consumers."*

C. **Market impact:** Achieves a specific desired market impact with a stakeholder you will attempt to move, whether it is consumers, sales channels, competitors, or influencers. In this example, the desired impact is to *"to delight and tighten their bond with Gray's."*

D. **Performance result:** Drive a specific performance result linked to the market impact, either making the brand more powerful or more profitable. In this example, *"to drive usage frequency and higher share."*

Pick your resources and apply against a capability. Look for an accelerator that is happening in the marketplace that can supercharge your investment. Choose a market impact that moves consumers along their journey, tighten the bond with consumers, or solidify the brand positioning. And, the performance result harnesses more power or profit.

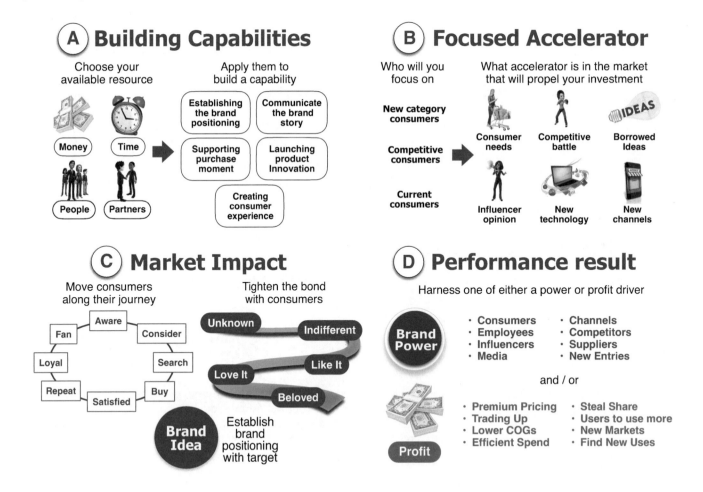

Writing your brand strategy statements

Using the cheat sheet for brand strategy statements we showed in Chapter 2, start by investing in capabilities, choose the target and focused accelerator. For the market impact, will you attract, inform, close, service or delight consumers. What do you want them to do? For performance result, choose one of four ways to get more powerful or wealthier, by pushing penetration, frequency, pricing or enter new markets.

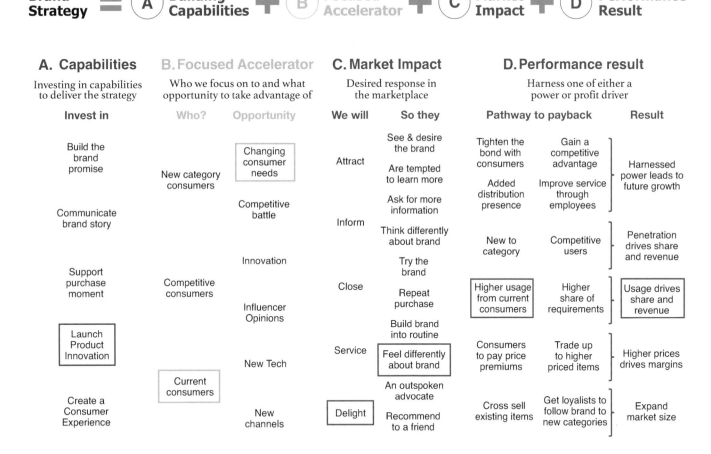

Structuring your brand strategy statement

Build a new products pipeline **(A)** that meet the changing flavors needs of our loyal consumers (B) to delight and tighten their bond with Gray's **(C)** to drive usage frequency and higher share **(D)**.

Our A + B + C + D strategy statements can run your brand

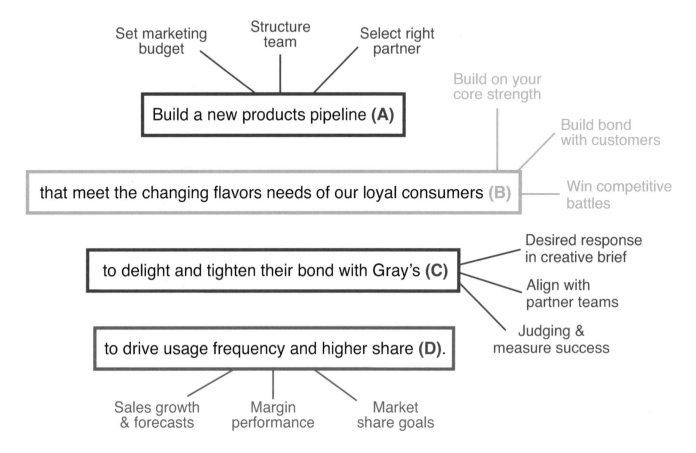

With these chunky strategy statements, you can decide on your team's budget and structure based on the skills you need and select the right execution partner. The strategy helps determine how to build on your core strength, bond with consumers, or win competitive battles.

You will have the desired response on your creative brief, you can align with your sales team, and you will know how to judge the work you see. It will help you set your sales forecast, impact your profit margins and set your market share goals.

While it takes much work to get to this strategy statement, it will pay off for you. This strategy statement will show up on each strategy page of your plan, it will be at the top of your creative brief, and it should be what you use to see if your execution delivers on the strategy.

Turn chunky strategic statements into a strategy headline

The method I use creates a very long strategic objective statement first, before writing a pithier version of the strategic statement. You will notice the wording feels quite chunky and far too long. Once you have three steadfast strategic objective statements, you can narrow them down to a headline.

Strategic Statement	Strategy Headline
Communicate Gray's new "guilt free" positioning to new consumers (a) that meet the changing needs of "proactive preventers" (b) to attract and tempt them to try Gray's (c) and drive higher market share. (d)	Drive trial by communicating Gray's "stay in control" positioning
Continue to dominate healthy cookie segment (a), owning "great tasting lowest calorie" claims (b) pointing out Nabisco's 30% higher calories (c) to help maintain Gray's loyal fan base (d).	Attack Nabisco's 'healthy' credibility by having 60% higher calories
Use a salesforce blitz to reach new retailers (a) in the convenience channels (b) to drive new purchase moments for our "on the go" consumers (c) and a higher share of requirements. (d)	Fix Gray's distribution gaps with a sales force blitz to convenience customers

How to lay out each strategy

Your effort in writing these clunky statements will not go to waste. Once you have decided on your top three strategies, you can lay out a specific slide to explain each strategy within your presentation.

- Include the chunky strategic statement (told you it would not go to waste) and the headline at the top.
- The goals measure the ideal result of this strategy. The goals should measure the ideal strategic outcome that measure market impact (awareness, trial, repeat, loyalty, share of requirements) and performance result (sales, share, costs, pricing, profit) you wanted to achieve in your strategy statement.
- List three tactical programs where you will invest your resources. These should all be guided by the strategy.
- Insert a "watch out statement" to proactively address any issue I feel could derail my presentation. The watch out statement shows you are proactively addressing the biggest pushback you could receive and answer it before being asked. This helps avoid getting a question that could derail your presentation.

Example of the ideal strategy slide

For each of your strategies, I recommend doing a separate page. You need to get senior management buy in to each strategy. In the next chapter, I will show you one-page execution plans for brand communications, innovation, and a sales plan. This allows your experts to follow the specific execution plan.

You have completed these two elements.

Market impact or performance result (C +D)

Top 3 programs where you invest

Strategy #1: Drive trial by communicating Gray's "stay in control" positioning

Strategic Objective:

- Communicate Gray's new "guilt free" positioning to new consumers that meet the changing needs of "proactive preventers" to attract and tempt them to try Gray's and drive higher market share.

Goals:

- Increase penetration from 10% to 12%, specifically up from 15% to 20% with the core target. Monitor usage frequency among the most loyal to ensure it stays steady.

Tactical Program:

- Ensure all programs target "Proactive Preventer", who is 35-40 female, works out 3x a week.
- Use "guilt free treat" message across advertising, packaging, in-store and events, which has tested as the most motivating and own-able message for Gray's.
- Recommend a balanced consumer marketing mix of advertising to drive positioning and sampling to drive trial. More details are outlined on the next strategy.

Watch out:

- At this point, we believe the product taste and consumer habits around healthy eating can help drive frequency of use.

Proactively address biggest pushback you could receive and answer it before being asked.

We offer **brand templates** you can use to run your brand. We include PowerPoint templates for strategic brand plans, marketing plans, deep-dive business reviews, brand positioning presentations, and creative briefs. For more information: **https://beloved-brands.com/brand-management-templates/**

The most common brand strategy statements

In terms of marketing communications, here's how to structure your strategy statements for communicating your brand positioning to new users, trying to drive frequency among current users, and a new product to get lapsed users to come back. Here are strategy statements about new products to current and competitive users. You can use the existing sales team or create a new sales team to reach new channels for the purchase moment. As you add in your strategies, these are just a starting point for you.

Brand Strategy = **(A) Building Capabilities** + **(B) Focused Accelerator** + **(C) Market Impact** + **(D) Performance Result**

Communicate positioning to new category users
→ Communicate Gray's new "guilt-free" positioning **(A)** to a growing "proactive preventer" consumer who is new to the category **(B)** to attract and tempt them to try Gray's **(C)** resulting in a higher market share. **(D)**

New product launch to drive usage frequency
→ Build a new products pipeline **(A)** to meet the changing flavors needs of our loyal consumers **(B)** to delight and tighten their bond with Gray's **(C)** to drive higher usage frequency and higher share. **(D)**

Use sales team to get into new channels
→ Use a salesforce blitz **(A)** to reach new retailers in the convenience channels **(B)** to drive new purchase moments for our "on the go" consumers **(C)** and a higher share of requirements. **(D)**

Communicate to current users to drive frequency
→ Advertising **(A)** to current consumers with a proactive preventers mindset **(B)** informing them of the health benefits of adding Gray's to their brushing routine **(C)** using increased frequency to gain share. **(D)**

New products or claims to steal competitive users
→ Launch milder flavours **(A)** to competitive consumers who have previously rejected Gray's intense taste **(B)** to attract and get them to try Gray's again **(C)** to drive penetration and gain market share. **(D)**

Defence plan against competitors
→ Aggressive in-store communication and BOGO promotion **(A)** to hold onto current loyal consumers during the Crest MW launch **(B)** to remind them of Gray's superiority **(C)** and hold onto market share. **(D)**

Communicate new product format to lapsed users
→ Advertise Gray's new retail pack **(A)** to lapsed brand fans who no longer frequent the downtown bars **(B)** to get them to buy Gray's for their at-home celebrations **(C)** and create additional usage points. **(D)**

New sales team to enter new channel
→ Launch a new retail sales team **(A)** to gain new retail distribution points that gets lapsed brand fans **(B)** to purchase our new retail pack **(C)** to gain a higher share of wallet and gain share. **(D)**

Writing the plan with the power of threes

I believe in **"the power of threes."** As I said earlier, your brand plan should help you make decisions on where to focus and allocate your limited resources. As a guideline, for an annual plan, I recommend you focus on the **top three strategies**, then focus on the **top three tactics for each strategy**.

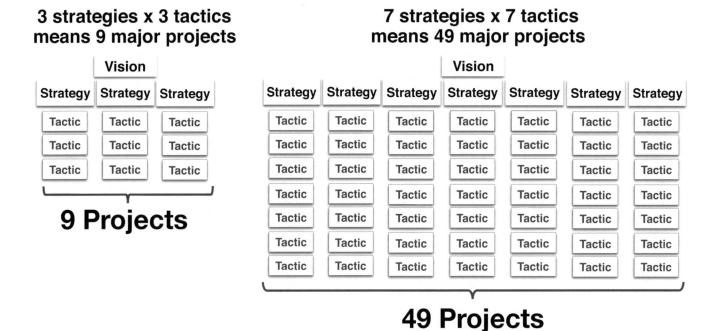

That means nine significant projects for your brand to focus your limited resources against during the year. Compare the subtle difference with what happens when you try to do five strategies with five tactics: the plan quickly explodes into 25 projects, and seven by seven leads to 49 projects. That would cripple your brand's limited resources.

What if you never get to the forty-ninth project, but it was the most important project? With fewer projects, you will be able to execute everything with full passion and brilliance.

I see too many marketers with a long list of things they need to do. They are so busy; they have no time to think about what matters to their brand. They have very little passion for any one particular project; they are trying to get everything done. This thinking is not the ideal behavior a brand needs to become a beloved brand.

Summary definitions of the brand plan

✓ **Brand Vision:** "Where could we be?" Put a stake in the ground that describes an ideal state for your future. It should last for five to 10 years to give everyone clear direction. Write your vision in a way that scares you a little and excites you a lot.

✓ **Brand Purpose:** "Why does your brand exist?" It's the underlying personal motivation for why you do what you do. The purpose is a powerful way to connect with employees and consumers, giving your brand a soul.

✓ **Values:** "What do you stand for?" Values should guide you and shape the organization's standards, beliefs, behaviors, expectations, and motivations. A brand must consistently deliver each value.

✓ **Goals:** "What will you achieve?" Specific measures include consumer behavioral changes, program metrics, in-market performance targets, financial results, or milestones on the pathway to the vision. Use goals to set up a brand dashboard or scoreboard.

✓ **Situation Analysis:** "Where are we?" Summarize the drivers and inhibitors you currently face, and the threats and untapped opportunities in the future.

✓ **Key Issues:** "Why are we here?" Look at what is getting in your way of achieving your vision. Set up the issues as questions, using strategies to answer each issue.

✓ **Strategies:** "How can we get there?" Look for market opportunities you see with consumers, competitors, or situations. Strategies provide clear marching orders that define your investment in strategic program, the focused opportunity you see, the desired market impact and performance result that benefits your business.

✓ **Tactics:** "What do we need to do?" Framed entirely by strategy, tactics turn into action plans with clear marching orders to your teams. Decide on which activities to invest in to stay on track with your vision while delivering the highest return on investment (ROI) and highest return on effort (ROE) for your business.

We offer **brand management training** *that will make your team smarter. We build their marketing skills around strategic thinking, brand positioning, brand plans, marketing execution, and brand analytics. As a result, you will see your team making smarter decisions on the brand plans and marketing execution. Find out more information on our website at* **beloved-brands.com**

Brand Plans

How to build a brand's execution plans

Build capabilities through your execution plans

Invest resources in solidifying your capabilities to deliver your strategy. The execution plan serves as an organizing tool, so everyone has specific marching orders on the particular strategy related to their functional expertise. As you cascade strategies throughout the organization, use our five consumer touchpoints to guide the capabilities you need to invest in to deliver the strategies on your brand.

Brand Promise	Brand Story	Innovation Surprise	Purchase Moment	Happy Experiences
Logos or Tag Lines	Creative Advertising	New Product Launches	Point of Purchase	Sampling and Trial
Packaging	Paid Media	Format Line Extensions	Sales Materials	Employee Behaviors
Content Strategy	Earned or Social Media	Claims	Account Management	VIP Loyalty Programs
Home Page Messages	Events & Sponsorship	R&D Exploration	E-Commerce	Active Influencers

- **Brand promise:** To deliver the brand positioning, create an execution plan related to the development of a brand book, logos, slogans, look and feel, packaging, content strategy, sponsorships, and the homepage.

- **Brand story:** To communicate your brand's story, look at creative advertising options, as well as paid, earned, shared, and owned media. Align advertising, social media, search, PR, and content management.

- **Innovation:** Use execution plans to steer the product development team on new product launches, line extensions, claims, acquisitions, partnerships, market research, and product exploration.

- **Purchase moment:** Develop execution plans with your sales team, related to specific channels, consumer promotions, coupons, pricing, trade spend, point-of-purchase merchandising, sales materials, account management, sales force deployment, customer marketing, and e-commerce.

- **Consumer experience:** Possible execution plans include the creation of service values, service behaviors, employee training, sampling, loyalty programs, events, websites, and influencer programs.

Brand communications plan

The brand communications plan answers seven questions. These questions steer and inspire the creation of the brand story work, so the brand communications work will establish your brand positioning, and motivate consumers to see, think, feel, do, or influence. The plan must answer the following questions:

1. What do we need our advertising to do? (Brand strategy statement)
2. Who is in our desired consumer target? (Most motivated people to buy what we do)
3. What are we selling? (Our main consumer benefit we stand behind)
4. Why should they believe us? (Support points to back up the main benefit)
5. What is our organizing brand idea? (Brand soul, essence or DNA for the brand)
6. What do we want people to see, think, feel, do, or influence? (Desired consumer response)
7. Where will our consumer be most receptive to see and act upon our message? (Media plan)

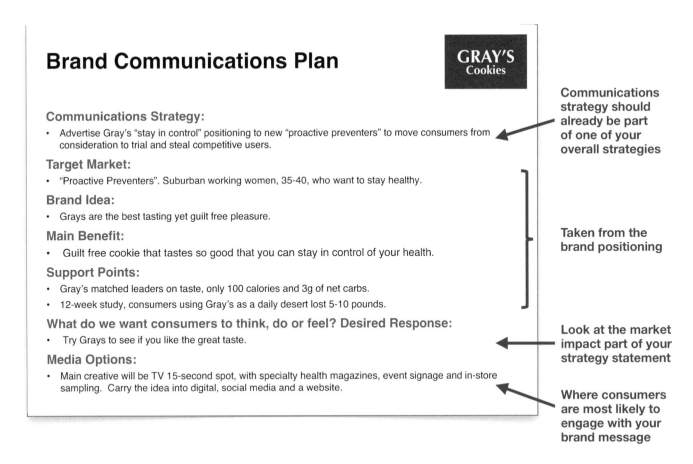

Brand Communications Plan

GRAY'S
Cookies

Communications Strategy:
- Advertise Gray's "stay in control" positioning to new "proactive preventers" to move consumers from consideration to trial and steal competitive users.

Communications strategy should already be part of one of your overall strategies

Target Market:
- "Proactive Preventers". Suburban working women, 35-40, who want to stay healthy.

Brand Idea:
- Grays are the best tasting yet guilt free pleasure.

Main Benefit:
- Guilt free cookie that tastes so good that you can stay in control of your health.

Taken from the brand positioning

Support Points:
- Gray's matched leaders on taste, only 100 calories and 3g of net carbs.
- 12-week study, consumers using Gray's as a daily desert lost 5-10 pounds.

What do we want consumers to think, do or feel? Desired Response:
- Try Grays to see if you like the great taste.

Look at the market impact part of your strategy statement

Media Options:
- Main creative will be TV 15-second spot, with specialty health magazines, event signage and in-store sampling. Carry the idea into digital, social media and a website.

Where consumers are most likely to engage with your brand message

Innovation plan

Use your brand idea to guide the product development team to manage innovation ideas at the exploratory stage, (beyond five years), pipeline ideas (two to five years) and go-to-market launch plans (within the next two years). As the brand leader, you need to influence, manage, and even direct your product development team to ensure they focus on the brand strategy.

Innovation process

Organize your brand's innovation using a **stage-gate innovation process**.

Innovation Plan

Innovation Strategy

- Leverage stage gate process to gain approvals and consumer acceptance. Continually launch new flavors, expanding the Gray's line up. Leverage 2 innovations to build the Gray's lineup around key flavor trends.

Consumer Needs

- **Target Market:** Suburban working women, 35-40, who are willing to do whatever it takes to stay healthy. They run, workout and eat right. For many, food can be a bit of a stress-reliever and escape. **Consumer Insights:** "I have tremendous will-power. I work out 3x a week, watch what I eat to maintain my figure. But we all have weaknesses and cookies are mine. I just wish they were less bad for you." **Consumer Needs:** new flavours, convenient formats, recycling.

Brand Strengths

- **Market Reputation:** Gray's is the market leader of healthy cookies, known for taste and health.
- **Manufacturing & Skills:** Long-standing recipe with access to high end ingredients, North American manufacturing.
- **Sales & Distribution:** Strong distribution at grocery; weak at drug/mass and convenience.

Brand Idea and Brand Positioning

- **Brand Idea:** Grays are the best tasting yet guilt free pleasure. **Brand Positioning Statement:** Gray's Cookies are the guilt free cookie that tastes so good that you can stay in control of your health. Gray's matched leaders on taste, only 100 calories and 3g of net carbs. And, in a 12-week study, consumers using Gray's as a daily desert lost 5-10 pounds.

Internal beacon to inspire the team

- Healthy doesn't have to taste bad. We need to make healthy, low carb cookies that never settles on taste. Continue to push the taste profile to ensure we are as good as the non-healthy cookies.

Project status:

- Launch Lemon in 2024, Carrot in 2025. Explore new formats and diet claims that will motivate consumer target and be ownable for Gray's.

The best innovation is well planned, not random hope. It is crucial to make innovation planning a core practice within your organization and embed an innovative spirit into the culture. Use a stage-gate innovation system with regular brainstorming, and consistent stages of approval, that have diligence and oversight on decisions.

Three stages of the innovation process

1. **Identify new opportunities** through continually observing and finding unmet consumer needs, market trends, and pain points, which new product ideas can solve. Use regular brainstorming to build a robust pipeline of ideas. From the best innovation ideas, develop concepts to test with consumers, measuring new ideas on uniqueness, motivation to purchase, ownability, potential size, and strategic fit with the brand. Listen to consumer feedback to optimize, adjust, or pivot the learning into new ideas.

2. **Build an innovation pipeline**, pushing the best ideas through concept refinement, using market testing and a decision process with management. Approvals include execution plan and milestones from production to launch. Drive a robust pipeline, with a balance of lower risk launches and higher risk exploratory ideas. On the next page, I introduce our Innovation checklist that allows you to capture the key decision-making factors to consider when judging whether innovation will be successful.

3. Create a **go-to-market launch plan** with project management, including name, logos, packaging, production, and channels. Build marketing support for advertising, launch presentations, and retail plans.

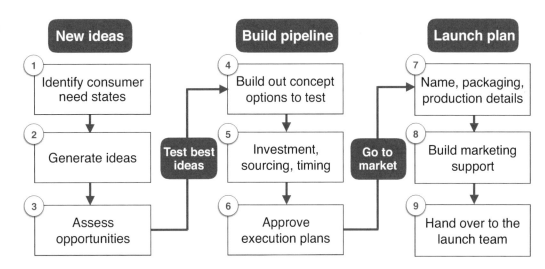

Range of Innovation

Brands have a range of innovation options starting with product extensions which are most straightforward and lowest risk, but likely lower gains. At the other extreme, blue ocean exploratory is the highest risk and challenging, but it could bring the highest gains.

- **Product extensions:** Identify new consumer needs that your brand can handle. Broaden portfolio to neutralize competitors or gain a share of shelf. Keep the brand fresh with new benefits, flavors, and sizes.

- **Product improvements:** Identify where you are losing consumers; help isolate flaws and gaps in your brand that need fixing so that your brand moves ahead or catches up to competitors.

- **New formats:** Stretch brand into new subcategories/adjacencies or parts of the value chain to get into new parts of the store, new distribution channels, or new usage occasions.

- **Brand stretching:** Take brand assets into new business opportunities—bringing loyal users and brand idea.

- **Game-changing technology:** R&D-driven invention matched up to fit the changing needs of consumers.

- **Blue ocean exploratory:** Ideas that combine your technical capabilities, matched to pure unexplored consumer need states to create game-changing launches to move into fully protected blue oceans.

Selling and retail plan

Brand leaders should work side-by-side with the sales team to manage the consumer through the purchase moment. The brand plan should guide the sales team on specific strategy and goals. Given that your sales team owns the selling execution, you must gain the sales team's alignment and buy-in on the best ways to execute your brand's strategy through direct selling, retailer management, and e-commerce options. The programs include pricing, distribution focus, shelf management, promotional spending, customer marketing, customer analytics, and specific promotional tools.

Use a **"triple win"** to find the ideal retail programs, which match up with wins for your channel customer, your shared consumer, and your brand. Marketers must understand that sales leaders work through relationships, and need to balance the strategies of their customer with the desired strategies of your brand.

Your channel customers are trying to win in their market, satisfying a base of their consumers through your brands, while battling competitors who you may also be going through that customer. Your most successful programs will provide a win for your channel customer, as you will get much more support for your program.

Selling and Retail Plan

Sales Strategy
- Use a salesforce blitz to reach new retailers in the convenience channels to drive new purchase moments for our "on the go" consumers and a higher share of requirements.

Retail Customer Needs
- Gray's needs to close distribution gaps but must maintain in-store coop/display advertising investment to drive trial. Gray's is exceptionally strong in Food, yet equally weak in specialty channels, with only 16% distribution. Weak coop/display results for Gray's is directly linked to our lower trade terms being offered.

Consumer / Shopper Needs
- **Target Market:** Suburban working women, 35-40, who are willing to do whatever it takes to stay healthy. They run, workout and eat right. For many, food can be a bit of a stress-reliever and escape. **Shopper Insights:** "I read labels of everything I eat. I stick to 1500 calories per day and will find my own ways to that balance." **Shopper Needs:** added convenience channels and displays.

Execution: Merchandising, Assortment, Pricing / Promotion and Space
- **Merchandising:** Leverage key results, planogram recos and in-store specialty merchandising team.
- **Assortment:** Drive fair share of shelf for each flavor, leverage in-store sampling for new items.
- **Pricing/Promotion:** Tie price promotions to healthy eating moments (NYE, spring, back to school)
- **Space:** Sales blitz to increase distribution at specialty stores, holding shelf space at grocery, health stores.

Specific retail programs in place
- Q2 specialty blitz to grow distribution at key specialty stores.
- Q4 retail blitz focused on holding shelf space during competitive launches.
- Gain displays for back-to-school promotional lunch program.

Work collaboratively with your sales team. The worst marketers try to ram their ideas through sales, expecting them to follow your orders. Come up with ideas together. I recommend having quarterly meetings between sales and marketing with a collaborative look at the next 3 months, next 6 months, next 9 months and next 12 months, focused on merchandising, assortment, promotions, and your brand's shelf space.

Making tactical decisions - Return on Effort (ROE)

The principles of focus mean you have to limit the execution ideas to those that will best match your brand's limited resources.

Here is a tool that will allow you to assess the potential return on effort (ROE) for possible marketing activities. I call it the "big easy" execution decision-making grid.

Take each execution plan and hold a creative brainstorm. Put each tactical idea on a Post-It note. Then plot the ideas onto the grid as to whether the idea will have a big impact versus a small impact on your business results, and whether the tactical idea will be easy to execute versus difficult to execute.

The top ideas rise to the big easy quadrant in the top-right corner. The goal of this tool is to narrow down your focus to the best three activities for each plan while eliminating those ideas that are potential resource drains. While you may not always have access to the data to find the ROI before launching a program, you should be able to use your instincts and judgment to assess ROE (return on effort).

Three-step execution planning process:

Step One: Brief all the agencies at the same time

- Take everyone who works on the brand—agencies and internal support teams—through your brand plan and each of your execution plans. Give each agency a specific budget range with a potential high, medium, and low spend level. Be clear that you will not finalize the budget until after you see all the ideas presented. This process should spark a competitive fire to help generate the best ideas to earn your highest budget level.

Step Two: Review all ideas from all the agencies at the same time

- It is essential that everyone be in the room at the same time to see everything you see. Provide open and honest feedback for each agency. The first time you use this process, you will see a collection of disjointed ideas. It will not be any different than if you held separate meetings. It will be apparent that the agencies have not worked well together. Use your feedback to focus on the best ideas. You may openly start to offer higher budgets to the ideas you like best and take money away from ideas you do not want.

- After the feedback, the agencies will see how disjointed the work looks. The reality is that it would typically be up to you to piece everything together. Encourage your agencies to work together before step three. They should start to book meetings with each other to ensure they bring a more cohesive plan to step three. The reality is that agencies do not naturally work well together. This process will force them to collaborate.

Step Three: Bring it all together

- Agencies will take your feedback and focus on the best ideas from stage two. They will come together more cohesively, and you should to see how to enhance all the ideas and fit them together into a cohesive plan.

This process makes your job as the brand leader easier on execution. Your role is to make sure everything is on strategy and aligned. By seeing all the ideas in one meeting, it will make it easier for you to begin piecing the ideas together. It also forces your agencies to work together. In the old days, the main Agency used to present creative and media at the same meeting. This process tries to replicate some of that thinking while allowing you to still tap into specialists.

Step 1
Brief all agencies at the same time

Step 2
Review ideas from agencies at same time

Step 3
Bring all ideas together into plan

Avoid misfits within your brand plan

When you write a plan, think of it like conducting an orchestra. There are a lot of moving parts and, if you do not stay organized, the plan may begin to look like many scattered thoughts. When your plan is disjointed or looks like a collection of disconnected ideas, it will confuse and meet resistance, which are counter-productive to the reason why you create a plan. A smart brand plan should have a consistent flow in the writing as you move from the vision through to execution. Like an orchestra playing in perfect harmony, everyone is playing the same song.

When you write something that does not fit, it tends to stand out like, "a tuba player playing their own song." When I managed a marketing team, I came up with this analogy and started to call plan misfits "tubas."

From my experience, senior leaders are skilled at finding "tubas," which can derail your presentation, as the debate becomes more about why the "tuba" is there and less about the bigger aspects of your plan. Go "tuba hunting" by reading through your brand plan and eliminating the "tubas" before your management finds them.

The two worst types of "tubas"

The worst "tubas" are those elements of the plan that seems to 'die a quick death' in the document or they 'come from out of nowhere' with no analytical setup.

1. A reasonable idea is presented early on and dies a quick death never to be seen again in the plan.

If, early on in your plan, you say part of your brand vision or purpose is "to be the disruptive leader in innovation," then why is there no innovation strategy, innovation process or new products for the next four years? Sure, your vision sounds catchy. However, it appears to be a misfit "tuba" with very little to do with the rest of your plan.

2. A creative tactical idea presented late in the plan seems to come out of nowhere.

If the focus of your plan for a new product launch is to drive early trial, then why is there a significant investment in your tactical execution plan to create a VIP club for high-frequency users? If there is no analytical set-up of an opportunity or strategic set-up, then a tactic that comes out of nowhere late in the plan is a "tuba." It risks causing conflict or confusion. Aligning your agencies on execution

Given most of your great work will be done through others, you need to keep everyone aligned with your brand plan yet allow the creativity from your agencies to help bring your plan to life. The **three-step process** is designed to help brand leaders find the ideal balance of the control over strategy and the freedom of execution.

As the media has fragmented over the last few years, many brands have a collection of agencies, and the ideas come to the brand leader one at a time, creating a disjointed execution mess. Your brand need cohesion among partners to get a consistent delivery of your brand to the end consumer.

Brand measurement

You have to measure what matters. A good brand plan lays out key measurements and controls, including a marketing budget, sales forecast, and a profit statement for the brand.

Your brand plan should also include a brand dashboard with goals linked to financial performance (sales, margins, profit), brand health measures (market share, awareness, trial, repeat, loyalty) and execution performance tracking (advertising, innovation).

S. M. A. R. T. Goals

Specific, measurable, achievable, relevant, and time-bound.

Goal	2015	2016	Comment
Sales	$25MM	$30MM	Continue 20% growth rate
Share	0.8%	1.2%	New triple chocolate 0.5% share
Distribution	62%	72%	Increase coming mainly from fixing specialty.
Awareness	33%	42%	Below norm, 80% among niche, < 20% overall
Trial	34%	37%	New flavors have helped drive trial
Repeat	4%	5%	High quality taste converts high repeat
Gross Margin %	55%	57%	Launching new premium line up.
Profit %	19%	15%	Increased marketing spend in year 1 of launch
Ad Brand Link	62%	70%	Building on current brand equity in TV ad
Purchase Intent	70%	70%	Should hold strong as we trade up.
Customer Satisfaction	58%	60%	Halo impact from new premium line up.
Freshness Index	12%	20%	Increasing % sales from new launches.

- **Specific:** State exactly what you want to accomplish, including who, what, where, when, and why. Focus on distinct market impact results (market share, program tracking, brand funnel data, retail performance metrics, voice of the consumer, and product rating scores) and financial business results (sales, margin, spend, and profit), as well as significant milestones that move the brand towards your stated brand vision.

- **Measurable:** How will you demonstrate and evaluate the extent to which you have met the goal? The goal is usually tracked compared with last year, competitors, category norms, or milestones towards the end goal.

- **Achievable:** Set stretch goals with the ability to achieve the outcome. Use action-oriented verbs.

- **Relevant:** Link each strategy to a specific goal, as well as a 5-10 year goal tied to your vision, which can have an annual milestone.

- **Time-bound:** Set target "by when" dates linked to significant milestones or deadlines. Break them out quarterly, annually, and over a 5-year time horizon. A brand always needs specific deadlines for major spend projects, all advertising, production schedules, in market timing, as well as all launch dates.

Our brand plan presentation template

It is easy for a brand plan presentation to get out of control, with too many slides and a lack of flow. This makes it difficult for your senior management to follow along and buy into your brand plan. Based on what we have shown throughout our book, we have created an ideal process for how to lay out the slides in an ideal presentation. This includes the tools you have seen throughout the book. Our brand plan templates are available for purchase at **beloved-brands.com**

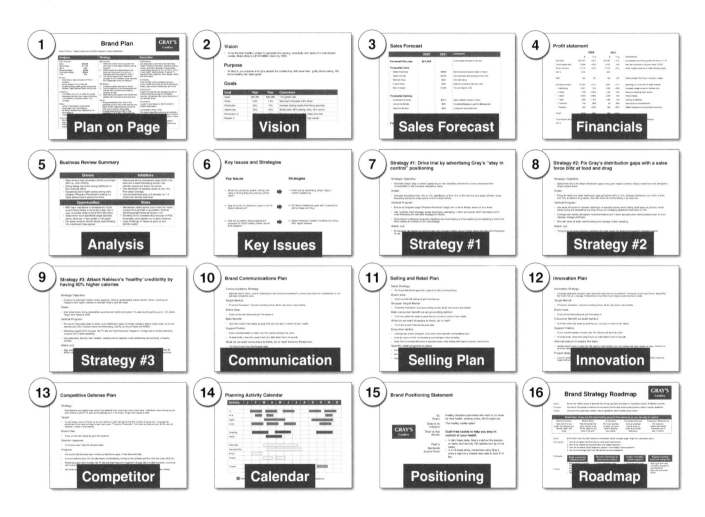

Brand Finance 101 to help manage your brand's profitability

Anyone who does not include "profit" in their definition of a brand has never run a brand before. To me, a product is a basic commodity you sell. A brand creates a bond that leads to a power and profit beyond what the product alone can achieve.

If you want to succeed in brand management, you have to understand brand finance. After all, you are running a business. If you only like the activity of marketing, then you should become a subject matter expert, because if you cannot work the finances of your brand, you will not get promoted beyond brand manager.

I will go through everything you need to know so you can manage the profitability of your brands. I will include all the essential formulas you need to know with examples to help follow along. Even if you are not a natural at finance, my hope is this chapter will help make you smarter at brand finance.

A quick dissection of the brand's financial statement

For many of us, we became marketers because we were attracted to the strategic, creative, and the psychological aspects of business. So if finance is not a natural skill, when your finance manager hands you the brand's profit and loss (P&L) statement, it can be intimidating. I come at this as a fellow marketer, not a finance expert.

To assess the performance of your brand, and begin knowing where to dig deeper, I recommend you break it down by looking at four key numbers.

1. As a leader of the brand, I start by trying to understand the growth rate. Most brand leaders have brand growth as their number one objective. You can do a quick calculation to figure out the average growth rate but, as you dig in, you should try to find out what happened each year to give you a better feel of the brand performance. There are two calculations you can use, either average growth rate or compound annual growth rate (CAGR).

In this example, the average growth rate is 7%, and CAGR % is 9.1%, both very high compared to the overall economic growth of 2-3%. My first instinct would be to look at the category growth to see if the brand is gaining or losing market share. Next, the year-by-year growth

Brand Financial Statement

	Year 3		Year 4		Year 5	
	$	g%	$	g%	$	g%
Net Sales	21,978	8%	24,616	12%	27,354	11%
Cost of Goods Sold	12,496	9%	14,754	18%	17,129	16%
Gross Margin	9,482	49%	9,862	4%	10,225	4%
GM %	43%		40%		37%	
R&D	200	3%	352	76%	352	0%
Marketing Budget	3,519	22%	4,266	21%	5,101	20%
Advertising	2,000	22%	2,000	0%	2,712	36%
Research	125	55%	60	-52%	100	67%
Packaging	133	66%	30	-77%	50	67%
Trade Expense	250	44%	1,000	300%	1,250	25%
Other SG&A	1,011	22%	1176	16%	989	-16%
Contribution Margin	5,763	22%	5,244	-9%	4,772	-9%
CM %	26%		21%		17%	

shows the growth rate has shot up to 12% and 11% over the past two years. I would make a mental note to expect to see this as an investment brand and determine whether the profit is paying off yet.

2. My eye is drawn immediately to figuring out the gross margin percentage, as a first signal of brand health or to try to understand the strategy behind the brand. Divide the absolute gross margin by the sales. You can assess the brand's health by comparing the margin percent over time to see the trend line, with other brands in your portfolio to evaluate the opportunity cost, or with other competitive brands in the category.

In this example, the gross margin percentage has fallen from 43% in Y3 down to 37% in Y5, which should prompt you to go a layer deeper to look at price and cost of goods. Regarding price, dig around to see if there has been an average price decrease, then look to see if it is due to an increase in trade spend, a shift in the sales mix to lower-priced items, or even a shift to lower margin items.

3. Next, look at the contribution margin percentage, dividing the bottom line contribution income by the overall sales. Some cost factors are outside the brand's control, such as foreign exchange, raw material cost increases, duties, and transportation costs. However, look out for factors within the brand's control. Was there a strategic decision to change to a higher cost of raw material? Was there increased quality control at the manufacturing site? Did you switch to a more expensive supplier or change the location of your production?

   In the example, an alarm bell goes off when I see the contribution margin percentage has fallen from 26% to 17% in three years. My first observation is the sales are up dramatically, yet both the gross margin percentages and contribution margin percentages are down. While the gross margin percentage is down, the gross margin dollars increased. However, in this case, the contribution margin dollars have gone down from $5,763 to $4,772. After two years of investment, the brand is not responding fast enough to cover that spend level.

4. Look at the comparison between the sales growth rate and the spending growth rate.

   While sales are growing at 12% over the past two years, spending is up 22%. The brand is not covering the spending increase. Dig in to understand if the payback was expected to be slower. If not, I would dig in to explain why it is not paying back: not the right message, competitive activity, or market dynamics.

With each of these four questions, view it as a starting point to dig in deeper and ask questions of the experts around you. From my experience, every P&L is as unique as a fingerprint. As the business leader, you run your brand's P&L.

---

1 — Start with the overall sales line, and explain year-by-year growth rates

	Year 1	Year 2	Year 3	Year 4	Year 5
Net Sales	19,483	20,383	21,978	24,616	27,354
Growth Rate		5%	8%	12%	11%

2 — Look at the Gross Margin %, by dividing the gross margin by sales

	Year 3	Year 4	Year 5
Sales	21,978	24,616	27,569
Gross Margin	9,482	9,862	10,225
Gross Margin %	43%	40%	37%

3 — Look at Contribution Margin %, dividing contribution margin by sales

	Year 3	Year 4	Year 5
Sales	21,978	24,616	27,569
Contribution Margin	5,763	5,244	4,772
Contribution Margin %	26%	21%	17%

4 — Compare the sales growth rate with the marketing spend growth rate

	Year 2	Year 3	Year 4	Year 5
Sales Growth	5%	8%	12%	11%
Spend Growth	5%	22%	21%	20%

Eight ways you can drive brand profits

1. Premium pricing
2. Trade loyal consumers up to a higher price
3. Lower cost of goods
4. Lower marketing and selling costs
5. Steal competitive users
6. Get loyal users to use more
7. Enter into new markets
8. Find new uses for the brand

Profit = (Price - Cost) x (Market Share x Market Size)*

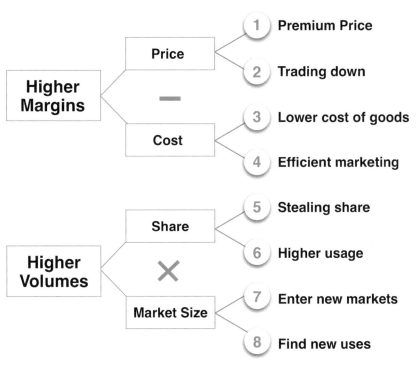

1 Premium Price	• High quality perception allows you to command a premium price
2 Trading down	• Good-better-best allows you to move loyalists up to premium versions
3 Lower cost of goods	• Economies of scale gives your brand power over suppliers
4 Efficient marketing	• Higher volume helps spend ratios. Use power over media to achieve
5 Stealing share	• Use your brand's momentum to gain tipping point on market share
6 Higher usage	• Get loyal users to use more by turning routine into rituals
7 Enter new markets	• Take brand idea and loyalists to follow into new categories
8 Find new uses	• Increase the number of ways your brand fits into consumer's life

Higher Margins: Price − Cost

Higher Volumes: Share × Market Size

177

1. How to use premium pricing

While many marketers think of price as a defensive response to counter inflation or a competitive reaction at the retail shelf, the smartest brand leaders use price as a weapon to drive brand value.

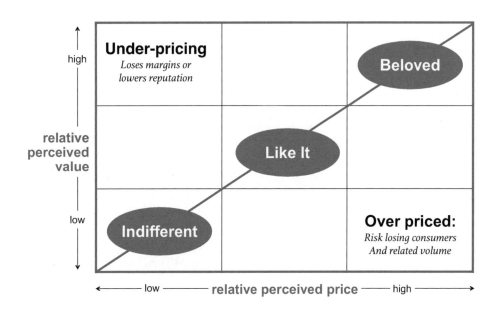

It is crucial to understand the price/quality relationship of your brand and look for ways to increase the perception of quality. When you find a unique position, which you know motivates consumers, it can differentiate you from competitors. Then you can use the motivation to tighten the bond with your consumers.

The chart shows a relatively long-term direct correlation between perceived value and price. An indifferent brand has low perceived value and will end up with a much lower price point. A beloved brand can use its emotional connection to drive perceived value and ensure the price premium is perceived as good value. For instance, consumers are undoubtedly willing to pay $5 for a Starbucks latte, $500 for an iPad or $100,000+ for a Mercedes. The same consumers will price shop on brands where they have no feelings. A beloved brand has an inelastic price, which means the quantity demanded does not change very much when the price changes.

- Price increase: Simply put, brands can execute a price increase when the market or consumers allow the brand to do so. A beloved brand will have an easier time pushing through a price increase as it can use the power of its brand versus consumers, competitors, or channels. When pushing a price increase through retail channel partners, brands usually require proof that the new price will work or that product costs have gone up. Factors that help the brand story include the health of the brand and market.

- Price decrease: Use this tactic when battling a competitor, in reaction to sluggish economic conditions or retail channel pressure. You can also use an aggressive price decrease when you have a cost advantage, whether that's manufacturing, materials or distribution. When you have that cost advantage, it may make sense to deploy a lower price to deplete the resources of your competitor.

Price changes always carry a risk of a competitive overreaction. Always consider various potential competitive reactions when doing your financial analysis. Be careful. As difficult as it is to implement a price change, it is almost impossible to change it back.

2. Trade the consumer up or down

Another strategy is to create a range of products at various price levels, with a good/better/best approach that allows the brand to reach up or down to a new segment of consumers. Make sure that you are doing this for the right reason or it could backfire on you.

- Trading consumers up on price: Make sure your brand can carve out a meaningful difference to create a second or third tier, so consumers can see an apparent reason to move up. Many brands will deploy a good/better/best approach to pricing. When your brand secures trust or a bond with the consumer, it will be easier to use your brand reputation and product performance to move loyal consumers up to the next level.

- Trading consumers down: When the brand sees a potential unserved market, it can trade consumers down when the move brings minimal damage to the brand image or reputation. In a tough economy, creating a lower-priced set of products can be a smarter strategy than lowering the overall price of your main brand. Once the economy bounces back, you can discontinue the lower-priced product option.

There are a few cautions around trying to trade consumers up or down. Be careful not to lose your focus on the brand's core business or image.

Stay focused because brands struggle when they try to be all things to everyone. When trading down, try to take costs out of the product to ensure margins rates stay consistent. For a mass brand going through retail channels, it can be challenging to manage multiple price levels. The products with lower sales may receive poor shelf placement and miss out on retailer-merchandising tools.

Financial calculations for a price increase will impact both revenue and profits. You should do an elasticity market research test to find out how your brand will perform.

In this example, the price goes from $2.50 up to $2.75, only a 10% price increase. I assumed the cost of goods remained flat and I used a forecasted sales decline on units sold. The sales revenue falls slightly, but the profit goes up by $7,500 or by 4.6%.

Price Increase Formulas

	Current	New	Profit impact of a price increase
Price	$2.50	$2.75	**((New Price - COGs) x new unit volume)**
COGs	1.00	1.00	**MINUS ((Old Price - COGs) x old unit volume)**
Margin	1.50	1.75	
Margin %	60%	64%	= ((2.75-1.0) x 90,000) - ((2.5-1.0) x 100,000)
Unit Forcast	100,000	90,000	= $7,500
Revenue	$250,000	$247,500	With a 10% price increase against a 10% volume
Profit	$150,000	$157,500	decrease, you will generate $7,500 more profit.

The marketer's role in increasing the perceived price:

While many marketers think of price as a defensive response to counter inflation or a competitive reaction at the retail shelf, the smartest brand leaders use price as a weapon to drive brand value.

Your pricing strategy starts with understanding your brand's price/value relationship and looking for ways to increase the perception of value. The marketer needs to gain that touch-feel for those perceptions.

To help drive the perceived quality of the products, marketers need to explain the product benefits in ways that match up to the customer's needs. Adding emotional benefits helps the brand to go beyond a commodity.

Using the brand positioning tools, marketers need to build a reputation for expertise reinforced by the consumer experience, past usage, or reviews/referrals for a similar situation.

When managing the perceived quality of the services, you need to go beyond the product. Look for innovative ways to make it faster, easier, or smarter for consumers. Look to replace activities the consumer can't do or does not want to do.

Make your consumers look better or look more brilliant. Happy experiences build trust that allows consumers to open up emotionally. With each happy experience, you can add cached value.

How your work impacts perceived value and pricing

How consumers perceive price

1. **Perceived quality of the products:** Explanation of the product benefits match up to the consumer's needs. Adding emotional benefits go beyond commodity.

2. **Reputation for expertise:** Re-enforced by experience, past usage or reviews/referrals for a similar situation.

3. **Perceived quality of the services:** Go beyond product to make the experience faster, easier, smarter. Replace activities the consumer can't do or does not want to do.

4. **Make your consumer look better or smarter:** They will pay more if it is easier for them to maximize their value.

5. **Current consumers:** Happy experiences builds trust that allows consumer to open up emotionally. With each happy experience, you can add cached value.

What you can do to add value

✓ Use claims and the emotional benefits that explain the value of your products

✓ Create a brand idea helps position your brand and build a unique and motivating reputation

✓ Work with sales team to explain the quality of the added services

✓ Explain how intuitive design or added teaching helps consumers get more or do more.

✓ Know who the best consumers are and why they are happy. Surprise & delight those who love the brand, with reenforcing messages to keep happy.

3. Use product costs as a strategic weapon

Marketers usually assume that managing the cost of goods (COGs) is someone else's job. However, product costs can be a useful strategic weapon that marketers should utilize.

- Decreasing the cost of goods: There are a few ways to drive down cost of goods (COGs). First, you can use your brand power and higher volumes to negotiate with suppliers. You can choose to use lower-priced raw materials, drive process efficiencies, or explore offshore manufacturing.

- Increasing the cost of goods: The most significant reason to increase cost of goods (COGs) is when upgrading to a premium market or an added benefit. Watch out for suppliers trying to pass along costs beyond inflationary rates.

When lowering your product costs, make sure the product change is not significantly noticeable. Where there is a noticeable product change, understand the potential impact on your brand's perceived performance or quality. When costs go up, make sure the increases can be covered through other parts of your profit statement, whether through price increases, volume increases, or cuts to your brand's marketing costs.

There are two ways to calculate the cost of goods. The first uses the unit costs, which includes the variable material and labor costs, plus the manufacturing overhead. Alternatively, you can use an inventory cost method, which takes the beginning inventory cost plus the cost for the year, then subtract the ending inventory cost.

4. Control the marketing and selling costs

Marketers are protective of marketing budgets. They usually want as much money as possible to carry out the activities on their priority list. The strategic brand leader should act as the owner/CEO by using budgets to manage the profit rather than act like a subject-matter expert trying to protect their turf.

- Marketing cost decrease: Many times companies look at cost-cutting to counter short-term changes happening within other parts the P&L (price, volume or COGs). However, many of the best-run brands keep the investment strong, aligning with the longer-term strategy instead of a short-term situational need.

- Marketing cost increase: Used when there is an opportunity to gain share against a competitor or as a defensive position trying to hold share. The brand should see an opportunity where significant revenue gains can cover off the lower profit ratios.

Use your strategic thinking to determine your marketing budget level. How connected your brand is with consumers determines where on the consumer journey you will focus. For an indifferent or liked brand, you should focus on driving awareness and purchase, which are usually high in cost. As you get to be more loved, you can concentrate on turning repeat purchases into routines. You can shift some of the marketing budgets over to create a superior consumer experience to reward your loyal users. The more loved a brand, the better the spend-to-sales ratios you should realize.

The degree of competitive warfare should impact the size of your budget. Craft brands or disruptive brands are different enough to avoid competitive battles. When a brand takes on a challenger stance, the budget should go up. Be careful of competitive warfare situations, as a competitor may overreact, leading to spiralling spend escalations. Like a price war, marketing investment wars can also drain resources and will be viewed as a failure when there is very little market share change after the war.

Also, consider your brand's core strength. If you use a product-led or brand story-led strength, you will have to invest in advertising to show how your brand is better or different. These brands will require significant investment. However, an experience-led brand should put the brand's limited financial resources into creating a consumer experience. Early on, you will have to rely on a slower build through word-of-mouth advertising rather than paid media.

Return on Investment (ROI) for a marketing investment

	Program	Formulas for ROI
Incremental Sales Volume	$5,000,000	**Gross Margin = Revenue - Cost of Goods Sold**
Cost of Goods Sold (COGS)	$3,000,000	$5 Million - $3 Million = $2 Million
Gross Margin	$2,000,000	
Gross Margin %	40%	**Contribution Margin = Gross Margin - Spend**
		$2 Million - $1.5 Million = $0.5 Million
Total Investment Spend	$1,500,000	**ROI = Contribution Margin divided by spend**
Contribution Margin	$500,000	$0.5 Million divided by $1.5 Million = 33%

Always bring an ROI mindset to your brand's marketing budget. In the example, the investment of $1.5 million generates an incremental sales of $5 million. After subtracting the cost of goods and the marketing investment, your brand makes $500,000 in additional profit. To calculate the ROI, take the profit and divide it by the investment. In this example, the ROI is 33%; if it holds, the investment will take three years to pay back.

5. Steal other users

The share and volume game is a traditional tool for marketers. Be careful when trying to gain share. As discussed in the competitive strategy section, attacking competitors can prove challenging. Many times, an attack can result in a spend escalation with neither brand making any gains. When you lead a share war without a substantive competitive advantage, there may not be any winners, just losers.

- Offensive share gains: Look to gain share using a significant competitive advantage against an opportunity in the marketplace, whether that is a first-mover advantage into new technology, an unmet consumer need, a changing retail channels, or a chance to steal share, using your brand's superior performance against a vulnerable competitor.

- Defensive share stance: Hold your market share or minimize the share losses until your brand can catch up on technology. The best way to protect your brand is to feed your loyal base of consumers who are less likely to switch.

6. Get users to use more

Going after usage frequency is a difficult strategy. It means telling consumers who have already decided how to use your brand; they should use your brand even more.

- A higher share of requirements: In many categories, even loyal consumers will work within a competitive set of favorite brands. You need to provide a reason, through product superiority claims, consumer experiences, or emotional benefits to persuade loyal consumers to use your brand for every occasion.

- Get current users to use more: Look for opportunities with loyal users to create a potential routine or ritual around your brand.

It is an excellent strategy to use when there is a real benefit to your consumer to use your product more often. Otherwise, consumers will see it as a shallow money grab by the brand. Driving routines or rituals can be difficult. Even with lifesaving medicines, the most prominent issue for frequency is compliance. The best frequency strategy is to link your brand to a part of their current life. Special K did a great job with "Use Special K for two meals a day for two weeks, and you will lose 5 pounds." McDonald's offered "Free coffee for 15 straight days" to drive the routine.

Compound Annual Growth Rates (CAGR)

	Year 1	Year 2	Year 3	Year 4	Year 5
Sales	$500	$600	$650	$625	$800
Annual Growth		20%	8%	-4%	28%

CAGR = ((Y5/Y1) to the power of (1/4 years) -1
= ((800/500) to the power of 0.25) - 1 = 12.47%

Average Growth Rate = ((Y5 - Y1)/Y1)/4 years
= ((800-500)/500)/4) = 60/4 = 15%

When calculating revenue growth, you can use average growth rate, yet a compound annual growth rate is a much truer version of what is happening. In the example above, the average growth rate is 15%, but the more accurate compound growth rate is 12.47%. If you are scared off by math, you can always use the CAGR calculator on the Investopedia website.

7. Enter new categories

When your brand has a strong base of loyal consumers, and you see an opportunity to take those consumers into a new peripheral category, you can open up new revenue streams for your brand. Make sure the new category fits with the brand idea, and you can transfer elements of your brand reputation into the new product.

As I showed in the Starbucks example, moving to snacks and sandwiches made sense for the brand, and allowed Starbucks to take their loyal morning coffee users into a new product category and a new part of the day. However, their entry into music and movies did not fit the brand. Instead, it distracted them away from the core brand. Special K has done a remarkable job in moving across various grocery categories, including cereal, breakfast bars, shakes, and water, while always staying true to "helping women control their weight.

Using the brand funnel to determine your sales forecast

Assumptions		10 million people, $5 per item
Awareness	90%	9 million people aware
Familiar	75%	7.5 familiar
Consider	50%	Half of people consider
Purchase	25%	2.5 million first purchase at $5 per
Repeat	10%	1.0 million buy a 2nd time at $5 per
Loyal	2%	200k buy a 3rd time at $5 per

Using the funnel for a forecast

Purchase:	$12.5 Million
Repeat:	$ 5.0 Million
Loyal:	$. 1.0 Million
Total Sales	**$18.5 Million**

8. Create new uses

Take the brand and create similar experiences into a new format or new offering. You need to make sure your current brand is in order before you divert attention, funding, and focus on a potential blue ocean expansion area. Be careful with this temptation because the legendary success stories (Arm & Hammer or one-a-day Aspirin) do not come along as often as you might hope.

Appreciation to Professor Ken Wong, who first introduced me to this financial model when I was in Marketing

10 financial questions to assess your brand's worth:

1. What is brand's compound annual growth rate (CAGR)? Explain the ups and downs over the past five years.
2. What are your gross margins and contribution margins over the last five years? Can you break it out by product line? Is there more pressure from price or the cost of goods?
3. What is your brand's marketing budget breakout? Variable direct costs versus indirect fixed dollars? What is the break between media and creative production? Consumer spend versus trade spend?
4. Have you completed any pricing elasticity studies? What did you learn about your brand? If you did increase your price, what did you see in the marketplace?
5. How is your brand's overall strategy impacting your brand's profits? How do your decisions on your brand's core strength, consumer connection, competitive pressures, and situation impact your financials?
6. How are your current brand/business performance metrics, brand's market goals, and financials linked?
7. Over the past five years, what are the programs that drive the highest and lowest ROI?
8. How does your business model impact your overall profit? What are you focusing on right now?
9. What are your forecasting error rates? Is there a seasonality impact? How do economic factors impact your brand's financials? How reasonable are your inventory levels?
10. What financial pressures do you face on an annual or quarterly basis?

Profit = Margins x Volume

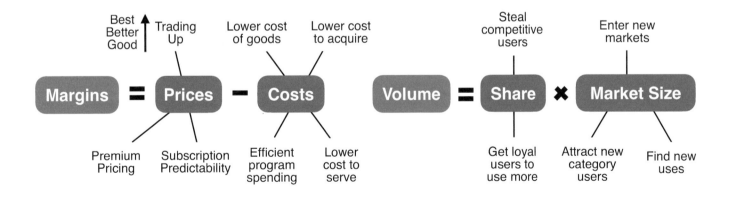

Monthly Performance Report

GRAY'S Cookies

Consumption Performance

Gray's hit a record 42% $ share in September, up 11% vya, while Private Label lost share.

For the latest 4 weeks, Gray's achieved a 42% dollar share (+11% VYA and a gain of 2.2 share pts via) and a 38% unit share (+12% and gain of 2 share pts VYA). The source of growth for the period is our new lemon flavor and increased share of the food channel. This keep's Gray's momentum going, with a YTD share going from 39% up to 41%. The significant growth continues to be the blueberry flavor, accounting for 48% of our overall consumption. We continue to see the new advertising driving increased future purchase intent, up from 67% in Q1 to 79% in Q4. The new lemon flavor now has 93% distribution accounts for 15% of Gray's overall consumption.

Brands	Latest 4 Weeks						Latest 12 weeks			YTD		
	Dollar % growth	Dollar Share	$ Pt growth	Units % growth	Unit Share	Unit Pts Change	Dollar % growth	Dollar Share	$ Pt growth	Dollar % growth	Dollar Share	$ Pt growth
Category	4%	100%	0	5%	100%	0	2%	100%	0	4%	100%	0
Gray's	11%	42%	2.2	12%	38%	2.0	14%	42%	2.1	11%	41%	2.0
Dad's	-6%	10%	-1.1	-4%	12%	-1.1	2%	11%	-1.1	-6%	10%	-1.1
Private Label	-2%	20%	-1	-4%	23%	-0.8	4%	23%	-1%	-2%	22%	-0.9

Consumption Drivers

1. TV advertising driving consideration and purchase intent.
2. Dad's cut spend, and is seeing consumption falling for second straight year.
3. Innovation behind lemon launch has helped steal share from Private Label (down 2% VYA)

Consumption Inhibitors

1. New TV ad has soft brand link: 42% vs norm of 55%. New edit options for Q4 media.
2. Q2 promo had strong sell in, but did not achieve coop and display of last year.
3. Lemon awareness is softer this year, over-shadowed by purple. Explore Lemon sampling.

Shipment Performance

Gray's sales up 15.7% vya for October, up 6% in Q3 and up 9.7% for the year.

Latest forecast has Gray's exceeding plan by 3%. Walmart sales lead way (+27% growth), Costco at risk (down 6%). Safeway sales soft in October, but on pace for a recovery year (+15%). The 48 count continues to be strong (up 25%) and blueberry continues strong sell-in, up 40% compared to lemon launch in 2016.

	October		Year to Date	
	Total Sales ($ MM)	% change vya	Total Sales ($ MM)	% change vya
Total Gray's	10	15.7%	112	9.7%
Top 5 Accounts				
• Walmart	2.59	+23%	25.0	+27%
• Costco	1.11	-11%	11.7	-6%
• Walgreens	0.85	+9%	7.2	+3%
• Kroger	0.55	+2%	4.4	+2%
• Safeway	0.41	-44%	5.3	+15%
• Publix	0.33	-9%	3.8	-7%
Top 5 Accounts				
• 24 count Blue	4.5	+2%	53.7	+5%
• 24 count Green	2.2	+1%	26.2	-2%
• 24 count Purple	1.5	+5%	17.3	+22%
• 48 count Blue	1.8	+73%	11.2	+11%

Shipment Drivers

1. Walmart growth outpacing Gray's overall sales 3-fold. Added promo plus increased display.
2. Lemon having strong year (+22%) following last year's launch. New food listings.
3. 48 count promo sell-in for Q3 stronger than last year. Ensure strong sell-through to hit forecast.

Shipment Inhibitors

1. Safeway had soft October (-44%) but continues to stay strong on the year (+15%).
2. Costco continues to be soft (-11% for Oct, -6% for year) as FDM customers launched 48 count.
3. Blueberry seeing cannibalization at shelf by retailers. Push re-list of blueberry at expense of Dad's.

How to write a monthly performance report

Every brand should have a monthly report to track how the business is doing throughout the course of the year. While these reports may feel tedious to write, the 3-4 hours it takes to dig in is a great discipline to help you maintain the touch-feel of managing the business results of the brand.

The monthly report helps steer everyone who works on the brand, to stay on track and deliver the commitments of the annual brand plan. There should be a consumption section and a shipments section.

The monthly report should answer the following CONSUMPTION questions:

1. What is your one-line story on what's happening on your brand? This is your elevator speech to the CEO.
2. What's the dollar, tonnage or unit share, on a 4-week, 12-week and year to date basis? Focus on the market share measures that the company uses—as it can vary. Using these three distinct time breaks helps clearly demonstrate the trend line.
3. How is the brand doing versus last year, vs. prior share periods, vs. the category or vs. the goals in your plan? Use both percentage growth and share point changes, and explain data breaks to tell a smarter story.
4. What is the competition doing? Look at their trends in the consumption, tracking results, brand funnel or any possible tactical actions you see happening in the marketplace.
5. What are the top three drivers of your brand growth? Look at consumption trends (e.g. by product sku, regions, channel, account, flavor, etc.), explanations of brand funnel scores, program results, retail challenges, or competitive moves. Develop a mini plan for how you are going to continue these drivers.
6. What are the top three inhibitors of growth? These inhibitors explain the weaknesses or friction you are seeing in your marketing programs, distribution gaps, competitive moves, or changes in consumer behavior. Outline a plan to counter these inhibitors, giving the assurance to senior management or ownership that you are on top of running the business.

The monthly report should answer the following SHIPMENT questions:

1. What's the one-line story that captures what's happening on the brand? Make sure you are aligned with your VP of sales, because they will have to answer to the CEO.
2. What's the overall sales for the month, the quarter and how will it impact the year-end forecasted sales call? Senior management might adjust their own forecast or change their short-term investment stance based on the brand's sales performance.
3. How are the sales by key account, by product skus or by regions? Track each by month, quarter and on a year-to-date (YTD) basis. This highlights the strength and exposes weakness.
4. What are the top three drivers of the brand for the month, quarter or the year? Highlight which accounts, product skus or regions are showing the most growth. Explain why and tell what you are going to do to maintain that growth.
5. What are the top three inhibitors of growth? Connect with your sales colleagues, ensuring they buy into the statement you will make in the report. Your answers should focus on both the short and long-term.

How to make marketing execution decisions

The best marketers play the most crucial role in the creative advertising process. They are generalists, not experts. They need to know enough to make marketing execution decisions but never enough to do the work.

With the increasing speed of advertising, marketers have taken one step in and often find themselves embedded in the creative development. If you are now doing the work, who is critiquing? And who is deciding if the work is good enough and if it fits your strategy? Even using internal agencies creates a potential risk or a bias. Marketers need to step back and let the creativity unfold.

There is a leadership advantage in being the least knowledgeable person in the room. While it may sound strange at first when you are a layer removed from the specialist who does the work, it allows you to think, question, challenge, and decide on choosing the ideal advertising. Focus on the strategy, but stay clear-minded enough to judge if the advertising is good enough or reject it if it is not.

It takes a unique leadership skill to inspire, challenge, question, direct, and decide without any expertise. As we engage experts, the respect that we show can either inspire greatness or crush their creative spirit. From my experience, the best advertising people I have worked with would prefer to be pushed rather than held back. The last thing they want is for you to ask for their expertise and then tell them what to do.

If you knew that being a better advertising client would result in better work, would you show up better? Being good at advertising is something you can learn. I will show you how to judge and choose the best advertising for your brand. Your advertising needs enough branded breakthrough to stand out from the market clutter so your brand connects with consumers. It must have a motivating message to move consumers along their purchase journey, whether you want them to see, think, feel, do, or influence.

Our Marketing PlayBox

The best creative marketing ideas come through in-the-box creativity.

As we introduced our Strategic ThinkBox to help you uncover the most significant key issues and strategies, we now turn to our Marketing PlayBox, with four dimensions to support our creative decision-making.

1. First, we want marketing ideas focused on the brand's desired target market.
2. Does the idea fit with the brand?
3. Does the idea express the brand's message?
4. Will the idea execute our strategy to move the consumers in ways that benefit our brand?

Our Marketing PlayBox will work with any marketing execution. This chapter will show how it works with advertising and product innovation.

The best advertising must balance being creatively different and strategically smart.

When ads are **smart but not different**, they get lost in the clutter. It is natural for marketers to tense up when the creative work ends up being "too different." Marketers look for past proof in all parts of the business as a sign that something will work. Push your comfort with creativity and take a chance to ensure your ad breaks through.

However, when it comes to advertising, when the ads start too similar to what other brands have already done, the advertising will be at risk of boring your consumers. The ads need to stand out more to capture their attention.

When ads are **different but not smart**, they will entertain consumers but do nothing for your brand. Your advertising must be smart enough to trigger the desired consumer response to match your brand strategy.

Smart

Strategy

Not Smart

Smart but not different

Solid strategy, but no creativity
Will do OK. Won't break through
clutter to make a difference.

Different and smart

Creativity helps breakthrough.
Solid strategy motivates
consumers to take action

Not smart and not different

Brand is lost and floundering.
Conservative creative against
a weak strategy.

Different but not smart

Creative for the sake of it.
Misses strategy: wrong target,
message, or desired response.

The same

Creativity

Different

How to predict advertising success using our ABC's model for marketing execution decisions.

Let's take this creative thinking to a predictive advertising model, changing the creatively different to branded breakthrough, and the smart strategy becomes motivating consumers.

The branded breakthrough is **"how you say it."** It uses creativity to capture the consumer's attention within the clutter of the market while linking your brand closer to the story. The motivating message is **"what you say."** You must communicate the main message to connect with consumers memorably so the ad sticks enough to move consumers to see, think, feel, or act differently than before they saw the ad.

To achieve branded breakthrough, you need ideas that attract attention and link back to the brand. To motivate consumers, you need ideas that communicate the message you know moves consumers, and you need that message to stick in the mind of consumers long enough to go through their path to purchase.

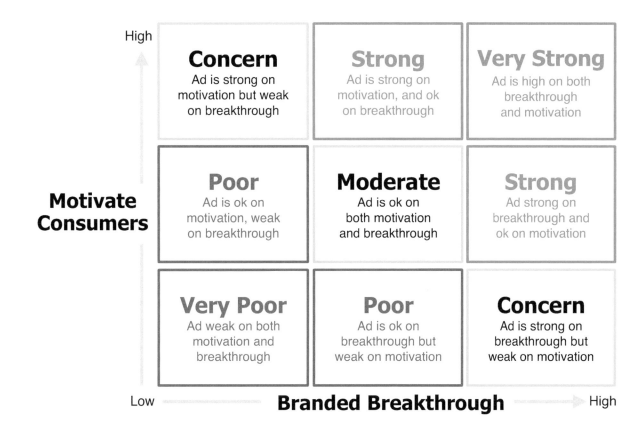

Branded Breakthrough + Motivate Consumers =
Attention + Brand Link + Communication + Stickiness

Our ABC's stands for Attention, Brand Link, Communication, and Stickiness.

When judging advertising, the most important thing I look for is to ensure the creative idea within the ad will attract attention, tell the brand story, communicates the main benefit, and stick in the consumer's mind. You have a red flag when you see a story, device, copy, or visual that does not fit with the delivery. You run the risk that the creativity of the ad works against your objectives.

✓ Is it the creative idea that earns the consumer's **attention** for the ad?
✓ Does the creative idea help to drive maximum **brand** involvement?
✓ Does the creative idea set up the **communication** of the main consumer benefit?
✓ Is the creative idea memorable enough to **stick** in the consumer's mind and move them to purchase?

Our creative brief defines the Marketing PlayBox that the creative advertising must play within.

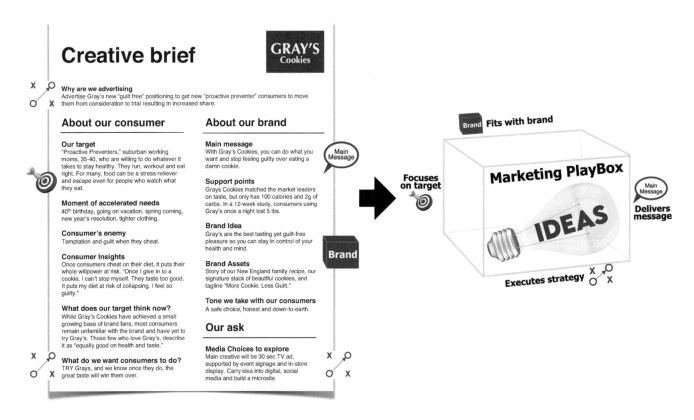

1. We want advertising focused on the brand's desired target market.

You will notice that half of our Creative Brief is about the consumer. To start, define the target with demographics, behaviors, and attitudes, and links how a cookie could fit into other parts of their healthy lifestyle. Most importantly, focus on the dimensions that matter to the target. Never spread your limited resources against a broad target that leaves everyone thinking your message is for someone else. Target the people most motivated by what your brand does best, and make your brand feel personal so consumers feel special. The best brands make consumers think, "This brand is for me."

Add consumer insights that provide little secrets hidden beneath the surface. Your communications experts will love working with consumer insights. These insights help explain the consumers' underlying behaviors, motivations, pain points, and emotions. Lay out the pain point of the consumer using the consumer enemy that we know torments our target market every day.

2. We need to make sure our advertising fits with the brand.

A smart creative brief uses a brand idea that organizes everything we do. Add brand assets that include past work that has worked, including visuals, slogans, copy points, logos, fonts, and colors. Don't cross the line by telling what type of creative you want. Stay confident that you have written such a great brief that you do not need to control the creative outcome. Give the expert enough freedom for them to come up with great ideas.

3. We want the advertising to deliver the brand's main message.

Highlight the main message you know will work based on the brand positioning work that leverages the functional and emotional benefits most motivating to consumers and ownable for the brand. Explore using our brand positioning template. Build advertising that gets consumers to do only one thing at a time, whether it's something you want them to see, think, do, feel, or influence their friends. You must connect the advertising objective with your brand strategy.

 Focuses on target

 **Fits with brand**

 Delivers message

 Executes strategy

Do not put so many messages into your ad; consumers will see and hear a cluttered mess. They will shut down their minds and reject your ad. They will not know what you stand for, and you will never build a reputation for anything. Start a conversation that shows what the consumers get or how they will feel. Do not just yell features at the consumer. Use your brand idea to simplify and organize your brand messaging.

4. The brand strategy must move consumers in ways that benefit our brand.

Ensure everyone is clear on the brand strategy by having one clear objective in the creative brief. Importantly, try to get consumers to do one thing. Don't try to do everything. Provide media choices to explore, but be willing to maneuver based on the creative ideas that come back.

Our ABC'S guides you through our Creative Checklist

When you see creative marketing ideas come back from your experts, our Creative Checklist will identify any gaps you have with the work. Specifically, what do you see that is outside of the Marketing PlayBox?Then, use your feedback to steer the ideas back in the box. Highlight the gaps you see while avoiding providing a solution. Let your creative marketing execution experts use their in-the-box creativity to discover new solutions that will fit the box.

1. Will the advertising idea capture the attention of the target? (A)

- You want advertising that builds a bond with the consumer. First, ask if it speaks directly to the consumer target. Then, does it leverage consumer insights to connect? Next, will the marketing idea deepen the bond with the consumers? Finally, can the ad help build memories and rituals?

2. Will consumers link the advertising idea back to the brand? (B)

- Look for marketing ideas that fit with the brand. First, does the marketing idea deliver the brand idea? Second, does it leverage your creative assets? Third, is there a fit with the tone of the brand? Finally, does the marketing idea meet brand book standards?

3. Does the advertising idea communicate the message to consumers? (C)

- You want marketing execution that has a motivating message. First, is the communication of the main benefit easy for consumers to understand? Second, does the idea naturally set up the main message? Finally, will the main message move consumers to see, think, act, feel, or whisper?

- Does the creative marketing execution help distinguish the brand? Indeed, you want ads that communicate the functional or emotional benefits. Creative advertising should help the brand own a competitive space that motivates consumers.

4. Will the advertising idea stick in the minds of consumers long enough to help move consumers along their purchase journey? (S)

- Find advertising that delivers the strategy. First, does the marketing idea match up to the objective of the brief from your brand plan? Then, does it achieve the desired consumer response? Will it have an expected market impact and brand performance?

Other factors we've added to our Creative Checklist

What does your gut instinct say?

You might be coming from a 3-hour meeting, and it takes work to change speeds as you head into a creative meeting. Relax, find your creative energy, let it soak in, and use your quick-twitch instincts. Do you love what the ad has the potential to do? Will you be proud of this ad as your legacy?

Does the ad deliver the strategy?

Slow down with some thinking time after the meeting. In a quiet place alone, make sure it delivers your strategy. Does the ad match up to the objective in the creative brief? Does it achieve the desired consumer response? Will it have an expected market impact and brand performance? Refrain from overthinking and talking yourself out of a good ad that works.

Will the ad build a bond with consumers?

Will it speak directly to the consumer target, leverage consumer insights to connect, deepen our bond with our consumers, or build memories and rituals?

Does the ad fit with the brand and distinguish it in the market?

Will it deliver the brand idea, leverage your creative assets, and fit the brand's tone? Does it use the functional or emotional benefits to own a competitive space that is motivating to consumers and ownable for the brand? Is the ad different enough to capture attention within the clutter? Does the creative naturally create the main message and move consumers to think, feel, or act?

How to handle yourself at the creative meeting

When you see new creative ideas, you only really have three choices: You can approve, reject, or change the ads. Marketers rarely approve creative ideas outright. And, there seems a reluctance or fear to reject outright.

Creative Advertising Checklist

Script #1: Re-discovering our recipe (60 sec video)

Rate each as **high**, **medium** or **low** to identify gaps you see in the advertising, to focus your feedback or challenges to the creative team.

ABC's Summary

- [L] **Attention**
- [M] **Brand Link**
- [L] **Communication**
- [L] **Stickiness**

Gut instincts reaction

[L] Do you love what the ad has the potential to do? Does the ad match the brief? Will you be proud of this ad as your legacy?

Delivers strategy

[M] Does the ad match up to the objective of the brief, from your brand plan? Does it achieve the desired consumer response? Will it have an expected market impact and brand performance?

Builds consumer bond

[L] Does the ad speak directly to the consumer target? Does it leverage consumer insights to connect? Will it deepen our bond with our consumers? Can the ad help build memories and rituals?

Fits with brand

[M] Does the ad deliver the brand idea? Does it leverage your creative assets? Does the ad fit with the tone of the brand? Meets brand book standards.

Distinguishes brand

[L] Does it use functional or emotional benefits to own a competitive space that is motivating to consumers and ownable for the brand?

Branded Breakthrough

[L] Is the ad different enough to capture attention within the clutter? Does the ad engage consumers with the brand? Is the brand a significant part of the climax of the ad?

Motivating message

[L] Is the communication of the main benefit in the ad easy for consumers to understand? Does the creative naturally set up the main message? Will the main message move consumers to think, feel or act?

@Beloved Brands Inc.

My feedback

Too many creative messages in the way

Far too many messages that get in the way, the grand daughter, going to be a lawyer, San Francisco, her own family, a family, old recipe, going to all these farms is getting in the way of the beer message.

New beer launch message needs to be front and centre

The new craft beer message is lost. I want a simplified message: you love our store; you will love our new beer. I'm not selling this to everyone, so over-explaining the history of our store is not needed.

Other scripts work better

I worry if you start dismantling the creative and re-structuring everything, it would be smarter to throw this one out, rather than encourage you to fix it.

Marketers erroneously believe their job is to change, modify, and rewrite the ads. Many come to creative meetings equipped with a pen and paper, ready to list numerous suggestions for each ad. Stop it. Refrain from offering your solutions. If you lack the skill to create an ad, what makes you think you can perform the more difficult task of fixing it? Use your feedback to pose new challenges for your agency to solve.

Yes.	Maybe.	No.
It feels like it fits with tweaks	Flaws in target, message, or tone.	Structure, target, tone feel unfixable
Tweak.	**Fix.**	**Kill it.**
Provide feedback on details that need fixing	Identify gaps and challenge agency to fix those gaps.	Focus on the positive of the other ideas

In your next creative meeting, utilize our Creative Checklist. Rate each item as high, medium, or low. Identify the most prominent gaps and provide directional feedback for the creative team to address. Like the creative brief that poses a challenge, let your feedback present a new challenge for the creative team to solve.

Embrace that your brand's greatness comes from the experts you engage. Focus on inspiring those experts to strive for their own greatness and apply it to your brand. The most talented creatives I've encountered prefer being pushed to deliver outstanding work rather than feeling held back and limited to producing mediocre work. The more you present them with your problems, the more astonishing their solutions will become. When you ask for their greatness, you may be shocked by the caliber of their work. Below are some suggestions on phrases to avoid and alternative expressions to consider using instead:

When *you see*	**Ad is not a fit with our target**	**Ad has a brand link concern**	**Main message problem**	**None of the ads work**
Don't *say*	"Turn the old man into a young mom, and his friend into a toddler… and change the golf course to a park."	"Put more brand throughout the spot" or "Make the logo bigger!"	"I have a few copy changes I want…" or "Can we put our 2nd claim in the ad?"	"Here's an idea I have that we can try…" or "Let's do a testimonial."
Do *ask*	"I like the structure of the ad, but can you provide other situations that would fit with our target?"	"How can we integrate the brand into the overall storytelling?"	"What is getting our way of the main message not coming through?"	"Which ad did you keep coming back to and what is it you liked?"

The 12 steps of the creative advertising process

Advertising strategy

(1) Brand Plan
Vision, purpose, values, key issues, strategies, and the brand communications plan.

(2) Strategy Pre-work
Build target profile, consumer insights, brand positioning, brand idea, objective.

(3) Creative Brief
Creates box ad must play in: objective, insights, desired response, benefit, RTB.

Inspiring creative team

(4) Creative Expectations
Chance to meet creative team to convey vision, strategy, inspire and focus.

(5) Tissue Session
Works when you are looking for new ad ideas. Be open and focus on big ideas.

(6) Creative Meeting
Be positive, focus on big picture, less on details. Give direction, but no solutions, make decisions.

Advertising decisions

(7) Feedback Memo
Details, challenges but without specific solutions. Use your feedback to create a modified box for team to solve.

(8) Ad Testing
Use ad testing—qualitative or quantitative—to confirm your pick, not make your decision. Eliminate blind spots.

(9) Gain Approval
Sell in the ad, be ready to fight any resisters to make sure the ad happens.

Delivering the advertising

(10) Media decisions
Get more specific on the idea media that will deliver the creative idea.

(11) Production
Manage the tone to fit the brand. Always, get more than you will need in post.

(12) Post Production
Talk directly with experts and leverage their knowledge

1. **Brand Plan work:** Establish a clear vision, purpose, values, key issues, and strategies to guide the brand communications strategy. The plan lays out the advertising strategy, investment, and desired response.

2. **Strategy pre-work:** Develop a strong brand positioning and brand plan using consumer insights, enemy analysis, and a well-defined brand communications plan before writing the creative brief. For a new campaign, I would test the brand concept to give us the confidence to know our brand strategy will work. This helps us isolate the focus on the creative expression of that brand concept.

3. **Focused creative brief:** Collaborate with your agency to create a strategic, focused brief with a clear objective, target market, desired consumer response, and main message. Think of the creative brief as creating a strategic box the ad must play within. I like one objective, one desired consumer response, one target tightly defined, one main benefit, and up to two main reasons to believe.

4. **Creative expectations:** Meet the creative team early to convey your vision, passion, and strategy, fostering a personal relationship for better advertising results.

5. **Tissue session:** Hold an informal session for high-risk campaigns, discussing conceptual ideas to guide and inspire the creative team without imposing your own ideas.

6. **Creative meeting:** How you show up at the first creative meeting is crucial to the entire project. You are now on the "hot seat," and you should feel the pressure. You are being judged as much as you think you are there to judge the work. Think of the first creative meeting like a first date. I have seen the relationship fizzle within seconds. Approach the first creative meeting positively, focusing on big-picture decisions, giving direction, and inspiring the team.

7. **Feedback memo:** Work it out with the agency ahead of time that you will give a feedback memo 48 hours after the creative meeting. This memo is your chance to gather your thoughts, balancing your creative instincts with your strategic thinking. Provide a detailed memo within 48 hours of the creative meeting, clarifying points and framing problems without offering specific solutions.

8. **Advertising testing:** The use of ad testing depends on timing, budget, or degree of risk. Where you have a new major campaign, test the ideas you feel have the best chance to express your brand positioning, communicate the main benefit, break through the clutter, and motivate consumers to purchase.

9. **Gain approval:** Keep your boss informed at every stage, own your vision, and find a way to make your favorite ad happen. However, you always need to sell in the ad! With every great ad I ever made, there were many resistors. However, with every possible bad ad on the table, I seemed to be the only resistor, who was trying not to make it.

10. **Media Decisions:** I always want to see creative ideas expressed as video, billboard, and long copy to see the possibilities. I might know the primary media, but I want to see the creative ideas before making firm decisions. Once I know our direction, I can finalize the media plan based on the creative direction, main messages, and creative assets you will build through the creative process.

11. **Production:** The production process can be a complicated element of the project. Remember, you have zero expertise in any production area. Do not even pretend you do. Your primary role is to deliver as close to the original script that was approved while managing the tone to ensure it fits your brand. During the shoot, try to get more options than you need, just in case, as it may look different in the final edit room.

12. **Post-production:** As you move to the post-production stage, you become even less of an expert. Many clients decide to stay close to their agency account person. I believe you should talk directly with every expert (editors) you work with. A personal approach will enable you to get the most out of each expert. Always remember that your brand's greatness happens through the greatness of others.

The ABC's of Product Innovation

While inventions are random, the best innovations must be well-planned. It is crucial to make innovation planning a core practice within your organization and embed an innovative spirit into the culture.

As we did with advertising ideas, we want innovative ideas that fit our Marketing PlayBox.

We can twist our ABC's tool to ensure the best innovations attract consumers **(A)**, build on the brand's strengths **(B)**, communicate the brand idea **(C)**, and achieve a successful entry into the market **(S)**.

1. Does the innovation idea attract consumers to create enough desire? (A)

- Focus on ideas that generate enough consumer demand to help the innovation reach volume thresholds to impact both the category and the brand significantly. It must create a market impact that will tighten the brand's bond with consumers, moves consumers along their journey, or adds to the brand's reputation.

2. Does the innovation idea build on the brand's strengths? (B)

- Focus on ideas that generate enough consumer demand to help the innovation reach volume thresholds to significantly impact both the category and the brand. It must create a market impact that will tighten the brand's bond with consumers, moves consumers along their journey, or adds to the brand's reputation.

3. Does the innovation idea communicate the brand idea? (C)

- Focus on ideas that communicate your brand idea so you can continue to differentiate your brand in the consumer's mind. When it fits with the brand idea, you can generate early trial from your brand's most loyal consumers to help provide an easy entry for the innovation.

4. Does the innovation idea provide a successful entry into the marketplace? (S)

- Focus on ideas that provide profitable units you can sell to generate initial success, prevent competitors from duplicating your new offering, and lead to a long-term return on investment and effort.

Use our Innovation checklist to stay on strategy

To help judge the various innovation options, we use an Innovation Checklist to stay on strategy and deliver the ABC's. Use the checklist to compare different innovation options. The assessment notes can close off any gaps that you are seeing.

Our innovation checklist looks at these factors:

- ✓ Financial projections includes revenue, margin, investment and headcount needed.
- ✓ Consumer demand to achieve volume thresholds
- ✓ Ownability in leveraging the brand idea to make for an easy entry
- ✓ Matches up with go-to-market of sales and distribution
- ✓ Builds on your strengths in manufacturing or servicing
- ✓ Profit payback and margin fit within the portfolio
- ✓ Competitive intensity of the category you enter
- ✓ Ability to be successful in the long run
- ✓ Expected market impact in tightening bond with consumers

On the next page, see how the innovation checklist allows you to assess whether launching Gray's ice cream makes sense for the brand.

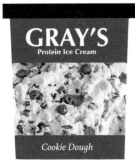

GRAY'S
Protein Ice Cream

Cookie Dough

Innovation Checklist
Gray's Ice Cream

When facing multiple ideas, use the checklist to narrow down the list to potential winners to explore further. Rate each as high, medium or low to identify gaps you see in each innovation, to evaluate whether to the move forward, reject, or seek solutions where there are gaps.

Financial Projection

Year 1 revenue ___$3 million___

Margin % ___25% vs 40% norm___

Investment needed ___$10 million___

Added headcount ___15 in sales___

Consumer demand

H Consumer response leads you to believe to trial/repeat will help achieve volume thresholds, making a significant impact on both the category and company.

Ownable for the brand

L Consumers see fit with your brand idea and ownable for the brand. Provides an easy entry to bring your most loyal brand fans to the new product to drive early trial.

Go to market

BRAND

L Uses sales team's talents, relationships, knowledge or experience. Distribution matches with your current methods for warehousing, shipping, and servicing.

Production / Processes

BRAND

L Fit with your current manufacturing so you can produce efficiently, to drive higher profits, needing fewer partners

Profitability

L Meets ROI hurdles, margin rates match current portfolio. Profitability allows for continuous investment in new innovation.

Competitive intensity

L Competitive intensity of the category you enter impacts your initial success, pricing, profits and the ability of competitors to duplicate your offering.

Long-run success

L Looking at differentiation to help separate brand, ownability of the brand, sales and profits, and fit with the strengths of the brand.

Market Impact

L Tightens consumer's bond with the brand, adds to the brand reputation. Sizeable opportunity to keep investing.

Assessment notes

Strong consumer feedback, but outside our expertise—production and shipping are more complicated. Category is extremely competitive, our sales people have no relationships with buyers. Recommend we approach ice cream companies to licence our brand name for % royalty

How to write a creative brief to set up brilliant execution

Creative brief

YOUR LOGO HERE

Why are we advertising
Smart briefs start with one very clear objective, while bad briefs try to accomplish too many things at once.

About our consumer

Our target
A good brief uses a combination of demographics, behaviors, and attitudes, and links how brand could fit into other parts of their life.

Consumer's enemy
Takes a consumer problem and dials it up into an enemy that torments them.

Consumer Insights
Consumer Insights come to life when you start them with the word "I" to force yourself to get in the consumer's shoes and then put them in quotes to begin to use the consumer's voice.

What does our consumer think now?
Use brand love curve from consumer strategy to capture how consumers currently feel about your brand.

What do we want consumers to do?
Get consumers to do one thing at a time, whether that means to see, think, do, feel, or influence others.

About our brand

Main message
A smart brief focuses on one main message, bringing the consumer benefit to life.

Support points
Use support points to close off lingering gaps. We recommend a maximum of two support points, as more just gets confusing.

Brand Idea
Brand idea organizes everything you do.

Brand Assets
Build creative and strategic assets. Stay confident that you have written such a great brief, that you do not need mandatories to control the creative outcome.

Tone we take with our consumers
Emotional zones your brand is trying to win.

Our ask

Media Choices to explore
A smart brief provides a range to see what the creative looks like first.

Before writing a creative brief, make sure you have done your homework on developing a winning brand communications strategy that combines the work of your brand positioning, brand idea, and the brand plan.

The briefing stage plays a crucial role as the bridge between your smart strategy and your brilliant execution. I believe brand leaders should control the strategy, yet give more freedom on execution. Too many marketers have this backward. They give up too much freedom on strategy then try to control the creative outcome of the execution.

Make the tough decisions to narrow the brief down to:

- One strategic objective
- One tightly defined consumer target
- One desired consumer response
- One main message
- Two reasons to believe.

I meet resistance when I show people that list. You should see the resistance that your 8-page brief will meet. When I see marketers writing a big, wide brief with too many objectives, a vague target, and cluttered messaging, I wonder if you have unknowingly created too much strategic freedom. While you might think writing a big, wide creative brief provides room for creativity, it does not. Your agency will see you as confused, and will likely just peel the brief apart, rewrite the brief how they want, then provide you with strategic options, instead of creative options. The problem is that you will be choosing your strategy based on which ad you like.

When I see marketers write a big, long laundry list of mandatories, everyone knows you are just trying to control the creative output. Do not create a tangled web of mandatories that almost write the ad itself, or you will trap the creative team into taking various elements in the mandatory list and build a Frankenstein-type ad. If you want great work – and I know you do – give your agency the creative freedom they need.

Transforming the Brand Communications Plan into a Creative Brief

Let's look at the seven questions of the brand communications plan I outlined in the brand plan chapter:

1. Who is in our consumer target?

2. What are we are selling?

3. Why should they believe us?

4. What is our organizing brand idea?

5. What do we need our advertising to do?

6. What do we want people to think, feel or do?

7. Where will our consumer be most receptive to see and act upon our brand message?

Do the strategic homework you developed through the brand communications plan, and begin to populate the 12 questions of your creative brief.

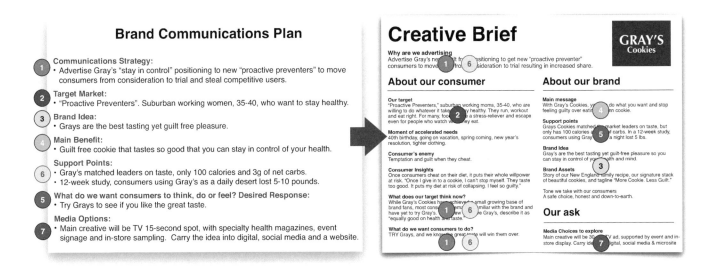

Creative brief

GRAY'S
Cookies

(1) Why are we advertising
Advertise Gray's new "guilt free" positioning to get new "proactive preventer" consumers to move them from consideration to trial resulting in increased share.

About our consumer

(2) Our target
"Proactive Preventers," suburban working moms, 35-40, who are willing to do whatever it takes to stay healthy. They run, workout and eat right. For many, food can be a stress-reliever and escape even for people who watch what they eat.

(3) Moment of accelerated needs
40th birthday, going on vacation, spring coming, new year's resolution, tighter clothing.

(4) Consumer's enemy
Temptation and guilt when they cheat.

(5) Consumer Insights
Once consumers cheat on their diet, it puts their whole willpower at risk. "Once I give in to a cookie, I can't stop myself. They taste too good. It puts my diet at risk of collapsing. I feel so guilty."

(6) What does our target think now?
While Gray's Cookies have achieved a small growing base of brand fans, most consumers remain unfamiliar with the brand and have yet to try Gray's. Those few who love Gray's, describe it as "equally good on health and taste."

(7) What do we want consumers to do?
TRY Grays, and we know once they do, the great taste will win them over.

About our brand

(8) Main message
With Gray's Cookies, you can do what you want and stop feeling guilty over eating a damn cookie.

(9) Support points
Grays Cookies matched the market leaders on taste, but only has 100 calories and 2g of carbs. In a 12-week study, consumers using Gray's once a night lost 5 lbs.

(10) Brand Idea
Gray's are the best tasting yet guilt-free pleasure so you can stay in control of your health and mind.

(11) Brand Assets
Story of our New England family recipe, our signature stack of beautiful cookies, and tagline "More Cookie. Less Guilt."

(12) Tone we take with our consumers
A safe choice, honest and down-to-earth.

Our ask

(13) Media Choices to explore
Main creative will be 30 sec TV ad, supported by event signage and in-store display. Carry idea into digital, social media and build a microsite

Dissecting the creative brief, line by line

I will dissect the creative brief, with a line-by-line review to demonstrate examples of smart and bad creative briefs. I will use some real case studies of bad briefs I have seen over the years to show you what not to do. I will use some of our principles I have talked about to show you a smarter brief. While each line in the brief has a role to play, the brief should have a natural flow, similar to the flow I talked about in the brand plan chapter.

1. Why are we advertising?

A bad brief has an unfocused objective:
• Drive trial of Gray's Cookies, steal market share from mainstream competitors while getting current users to use Gray's more often.

A smart brief has a focused objective:
• Drive trial of Gray's Cookies, using the positioning of "The good tasting healthy cookie."

Smart briefs start with one very clear objective, while bad briefs try to accomplish too many things at once. If you get this line wrong, it can destroy the entire brief. With the example above, the smart brief narrows the decision to one objective (drive trial). A clear objective helps steer the direction for the rest of the brief. The bad brief makes the mistake of trying to do two things at once.

I see too many brands put "drive penetration and usage frequency" at the top of the brief. It is the sign of a lazy mind. Do you realize how different these two strategies are? Can you see how much you will drain your resources when you try to do both with the same ad?

These two strategies have two separate targets, two different brand messages, and potentially two different media plans. Your agency will divide the brief in half, and come back with one ad to drive penetration and another to drive usage frequency. As a result, you will pick your brand strategy based on which ad you like best.

> **Penetration vs. usage frequency**
>
> • A **penetration strategy** gets someone new with minimal experience with your brand to consider dropping their current brand to try you once and see if they will like your brand. That will take a lot of hard work.
> • A **usage frequency strategy** gets someone already familiar with your brand, and you have to convince them to change their behavior about your brand. They will either have to change their current life routine or substitute your brand into a higher share of occasions.
>
> **Pick one strategy, not two**

If your brand has an issue with both penetration and usage, I recommend you write two separate creative briefs, with two independent projects, budgets, and media plans. From a brand plan viewpoint, I would also recommend you stagger these two strategies into different fiscal years to ensure you are not just dividing your limited resources and doing a poor job with both strategies.

Do you want to get more people to eat, or the same amount of people to eat more? Pick one.

2. Who are we talking to?

A bad brief has an unfocused target:
- 18-65 years old, including current consumers, new consumers, and employees. They shop at grocery, drug, and mass retailers. They like cookies and eat 14.7 cookies a month.

A smart brief has a focused and well-defined target bulls-eye:
- "Proactive Preventers." Suburban working moms, 35-40 who are willing to do whatever it takes to stay healthy. They run, work out, and eat right. For them, food is a stress-reliever and an escape. Even for people who watch what they eat, there is still guilt when they cheat.

One of the most significant correlations with brand success is for consumers to playback and feel, "This brand is for me." You can only achieve that by speaking directly with a precise, tight bullseye consumer target.

A smart brief uses a combination of demographics, behaviors, and attitudes, and links how a cookie could fit into other parts of their healthy lifestyle. These details paint a full picture of who we are talking to. In the bad, unfocused creative brief above, the target is pretty much everyone, so it will be hard for anyone to feel the advertising is speaking directly to them.

3. Needs of the consumer

A bad brief is too obvious and a bit of a sales pitch:
- Low calories, low fat, healthier cookie.

A smart brief speaks to the accelerated needs
- 40th birthday, going on vacation, spring coming, new year's resolution, clothes feeling tight

This is your chance to get into the consumer's head. At certain moments in our consumer's life, their physical and emotional needs will accelerate creating an openness for consideration of your brand. You can win by capturing consumers right at these moments when their motivation is high and their knowledge remains low.

4. What's the consumer enemy we are fighting?

A bad brief has the business problem as the lead:
- Gray's market share is still relatively small, held back by low awareness and trial. Product usage is not on par with the category.

A smart brief has a clearly stated consumer problem:
- Consumers struggle to fight off the temptation of cookies and feel guilty when they cheat.

The brief should reflect a consumer problem, not a business problem related to how consumers buy your brand. Think back to the target market chapter and use your consumers' pain point or enemy, which torments them every day. Think of how your brand will battle that enemy on behalf of your consumers.

In the example of a smart brief, the consumer's enemies are "temptation and guilt." When you put an emotional enemy in your brief, it allows the creative process to get into the emotional space right away. That is much more powerful than a functional problem such as losing weight or reducing calories.

In the bad brief example above, the focus on function rather than emotion is a classic flaw of leading with a business-driven problem that talks about a brand's problem with consumers.

5. Consumer insights

A bad brief has data over insights:
- Gray's product taste drives high trial (50%) compared to other new launches (32%). Consumers use Gray's 9.8 times per month compared to the category leader at 18.3 times per month.

A smart brief has deep, rich insights:
- Once consumers cheat on their diet, it puts their whole willpower at risk. They keep cheating. "Once I give in to a cookie, I can't stop myself. They just taste too good. It puts my diet at risk of collapsing. I feel guilty. However, I can't stop myself from cheating again."

Tell a story about the consumer, using insights to connect and show "We get you." As discussed in the Target Market chapter, Consumer Insights come to life when you start them with the word "I" to force yourself to get in the consumer's shoes and then put them in quotes to begin to use the consumer's voice. Express the insight in such a captivating way in your Ad that will make consumers stop and say, "Hmmm, that's exactly how I feel. I thought I was the only one who felt like that."

The smart brief above really goes deep to gain an understanding and build a story through the voice of the consumer. It captures their inner thoughts, uses their own word choices, and expresses their feelings. In the bad brief, there are no real insights. It is just a bunch of data points, without any depth of explanation or story. It will be hard for the creative team to write an engaging story with stats.

> The best way to express consumer insights is to start with the word "I" that gets in the consumer's shoes and then put the insight into quotes, to speak with the consumer's voice.

6. What does our consumer think now?

A bad brief provides data only, without a well-drawn conclusion:
- Gray's only has 35% awareness and 9% penetration. Over 42% of consumers say they like the taste. However, consumers only eat Gray's 3.6x per month.

A smart brief defines where consumers currently are with the brand:
- Gray's Cookies have achieved a small growing base of brand fans, but most consumers remain unfamiliar and have yet to try Gray's. Those who love Gray's, describe it as "equally good on health and taste."

You can use the **brand love curve** from the consumer strategy chapter to capture how consumers feel about your brand. Use the analytics from brand funnel analysis, the voice of consumer (VOC), market share data, loyalty data, and net promoter scores to determine where your brand sits on the curve.

The bad brief above just throws out random statistics; it fails to turn the data into stories that form a meaningful analysis. The smart brief draws an honest conclusion that your brand is at the unfamiliar/indifferent stage for most consumers. The statement also sheds light on what the few who love the brand say about it, suggesting what might motivate others.

7. What do we want consumers to do?

A bad brief tries to trigger too many responses:
• We want consumers to THINK Gray's Cookies are unique, to get consumers to FEEL they can stay in control, and then we want them to TRY Gray's and see if they like them.

A smart brief focuses on the desired response that comes from the strategic objective:
• Get consumers to TRY Gray's and believe the great taste will win them over.

The best advertising can only get the consumer to do one thing at a time, so you should focus your desired response to get consumers to see, think, do, feel, or influence others. Decide on what you want the desired response to be before you decide on the stimulus, which is the next question of the brief.

The bad brief above sets up an unrealistic attempt to get consumers to think, feel, and try – and all in one ad. The smart brief narrows the focus to drive trial, which aligns with the strategic objective of the brand plan.

Too many marketers already know what they want to say before they even know the response they want from their consumers. Start with the desired response, which comes from your brand plan, and only then can you decide what to say to achieve that response.

8. Tone we will take with our consumers

A bad brief uses clichés that are all over the emotional map:
• Optimistic, smart, down-to-earth, trusted, popular, and yet friendly.

A smart brief focuses on the emotional zones your brand is trying to win:
• A safe choice to stay in control. An honest and down-to-earth option.

With Gray's Cookies, the two emotional zones the brand positioning focuses on "stay in control" and "I feel good about myself." The related support words, including safe, honest, and down-to-earth, can help define the ideal emotional tone and manner of your brand.

The bad brief is all over the map with emotions. It seems half the briefs I see contain "smart, trusted, reliable and friendly." It has almost become clichés without thought. Using **our emotional zones** from the brand positioning chapter, you will see those words fall into five distinct emotional zones. These words would make your brand appear schizophrenic in tone.

9. What should we tell consumers? (Main message)

A bad brief tries to communicate too many things at once:
- Gray's Cookies are the perfect modern cookie, only 100 calories and less than 2g of fat. For those looking to lose weight, the American Dietitian's recommend adding Gray's to your diet. You can find Gray's at all leading grocery stores.

A smart brief focuses on one main message, bringing the consumer benefit to life:
- Try Gray's Cookies, the great tasting cookie without any guilt.

The smart brief above narrows down to one thing, the big idea of "great taste without the guilt."

The bad brief has a laundry list of seven unrelated messages. Most are just product features, instead of a primary consumer benefit. It is a marketing myth to believe that if you tell the consumer a lot of things, at least they will hear something. The truth is that if tell consumers too many messages, they will just shut you out and not listen to anything you say.

10. Why should consumers believe us?

A bad brief lists random claims about your brand:
- Gray's Cookies are the cookies recommended by doctors and pharmacists. Plenty of before and after photos, and consumer comments. Over 70% of consumers prefer Gray's to Dad's. Gray's cookies have been made in America since 1963, containing all natural ingredients. No one beats Gray's for fiber content.

A smart brief uses the support points to close off lingering gaps:
- In blind taste tests, Gray's Cookies matched market leaders on taste, but only has 100 calories and 2g of fat. In a 12-week study, consumers using Gray's once a night as a dessert lost 5 pounds.

Only use support points to close off any potential gaps in your logic. Listen to consumers for possible doubts they may have relative to your main message. Based on Logic 101, you can win any argument using two premise points to conclude. The same should hold true for a brand. Force yourself to use a maximum of two support points. The smart brief above focuses on two support points, which back up your main message. The bad brief throws out random claims that have nothing to do with the main message.

11. Brand idea

A bad brief throws out random features to anyone:
- Anyone could love Gray's Cookies, premium cookies that taste great. Over 70% of consumers prefer Gray's to Dad's. Gray's cookies come from a homemade recipe. Doctors and pharmacists recommend them. You can buy them at your local grocery store.

A smart brief uses the brand idea that organizes everything we do:
- Gray's are the best tasting yet guilt-free pleasure so you can stay in control of your health and mind.

The smart brief uses the brand idea that drives everything we do. The bad brief example above targets everyone and lists random features and claims. However, it does not contain any consumer benefits. If you only tell consumers what you do, and not what consumers get, you risk leaving it up to their interpretation.

12. Brand Assets

A bad brief throws out random features and ideas to control the creative:
- Avoid humor, as a sarcastic tone will not work with our target market. Real customer testimonials supported by before/after with our 90-day guarantee tagged on. Use our celebrity spokesperson. Increase credibility by having set in a pharmacy. Add our AMA doctor recommendation seal.

A smart brief uses distinctive creative and strategic assets to build behind:
- Story of our New England family recipe, our signature stack of beautiful cookies, "More Cookie. Less Guilt."

The smart brief builds creative and strategic assets. Stay confident that you have written such a great brief, that you do not need to control the creative outcome.

13. Media choices

A bad brief uses too many media choices, especially early in the process:
- TV, 30-seconds, and 15-seconds. Include 5-second tag for promotions. Print includes magazine and newspaper. Need separate display headers for Walmart. Need to use Facebook, Twitter, and Instagram. Must be able to use video on our website and YouTube channel.

A smart brief provides a range to see what the creative looks like first:
- Main creative will be a 30-second TV ad, supported by event signage and in-store display. Want to carry the idea into digital and social media, and build a microsite.

At the briefing stage, you might have ideas around what type of media you want to use, but it is difficult to know the ideal media until you see the creative idea. At this point, provide a potential media guideline, with a lead media option and possible media choices to support.

The unfocused bad brief above offers a laundry list of media choices, which will only spread your limited resources so thin that nothing will have the desired impact you hope for. When you try to be everywhere, you might end up nowhere.

At the briefing stage, ask to see each creative idea presented as a 30-second TV ad, a simple billboard, and a long-copy print ad. With this request, you will be able to see how each idea plays out across almost every possible media type.

Video	Billboard	Long Copy
• TV (15s, 30s, 60s)	• Outdoor/Mobile billboard	• Who are we story
• Movie Theatre Ads	• Digital billboard/header	• PR/Content Stories
• YouTube Video	• Magazine back cover	• Sales brochure
• Social media video	• Transit ads	• Newspaper/magazine
• Website video	• At-shelf or display sign	• Social Media content
• Demonstration video	• Trade show signage	• Radio

- The 30-second video script can be repurposed to fit TV ads of any length, movie theatre ads, viral videos, or a video on your website.
- The long copy print can be repurposed to fit with content blogs, news stories through PR, newspapers, magazines, website information, and sales brochures. It can even be atomized, broken down into digestible bits to populate a brand's social media content.
- The billboard can be repurposed for outdoor signage, digital display billboards, posters, in-store display signs, or even a magazine's back cover designs.

Mandatories

A good brief gives freedom to the creative team to explore:
- The line: "best tasting yet guilt-free pleasure" is on our packaging. 25% of the print must carry the Whole Foods logo as part of our listing agreement. Include our legal disclaimer on the taste test and 12-week study.

A smart brief has very few mandatories with none of them steering the creative outcome. Stay confident that you have written such a great brief, that you do not need to control the creative outcome.

Give some creative freedom to allow your agency the opportunity to look at the best way to express and deliver your strategy. The bad brief uses mandatories to steer the creative outcome with a prescriptive list that backs the agency into a creative corner. With this bad brief, for the agency to tick off each mandatory, they will create a messy, ugly "Frankenstein" ad to try to piece everything together.

The mini brief

Going too fast sometimes takes too long. With the explosion of media options, timing is everything. Unfortunately, there are too many "phone call briefs" happening. Even worse, no brief at all.

Without a brief, too many things could go wrong. When you see the creative options, you have to rely on your memory and instincts. When you try to present it to your boss, there is nothing to guide them through their decision-making. One round of rejection by your boss, and you will be wondering why you did not just take the 15-30 minutes to organize your thoughts and **write a mini brief.**

Mini brief

Why are we advertising
Tempt younger consumers (18-25) to try Gray's with a social media campaign on Instagram and Snapchat.

About our consumer

Our target
"Proactive Preventers," suburban working moms, 35-40, who are willing to do whatever it takes to stay healthy. They run, workout and eat right. For many, food can be a stress-reliever and escape even for people who watch what they eat.

Consumer Insights
Once consumers cheat on their diet, it puts their whole willpower at risk. "Once I give in to a cookie, I can't stop myself. They taste too good. It puts my diet at risk of collapsing. I feel so guilty."

About our brand

Main message
With Gray's Cookies, you can do what you want and stop feeling guilty over eating a damn cookie.

Support points
Grays Cookies matched the market leaders on taste, but only has 100 calories and 2g of carbs. In a 12-week study, consumers using Gray's once a night lost 5 lbs.

If your brand has a solid brand communications plan, you should be able to create a mini brief with a clear objective, consumer target and insight, the desired response, and the main message.

When I was a brand manager, I once did the dreaded phone call brief for the simplest of tasks. I was holding a "Brand Day" offsite to brainstorm new ideas for our plan. I called my trusted supplier, and asked for T-shirts with "Brand Day" on them, three colors for each flavor of Listerine. The box arrived on the morning of the offsite, and I had 20 T-shirts with "Brand A" on them. We had a big laugh at my expense. If something so simple could go so wrong, what might take you 10 minutes to could save you many hours.

All animations have been created by PRESENTERMEDIA and are used under a licensing agreement

Marketing Execution

Learning and appreciating each element of our ABC's of Advertising

As the marketer, your role is to get great ads into the market and keep bad ads out of the market. You make every decision on which ads will move forward, which ads need fixing, and which ads you should reject.

You need to hit the sweet spot where your brand's advertising is both different and smart. To be different, you need to achieve a branded breakthrough, using creativity to capture consumers. Gain their attention amid the market clutter and link your brand closer to the story. It's how you say it that breaks through the clutter.

To be smart, you need a motivating message to communicate the main message memorable to connect with consumers, and make the ad stick enough to move them to see, think, feel, or act differently than before they saw the ad. It's what you say that moves consumers.

The blind spot of the marketer is to play it safe with work that is smart but not different. You have to recognize that you have this blind spot so that you allow your creative expert to take you on a journey. If you have control over the strategy, you need to give some freedom on the execution.

For you to understand that journey, I want you to understand and appreciate the four elements of our ABC's model with principles for achieving attention, brand link, communication, and stickiness. I will show examples of some of the best ads in the history of advertising that support those principles. I am not teaching you how to write advertising. That's your creative expert's job. I hope that by appreciating how it works, it will challenge your thinking about your brand's advertising.

Ads that get attention

The best way to earn the attention of consumers within the cluttered media world is to take a risk. Do something creatively different from what consumers expect, which entertains, takes advantage of the media, and is shareable for consumers to influence others.

1. Be incongruent with what consumers expect

This technique is an excellent choice to help brands stand out from the clutter. Consumers notice when you are so different from what they expect or so different from what they are watching at the moment. Many brand leaders are afraid of this technique because it is a higher risk, less certain type of creative.

A great example of being incongruent is the **Hathaway Shirt** "Man in the eye patch" print ad. The eye patch is a simple addition to a very dull visual of a man in a shirt. David Ogilvy picked up a few eye patches on the way to the photo shoot. This unorthodox visual made the ad stand out and the brand famous. It was a lasting brand visual for decades.

Another fantastic ad is the "Think small" campaign for the **Volkswagen Beetle**. When every other car was going big, the VW Bug went small. The ad does two things to capture our minds. First, it plays on the commonly known phrase, "Think big." Second, the extreme use of white space, with a barely visible car, is equally arresting. It delivers a message of simplicity and minimalism, with the advantages of a small car down below. AdAge magazine ranked this ad as the best ad of the twentieth century.

The man in the Hathaway shirt

AMERICAN MEN are beginning to realize that it is ridiculous to buy good suits and then spoil the effect by wearing an ordinary, mass-produced shirt. Hence the growing popularity of HATHAWAY shirts, which are in a class by themselves.

HATHAWAY shirts wear infinitely longer—a matter of years. They make you look younger and more distinguished, because of the subtle way HATHAWAY cut collars. The whole shirt is tailored more generously, and is therefore more comfortable. The tails are longer, and stay in your trousers. The buttons are mother-of-pearl. Even the stitching has an ante-bellum elegance about it.

Above all, HATHAWAY make their shirts of remarkable fabrics, collected from the four corners of the earth—Viyella, and Aertex, from England, woolen taffeta from Scotland, Sea Island cotton from the West Indies, hand-woven madras from India, broadcloth from Manchester, linen batiste from Paris, hand-blocked silks from England, exclusive cottons from the best weavers in America. You will get a great deal of quiet satisfaction out of wearing shirts which are in such impeccable taste.

HATHAWAY shirts are made by a small company of dedicated craftsmen in the little town of Waterville, Maine. They have been at it, man and boy, for one hundred and twenty years.

At better stores everywhere, or write c. f. HATHAWAY, Waterville, Maine, for the name of your nearest store. In New York, telephone OX 7-5566. Prices from $5.95 to $20.00.

The common link is the use of incongruent visuals and copy to draw our attention. We can learn a lot from historical ads. With the modern-day clutter of digital media, this is a recommended technique to use to gain the consumer's attention.

2. Entertain consumers

Another technique to gain attention is to make viewers laugh, cry, or dance. People engage media to be entertained. Make your ad part of the entertainment. Be aware of the evolution of the art of creativity to make sure you match the latest type of entertainment. As much as movies, TV, or music evolve, so should your ads.

SMELL LIKE A MAN, MAN.
Old Spice

The **Old Spice** "Smell like a man" campaign's quirky, over-the-top humor is so different, it captured immense attention and helped P&G reinvigorate the Old Spice brand. The ad uses a series of quick cuts, putting the actor in crazy circumstances. His dry, over-the-top delivery adds to the humor.

I love **Budweiser's** "Wassup" campaign because it just makes you laugh. The ad offers zero message, but everyone knows Budweiser, so it is a great way to stay top of mind. The ad is highly entertaining and easily breaks through the clutter of other beer ads. The "Wassup" phrase became part of pop culture, especially among Budweiser's 20-something core target.

3. Use media choice to your brand's full advantage

on your right

ⓐ astral

Put your ads where your consumers are willing to see, listen, and engage, matched with creativity to take advantage of the media choice.

For the last decade, **John Lewis**, the UK department store retailer, has owned the most beloved Christmas ad of the season. It has become such fan favorites the media has leaked the launch date and song choice. These ads generate 50 million views online per year. While retailers struggle around the world, John Lewis used its emotional bond to fuel continuous growth. Advertising testing for John Lewis ads with Facial coding shows the ad has a high positive valence, with a gradual build in smiles, peaking at the end of the ad. The ad is in the top 5% of likeable and top 25% to generate short-term sales.

With such an impulse product, **McDonald's** has become the master of outdoor ads, with a playful spirit, designed to trigger your hunger for McDonald's products.

4. Content people want to share

Over the last decade, everything has become about creating content that is so engaging consumers want to share it on social media. The key is to use high impact storytelling ads that are highly entertaining, deeply emotional, or inspiring enough to engage and captivate consumers.

One of the best viral ads is for **Dollar Shave**. The brand created a hilarious, edgy, low-budget YouTube-driven video, which has generated millions of hits. The tagline for the ad is "Our blades are f**king great," which will undoubtedly alienate many people. However, it will inevitably make the younger male audience quickly love them. The ad tells a quirky story of why the brand doesn't waste

money like Gillette does, setting up the idea its razors are much cheaper than Gillette's. The ad helped launch the brand, which Unilever bought five years later for $1 billion.

One of the first viral videos is **"BMW Films,"** which launched in 2001. BMW gave $1 million to famous directors to make short movies, which had only one stipulation: you must involve the BMW car. These 10-minute videos included stars like Madonna, Clive Owen, Gary Oldman, Don Cheadle, and Dakota Fanning. Even though the videos launched in the early days of YouTube, they have generated over 100 million views.

One of the more modern approaches was **Red Bull's** live coverage and subsequent viral videos of Felix Baumgartner jumping out of a rocket ship 24 miles above the earth. The video fits very nicely with the target market and the brand. Red Bull is a brand sponsor of many extreme sports, with this being the most extreme sport possible. While, legally, Red Bull is no longer allowed to say, "Red Bull gives you wings," this event positively screams the brand idea, loud and clear. With millions watching the live streaming video online and over 100 million watching videos on YouTube, this stunt was a huge attention getter for Red Bull.

In sports, Red Bull has taken their attention seeking abilities to Formula 1 racing, where Red Bull Racing now have the #1 racing team in the world.

Ads with high brand link

The best brand link comes when you connect your brand closer to the ad's pinnacle moment. Understanding your brand from the consumer's perspective, tapping into relatable consumer insights, and making your brand the story's focal point will lead to strong brand link scores.

However, there are some misconceptions about creating a strong brand link that need to be debunked. Higher brand link drives both short-term sales and consumer motivation.

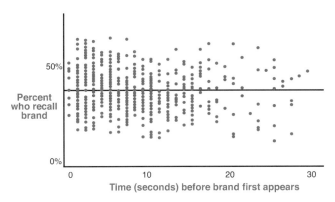

The first brand link myth: "Make sure the brand name shows up in the first few seconds of your ad."

While this idea may seem logical, it's not accurate. Milward Brown's advertising tracking data reveals that the timing of the brand name's first appearance in an ad doesn't affect brand link. The chart to the left, displaying a line at about 40% (the average brand link of all ads in Milward Brown's database), demonstrates that the likelihood of scoring above the average brand link is equal regardless of whether the brand appears in the ad's first few seconds or at the 25-second mark.

In the digital advertising or YouTube pre-roll ad context, waiting until the end to reveal your brand may not be feasible due to viewers' limited attention spans. Simply displaying the brand visually or as an overlay doesn't suffice unless it contributes to the story.

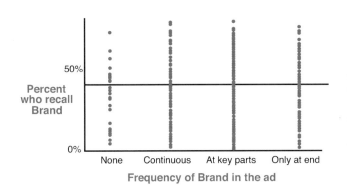

The second brand link myth: "The more often you show the brand, the higher brand link scores."

Milward Brown's chart on the left indicates that there's no correlation between the frequency of the brand's appearance in the ad and the resulting brand connection. The data examines four options for the brand's display frequency in the ad: none, continuous, at crucial points, or only at the end. As with the first misconception, there's no link between the number of times the brand name appears and the strength of your brand connection score. When the brand seamlessly integrates with the ad, it results in a 55% increase in consumer purchase motivation.

1. Make your brand a central part of the story

From my experience, it is not how much branding you use, but preferably how closely connected the reveal of the brand is linked with the climax of your ad.

"Got milk?" launched a hilarious and engaging storytelling ad with an elaborate tale of an Alexander Hamilton expert. He finds himself on a radio show, ready to answer an easy trivia question about Alexander Hamilton. However, after taking a big bite of his peanut butter sandwich, as he is about to answer, he realizes he is out of milk. With an elaborate story, the reveal of the brand comes at the climax of the story. The "Got milk?" campaign lasted over 20 years.

2. Resonate with meaningful consumer insights

Using consumer insights to tell a compelling human-interest story is a great technique to closely connect with your target market, then closely link your brand to the insight.

The **Always** "Like a girl" campaign is an inspirational video that connects with true insight about the perception of how girls run changes as they hit puberty. The ad starts by asking older teens and 20-somethings to run like a girl, and they depict a negative stereotypical overly feminine running style. Then, it asks 10-year-old girls to run like a girl, and they run in a highly athletic manner. It asks what changes to make the older girls see running as a negative. The ad challenges viewers to rethink their stereotypes. It inspires girls with an uplifting message to be themselves and encourages them to believe that, "running like a girl" is a good thing. The Always brand closely lines itself to the insights about the changes happening at puberty, just as moms and daughter will be choosing the feminine hygiene brand they will use. Without saying a word about Always products, the ad positions the brand as different from its competitors. This is the 7th most watched ad on YouTube and 2nd most among women

3. View the brand through the eyes of your consumer

Use emotional stories to demonstrate how the consumer engages your brand.

Google had a Super Bowl ad that tells the story of an American student who goes to Paris, meets a girl, maintains a long distance relationship, gets married, lands a job in Paris, and then has a baby. Every part of the story is told by Google searches, which surprise the consumer as they follow the story. The ad shows how much we can use and rely on Google for anything we need in life.

Google India launched a beautiful viral ad, which earned millions of YouTube hits. The first time I saw the ad, I cried, even though I could not understand the language, I realized the great storytelling was obvious enough to follow.

The ad starts with an elderly Indian man, who tells his granddaughter a story of how he lost touch with his childhood best friend after the partition of India in 1947. With the details of her grandfather's story, the granddaughter locates his childhood friend in Pakistan and connects with the other best friend's grandson, who is willing to help her to plan a surprise visit for her grandfather's birthday. Every element of the search and the travel arrangement is done through Google.
The brand weaves naturally throughout the ad.

4. Own the story of the brand

When telling the story of your brand, make sure to amplify what sets you apart from anyone else. Create a strong visual cue, which you can build over time, big enough to repeat and repeat and repeat.

During the turbulent times of the early '70s, **Coke** assembled people on a hill to sing "Teach the world to sing." Everyone in the commercial was holding a bottle of Coke. This ad spoke to a generation looking for peace and harmony. The ad is one of the best ads of all time.

A great example of a high brand link is the **McDonald's** Big Mac jingle with a descriptive "Two all beef patties…" song about the brand. It broke through and remains stuck in the consumer's mind.

Ads that communicate

Communication is not what is said, but what is heard. The best brand communication happens when you focus on the one benefit that moves consumers, by creatively amplifying, telling the story behind your brand purpose, using extreme demonstrations or powerful visuals.

As I said in the creative brief chapter, stop thinking of your ads like a bulletin board where you can pin up one more message. Start thinking as though you are shouting through a bullhorn in a crowded square. Tell me the ONE message you need to make sure the consumer hears.

The Milward Brown data show the more messages you put in an ad, the less likely the consumer will recall your main message. Looking at the chart, it shows when an ad

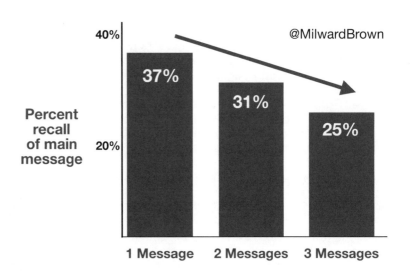

has one message, the average main message recall by consumers is 37%. For ads with two messages, the main message recall goes down to 31%, and for three messages, the main message recall goes down to 26%. On top of that, the recall of the third message recall is only 11%, almost worthless to the advertising.

Focus on one message, starting with the brief, and you will increase your message communication scores. Here are four techniques to look at increasing your brand communication:

1. Creatively amplify your brand's consumer benefit

Bring the idea to life by exaggerating the worst version of the consumer's enemy, to help set up your brand as the solution that will move consumers to buy. This technique results in some of my favorite Ads.

A great example of amplifying your consumer benefit is the **Snickers** Super Bowl ad with Betty White playing football with a bunch of college-aged guys. After a bad play by Betty, one of the buddies yells at her that she is "not playing like her normal self." He then hands Betty a Snickers bar and Betty turns back into the college-aged football player. The ad uses the consumer insight of, "You're not you when you're hungry" to set up the consumer benefit of how Snickers satisfies your hunger. This technique is a great combination that would fit many brands.

Berlitz used a scenario of a German Coast Guard operator who takes on an SOS distress call of a boat that was "sinking." His response, "What are you thinking about?" is an incredibly fun way to highlight the importance of language training.

There is also a great **Ikea** ad about a woman who throws out her old lamp, suggesting she should go to Ikea and get a new lamp instead. While the ad tries to get you to feel sorry for the tired, old lamp, as it sits by the corner of the driveway in the rain, along comes a strange Swedish man in the pouring rain, who suggests "Why do you feel sorry for this lamp? It's just a lamp. New is always better." This ad is an excellent demonstration of how disposable furniture is, and how good it feels to replace the old, tired options.

2. Tell the story behind your brand purpose to move consumers and employees

Use your brand's values, beliefs, and purpose to express your brand's background story in an engaging way that will move the consumer.

Apple's "Think different" campaign relaunched the Apple brand in 1997, with a script that said, "The crazy ones are crazy enough to change the world." This ad showed some of the most famous people in history, including Albert Einstein, Bob Dylan, Gandhi, John Lennon, Amelia Earhart, and Muhammad Ali. To me, the ad was just as much of an internal brand message designed to inspire the internal Apple culture to push for greatness to believe they are crazy enough.

The Crazy Ones — Apple TV ad

Here's to the crazy ones. The misfits. The rebels. The troublemakers. The round pegs in the square holes.

The ones who see things differently. They're not fond of rules. And, they have no respect for the status quo.

You can quote them, disagree with them, glorify or vilify them. About the only thing you can't do is ignore them. Because they change things. They push the human race forward.

While some may see them as the crazy ones, we see genius.

Because the people who are crazy enough to think the world can change are the ones who do.

In the 1960s, **Avis** used the "We try harder" brand idea to show various ways how as the #2 brand, they have to work harder than Hertz, the leader. They have to be nice, clean the ashtrays, make sure the tires are filled up, leaving you to wonder if Hertz cared about those details. This message is the perfect internal rallying cry to inspire the internal staff to try harder and be better. America always loves an underdog story. Embrace the copy of these great ads. It is fantastic.

While nearly every Super Bowl ad is loud and funny, **Dodge Ram** used a quietly dramatic ad, using Paul Harvey's famous radio show recording called, "God created a farmer." The ad is set against gorgeous photos of hard-working farmers, telling a classic working-class America story. It is a highly inspiring, optimistic story that will give you patriotic goose bumps.

3. Extreme demonstration of the consumer benefit

Find a creative extreme torture test to showcase your brand's most motivating consumer benefit.

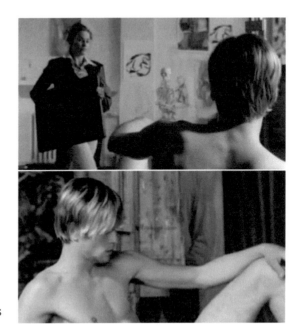

A great example of an extreme demonstration is the **Impulse perfume** ad from the UK. One of the most difficult creative challenges is to demonstrate the impact of a perfume scent visually. The ad tells the story of a nude male model in an art class. While he is at the front of the room, in walks a female student who walks past him, and he obviously smells her perfume, and becomes "aroused." While we don't see anything, it has become visibly evident to everyone in the art class.

Rolls-Royce used a highly creative demonstration to show how quiet their cars are, with a print ad with the headline, "At 60 miles an hour, the loudest noise in the new Rolls-Royce comes from the electric clock." This type of copy line makes the consumer think.

Back in the 1960s, **Timex** watches used highly engaging torture tests, including smashing a watch or holding a watch underwater, in order to demonstrate how a Timex watch "takes a licking and keeps on ticking."

4. Move consumers through a powerful visual

Take what should be the obvious benefit and bring it to life through a glorious visual demonstration.

One of my favorite ads is the **Honda** spot that utilizes a chain of colliding parts taken from a disassembled Honda Accord in a falling domino effect. As an engineering dominant company, the main consumer benefit of precision is a perfect fit with the Honda brand. The spot took 600+ takes to get it just right. It only aired 10 times, during high-profile sporting events. The ad helped the Honda UK business turn around from a declining brand to 28% sales growth the next year.

Ads that stick with consumers

Ads that stick need to be memorable enough to move consumers. Surround your consumer with your creative idea, invest in your assets, engage emotionally, and build a deeper love with those who already love you.

1. Continue to build your creative idea

A goldfish will get bigger with a bigger bowl. The same holds for creative ideas. Build your creative idea over time, across various media, over many products to different targets and through multiple stories, each time adding to the idea.

The best example of growing your creative idea is the **Nike** "Just do it" campaign, which turns 30-years-old in 2018. Nike's creative idea of "Just do it" reflects the strategic brand idea of, "Nike pushes you beyond your athletic boundaries." Nike has made the most of TV advertising, layering in new stories supporting the "Just do it" creative idea. Here are some of the best Nike TV ads:

- Michael Jordan's **"Failure"** ad has him speaking about the many times he has been entrusted with the last shot, only to fail to deliver.
- With **"Jogger"** from the 2012 London Olympics, Nike used a heavy-set kid jogging at 6 a.m., to show how not all of us are superstars and challenges the average athlete inside all of us.
- Nike launched their most controversial ad, in support of **Colin Kaepernick**. From a PR perspective, one simple tweet by Colin Kaepernick touched off a huge Twitter storm.
- **"If you let me play sports"** from the early 1990s, an emotional ad that speaks to all the life benefits for girls who play sports. Adolescent girls deliver the copy lines of "If you let me play sports, I will have more confidence, be more likely to leave a man who beats me or suffer less depression."
- Dream Crazier featured **Serena Williams**, sent an extremely powerful and inspiring message to women about the double standard women face when trying to go beyond what you can ever expect.

2. Emotionally transform your brand

As you move from a functional to an emotional consumer benefit, from logic to passion, the advertising will begin to stick in the hearts of your consumers.

Dove's "Real Beauty" ad shows the transformation of a woman's face as they touch up her makeup, hair and then show computer editing adjustments to create the perception of the perfect woman. They adjust her cheekbones, her eye shape and thin out her chin. The message is, "No wonder our perception of beauty is distorted." This campaign connected on a deep level with women, and it helped transform Dove from a functional brand (Ph balance) into an emotional brand that speaks on behalf of women.

Before this campaign, Dove had used a highly functional "Ph balance litmus test" to battle Ivory soap. Dove never managed to beat Ivory while focusing on functional benefits. However, once Dove launched the "Real Beauty" ad, the brand unleashed its full potential and helped Dove soar past Ivory.

Building emotion into advertising directly impacts a brand's persuasion score

While brand leaders are always trying to find a winning claim, there is proof of a correlation between the feel-good emotions you create with both consumer persuasion scores and overall brand appeal scores.

Milward Brown advertising research finds a direct correlation between how involved consumers are in the ads with the degree of the positive emotional feelings your advertising evokes in consumers. The chart shows that as the feelings go from low to medium to high, the scores for both persuasion and brand appeal also go up.

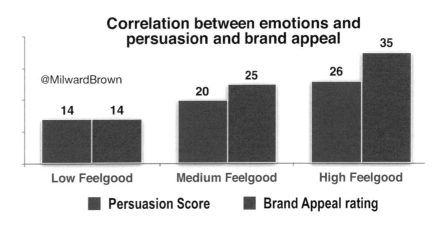

Correlation between emotions and persuasion and brand appeal

@MilwardBrown

	Persuasion Score	Brand Appeal rating
Low Feelgood	14	14
Medium Feelgood	20	25
High Feelgood	26	35

■ Persuasion Score   ■ Brand Appeal rating

3. Investing in your brand assets adds up

Build creative and brand assets, using new executions to always add a penny to your brand to the creative advertising idea. The best sticky ads are a combination of new, relevant, credible, and different.

There are **two types of assets** you should build behind:

- **Brand assets:** Look at the image scores or main messaging scores in your brand tracking, then continue to build those brand associations and messaging into the campaign over time. They become the heart of the brand's truth and reputation.
- **Creative assets:** Those images, icons, or devices of the ads, which consumers remember and internalize. You want to understand what's breaking through and continue to use those creative assets in future executions. Using these assets starts to give your brand a sense of consistency in execution.

A great example is **Apple's** "I'm a Mac … and I'm a PC" ads. They made over 70 different versions of the comparative story, with each ad showing another reason why PCs are complicated while the Mac offers simplicity. The visual of the two people made a perfect representation of the two brands.

4. Build a deeper love with those who already love you

Tell elaborate stories that showcase why your consumers who already love you should love you even more.

Six months after 9/11, **Budweiser** used their famous Clydesdale horses branding device with a Super Bowl ad that showed the horses walking through town after town across America. Then it shows the horses slowly approaching the New York skyline, and they kneel in front of Manhattan to honor those lost in the Twin Towers.

Filled with American patriotism, for the brand lovers who know the story of the brand, it links nicely with the history of the Clydesdales, when they marched from St. Louis across America in 1934 to deliver a keg to the U.S. President at the White House after he lifted the prohibition on alcohol.

New, relevant, credible, and different ads stick

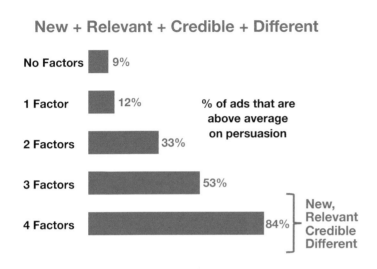

New + Relevant + Credible + Different

No Factors 9%

1 Factor 12%

% of ads that are above average on persuasion

2 Factors 33%

3 Factors 53%

4 Factors 84% — New, Relevant Credible Different

Everything in the ABC's model adds up. The ideal advertising should be **new, relevant, credible and different.** As we show in the creation of a brand idea, you want to find the space that is simple to gain entry on the first encounter. Your ad should be interesting enough to entice consumers to consider, unique to make consumers think, motivating to tempt and move consumers, inspirational to your team behind the brand, easily layered across every consumer touchpoint and ownable for the longevity of the brand.

Milward Brown advertising research finds a direct correlation between brands which fulfill all four criteria of new, relevant, credible, and different and brands with the highest opportunity to persuade consumers to buy. The research shows the higher the number of criteria your ad satisfies, the greater your opportunity to persuade.

Summary of the ABC's model

Attention	Brand Link	Communication	Stickiness
1. Be incongruent with what consumers expect. 2. Entertain consumers. 3. Use media choice to your brand's full advantage. 4. Create shareable content.	1. Make brand central to story. 2. Resonate with meaningful consumer insights. 3. View brand through eyes of your consumer. 4. Own the story of the brand.	1. Creatively amplify brand's benefit. 2. Tell the story behind brand purpose. 3. Extreme demo of consumer benefit. 4. Move consumers through a powerful visual.	1. Build up your creative idea. 2. Emotionally transform brand. 3. Invest in your brand assets. 4. Build a deeper love with those who already love you.

How to make media decisions to break through the cluttered media world

Media is a business investment to showcase your brand story through creative execution to help connect your brand with consumers where consumers are most willing to engage, listen, think, feel, and act in ways that pay back your brand.

There is power in using media to surround your consumer. Milward Brown data shows that TV + online video significantly outperforms TV alone or video alone. And, even the younger generations still see traditional media choices such as outdoor and print ads. We come at this from lens of the brand leader, not a media expert.

Here are six questions to help build your media plan:

1. What is the size of your brand's media budget?
2. What is your brand's core strength?
3. How tightly connected is your brand with your consumer?
4. Where can you best impact the consumer journey?
5. Where will your consumers be most open to engage, listen, think, feel, and act?
6. What media choices will best deliver your brand's creative execution?

Summary of our six media planning questions

1. What is the brand's budget size?

Start with the size of your business and the related gross margins available to spend. Look at the past media ROI and creative advertising results as a projection for success. Identify the brand or business impact from previous campaigns, and match up to potential strategy you are looking at this time.

2. What is your brand's core strength?

Explore the differences of whether your brand is a story-led, product-led, experience-led or price-led impacts and how it impacts your main message. Generally, story-led and product-led need significant budgets, to reach a large audience. Experience-led brands are a slower build and rely on word of mouth. Price-led brands needs efficient media choices to quickly trigger the transaction.

3. How tightly connected is your brand with your consumer?

Where does your brand sit on the brand love curve? Where you sit impacts the communication focus getting consumers to see, think, buy, feel or influence. You should filter based on the degree of competitive threats you face in the market. The higher the competitive battle, the higher the advertising spend.

4. Where can you best impact the consumer journey?

Understand how your consumer moves from awareness, consideration, search, buy, satisfy, repeat, loyal and to becoming a brand fan. Match up to the communication focus of the strategy to the stage where you can have the greatest impact, related to your overall brand strategy in the brand plan.

5. Where are consumers most open to engage, think, listen, feel, and act?

Who is your target consumer? What part of the consumer's life are they most willing to watch, listen, learn, engage, decide and act? How can you align with their day-in-the-life or moments during the week or year. For significant purchases, you can align to special life-changing moments. Are there adjacent or related products/services linked to your brand?

6. What media choices will best deliver the creative execution?

Your brand idea should drive the creative idea, which then drives your priority for gaining attention, brand link, communication or stickiness. Stay open on media during the creative development process to ensure your creative can fit with the best media choices.

| Brand story | Home Page | Explainer Videos | Search Engine | Social Media | Paid Media | Influencer Marketing | Sales Material | Trade Shows |

1. What is the size of your brand's media budget?

Balance the media choices by looking at media efficiency, quality, impact, and fit with the brand. The efficiency of media math starts with reach and frequency.

- **Reach** is the number or percentage of different households or people exposed to the ad at least once, over a specific period.
- **Frequency** is the number of times that household or person will be exposed to the ad within a particular period. Be careful to avoid relying on efficiency alone, as you need to balance it with the quality of the media choices.

I always set aside about 10 percent of my media budget to create a high impact to generate early attention to a new campaign or product innovation.

Use your **strategic thinking** to understand how much you can invest. You need to focus your limited resources on a distinct opportunity point you have identified based on a potential change in the market. The reasons you would strategically invest in media include:

- Discovery of a new brand message you know will motivate consumers to buy your brand.
- Identified change in consumer needs, motivations, or behaviors, which will benefit your brand.
- Shift the competitive dynamic, with an opportunity to make gains or a necessity to defend.
- Continue to fuel brand growth with a window to drive brand profits.
- New distribution channel you can use to move consumers through before competitors do.
- The launch of a breakthrough product innovation offering a competitive advantage to your brand.

To make the media investment pay off, you need to be able to drive a performance result that pays back with an increase in brand power you can use in the future or an immediate increase in brand profit.

Six factors to guide you on the size of your media investment:

1. Brand profit situation, looking at margin rates and the size of the business.
2. Past media ROI projected forward as a forecast of the potential.
3. Impact of your current creative advertising tracking results
4. Future investment opportunities or future threats to battle.
5. The degree of competitive pressures in the marketplace and their levels of media spend.
6. The comparative opportunity cost for investing elsewhere.

Media budget levels

There is a term called zero-based marketing budgeting, which starts each new year, assuming all brand budgets are zero, and the brand must prove their case to earn its budget level.

While it makes perfect sense in theory, with 20 years of experience with marketing budgets, this is not an easy concept to implement. One risk I see is that a zero-based budget could lead to short-term and highly transactional advertising.

A brand needs to balance brand-building activities, which add to the long-term connection with consumers with transactional call-to-action messaging intended to trigger purchases. For instance, if you tell me "Buy two, get one free" for five straight years, your consumers will eventually forget why they should buy your product at all, let alone two. There is a degree of uncertainty in making investment decisions. Get comfortable with your instincts to balance the degree of ambiguity to make the smart decision.

When you feel the risk/reward of the media investment is unknown, it might be wise to start with a smaller investment level. Use what I call a **"blowfish" media plan** so that, among those you target, you appear to be a large brand. Pick a tight target market with a limited media choice or geographic focus to replicate how a more substantial media investment would appear. When the unknown is very high, get smarter by using test markets with various media spend levels to gain the necessary consumer response data before you make a full investment.

Use a **medium investment leve**l when your brand faces only a couple of the media investment factors listed above, yet your brand has the size and margin to invest. With this level of spend, you should use a selective media plan by making smart choices of the target market who you know will respond to those media choices proven to pay back.

Use a **high investment level** when your brand faces many of the investment factors, including profitable brand, reliable messaging, product innovation, and an intensely competitive situation. You can afford to take a mass approach. However, just because you have a lot of money does not mean you should waste it. I still recommend using one lead media choice and then use support media to supplement. Figure out your lead paid media and your lead earned media to provide focus and alignment with your strategy.

One important consideration with any investment plan is to balance media spending and the creative production costs. Your brand's working dollars are those investments that directly reach and influence the consumer. You can directly see the impact and measure the payback. Media is considered working dollars. This costing method is one of the reasons you do not want to spread your brand across too many media choices. If most of your brand's advertising budget is spent making TV ads, billboards, and radio ads or paying for talent in the ads, then you will not have enough spending left to reach the consumer.

2. What is your brand's core strength?

Deciding whether your brand will be story-led, product-led, experience-led, or price-led impacts your brand message and related media choices.

If your brand is **product-led**, focus on standing out with trend influencers and early adopters. Use an interruptive and visual media choice, such as TV or online video, to demonstrate and explain what makes your product better. You can share the video demonstrations on your brand's website or through social media. Invest in search to help consumers who may have questions and need more information. Mobilize expert influencers to trigger trend influencers and early adopters to make informed purchases.

For **story-led brands**, use media to create a movement behind your idea, purpose, core belief or a stance. Connect with like-minded consumers who could become potential early brand lovers and influence their network to turn your brand into a movement. Bring your brand's concept, purpose, or story to life using emotional storytelling media, such as TV, long-copy print, storytelling content built to share. This approach allows those early brand lovers to spread awareness with influence and gives your brand an active voice on social media.

Core Strength	Communication
Product	What we make is best or better
Story	Our story, idea, purpose makes us different
Experience	Our people make us better
Price	Same quality at a lower price

When your brand's strength is the **consumer experience**, building your brand awareness takes time. Be patient. The slower build will be well worth the time invested once you hit a tipping point. Start by engaging key influencers and expert reviewers (industry critics) early on to reach the trend influencer consumers who will build word-of-mouth within their network. Build and manage the online customer review sites (Yelp, Trip Advisor) to entice other users to try your brand's fantastic experience. Consider allowing your staff to share their personal, authentic "wow" stories to become part of the brand's communication. It is your great people who make the difference. The voice of the consumer will make or break the brand early on.

When you are a **price-led brand**, you need high sales volumes to cover the lower margins. The most successful price brands invest in call-to-action, efficient media options, such as 15-second TV, digital display, or radio ads. Use traditional and online price tools, such as flyers or online coupon sites. Use the point of sale media to trigger transactions.

3. How connected is your brand?

Use the brand love curve to focus your media objectives and strategy. For **unknown** or **indifferent brands**, invest in the early part of the consumer journey, with media focused on building awareness to establish the brand positioning in the mind of consumers to separate your brand from the pack. You also need to get your brand into the consumer's consideration set.

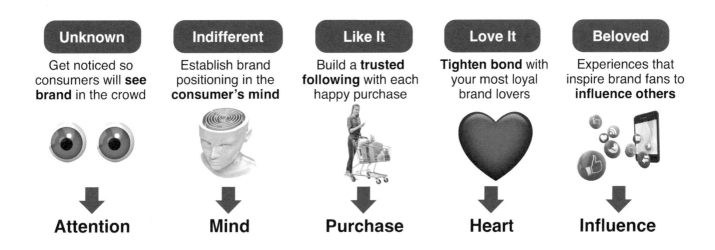

Unknown	Indifferent	Like It	Love It	Beloved
Get noticed so consumers will **see brand** in the crowd	Establish brand positioning in the **consumer's mind**	Build a **trusted following** with each happy purchase	**Tighten bond** with your most loyal brand lovers	Experiences that inspire brand fans to **influence others**
Attention	**Mind**	**Purchase**	**Heart**	**Influence**

Brands at the **like it** stage must separate themselves from others, to build momentum and create a following. Focus on closing the deal, by motivating consumers to buy. You can use search tools and deal-closing claims at the point of sale to resolve any remaining doubts. You can utilize your own e-commerce website or sites such as Amazon, Expedia, or Groupon.

Brands at the **love it** stage must turn your consumer's repeat purchases into higher usage frequency and become a favorite part of your consumer's day. The creative must instill emotional benefits, linked closely to the consumer's life moments. An excellent tool to use is to map out the "day-in-the-life" of your target consumer and place messages where they are most likely to engage. Use consumer insights to make the messages personal to make consumers feel special and attached to your brand.

At the **beloved brand stage**, you should begin shifting to a maintenance media plan, enough to maintain your brand's leadership presence and perception. Stay aware of the competitive activity, which may force you to adjust your budget levels. At this point, you can shift some of your media resources into enhancing the consumer experience, to retain your happy consumers, and to drive a deeper love to harness an army of brand lovers. You can begin creating shareable experiences for your brand lovers to share with their friends.

4. Where can you best impact the consumer journey?

Old-school marketing used to yell their messages at every possible consumer using mass media, then move consumers naturally through the brand funnel from awareness to purchase and loyalty. With so few media choices, consumers could not escape the advertising. If consumers did not respond the first time, show it to them again and again. Back in the 1970s, it was all about the interruption of consumers, with brands focused primarily on day-after brand recall. Many times, the more annoying the ad, the better it would work. This media planning is not quite the sophisticated media strategy brands need today.

New-school marketing whispers to the most loyal brand fans, hoping they drive awareness with influence to their friends. The word of a friend will bring more influence to their purchase decision than a random TV ad. As the brand moves to the masses, consumers look for the advice of trusted peers whom they respect to know enough about the latest and greatest of the category. They also look to the brand lovers, giving them evidence the brand does deliver what it promises.

In the **brand strategy section**, I showed you how brands evolved from a craft brand to a disruptor, to a challenger brand and finally to a power player. One significant distinction is what type of consumers they focus on. I introduced the idea of a consumer adoption curve, which leverages four types of consumers:

- Trend influencers
- Early adopters
- Early mass
- Late mass

I will use this thinking to show how brands can use influencers to trigger each type of consumer, as the brand evolves from the entry-level craft brand to the power player mass brand.

The role of influencers on the consumer adoption curve

The **trend influencer consumers** always want leading-edge stuff and are first to try within their social set. They stay aware of what the wise experts are saying, whom they trust or rely upon for knowledge. For brands competing in the car, sports, technology, fashion, entertainment, or foodie markets, there are leading expert reviewers or bloggers who have become the voice of the marketplace. Marketers who have a real revolutionary addition to the category should target and brief these wise experts to ensure they fully understand the brand story and point of difference. This information increases their willingness to recommend new products.

The **early adopter consumers** rely on their trend influencer friends for the details of new brands. However, they will also look to social icons as a secondary source for validation. These social icons could include movie stars, singers, or famous athletes. If the social icons are using the new product, this assures the early adopter the new brand is about to hit a tipping point. These consumers always want to stay ahead of the curve, so that they will adopt it now.

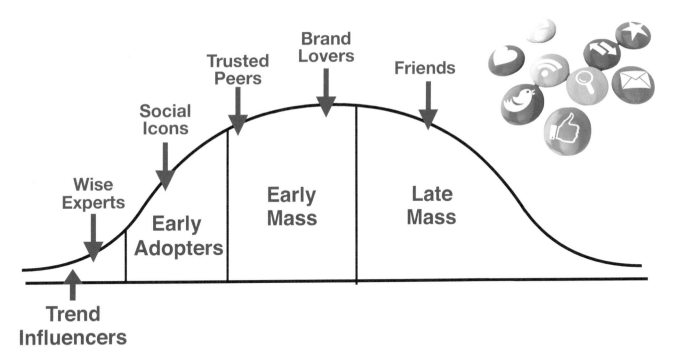

Early mass consumers look for the advice of trusted peers whom they respect within their network. These are the people we go to for advice on a given subject. The early mass also looks to early brand lovers for validation of proven success; This satisfaction level gives them evidence the brand does deliver what it promises. **Late mass audience** is slow to adopt; they look to friends for recommendations but only when they feel comfortable enough to buy the brand.

OmniChannel Marketing moves consumers along their journey

We revisit the consumer journey from the consumer strategy chapter. The stages of our brand love curve match up with the actions of attract, inform, close, service, and delight.

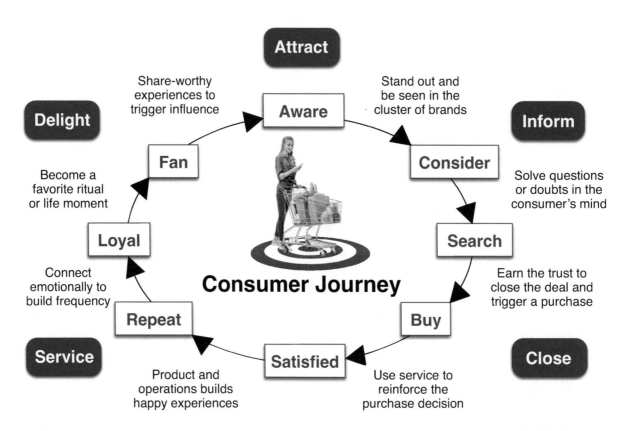

In the early stages of the consumer journey, when a brand is unknown, it must stand out to attract attention. Mass media options, including traditional TV, out-of-home advertising, and digital platforms, are necessary.

As more consumers turn to search for validation, the focus shifts to answering questions and resolving doubts. Leveraging your website or salespeople can earn the trust consumers need to finalize a purchase. Providing excellent service can reinforce their decision and create positive experiences that lead to repeat purchases.

In the later stages of the journey, a brand must connect emotionally to become an integral part of a consumer's life. Delighting your most loyal brand fans creates shareable moments and encourages them to influence their friends. The best brands understand how their most engaged fans can generate new awareness.

An omni-channel vs a multi-channel approach

For years, our approach to multi-media was primarily focused on combining a lead medium with several supplementary options such as TV, radio, and out-of-home. But as the landscape evolves, brands are pivoting to a more holistic Omni-Channel strategy. It's essential to grasp how diverse media elements integrate, guiding consumers seamlessly through their journey.

First, let's illustrate the interplay of brand building, sales activation, and user-generated content. The following diagram showcases their combined influence on the consumer's journey.

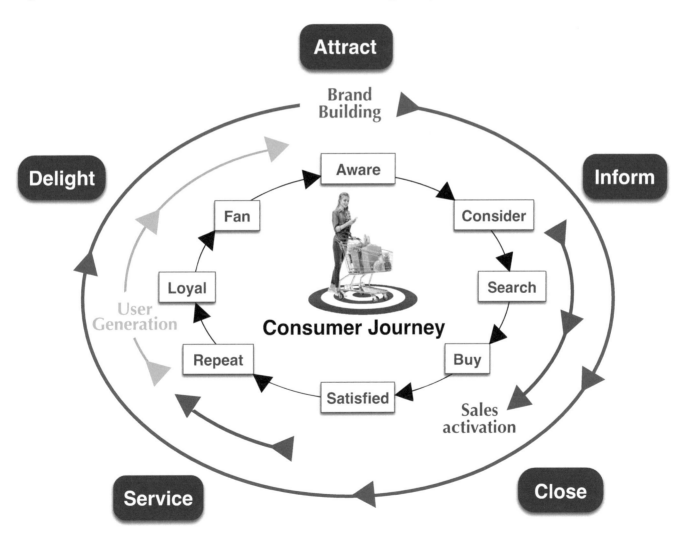

Brand Building

Brand building begins gradually but gains momentum, driving substantial growth over time. Contrary to the misconception that it's solely for the top of the funnel, brand building engages new consumers for awareness and employs compelling narratives throughout the entire consumer journey. Effective advertising should resonate deeply, emotionally aligning with the brand's positioning and distinguishing itself with unique creative assets. Paid media, with an "always-on" strategy, ensures extensive reach, further enhanced by standout placements. For consumers desiring more information, seamlessly integrate owned media.

I love anthemic advertising in brand-building to solidify brand positioning, foster emotional connections with target audiences, strengthen brand identity, and nurture consumer bond. Over time, brand-building yields a sustainable competitive advantage and brand affection, translating to growth in sales, market share, and profit.

Sales Activation

Sales activation yields immediate results, particularly during trial or repeat phases. Early in the consumer journey, focus on high-need consumers during their pinnacle moments of interest. Ads should present credible information, guiding consumers from consideration to purchase. Subsequently, use service and other incentives to promote repeat purchases. Such strategic journey management prevents excessive discounting, thus safeguarding profitability. Encompass the consumer with a blend of paid, earned, owned, and shared media.

Short-term transactional advertising aims for quick outcomes, such as boosting sales, amplifying website traffic, or amassing leads. These campaigns often play on desires and impulses, using promotions, discounts, or limited-time offers to instill urgency and spur immediate consumer actions. However, while short-term advertising can generate swift returns, over-relying on this method might erode brand equity and hinder long-term growth. If all you do is say "buy me now" consumers will not know why they should ever buy you.

User Generation

User generation capitalizes on the bond between a brand and its most ardent fans, converting their advocacy into impactful awareness. To metamorphose satisfied customers into brand advocates, one must exceed their expectations, encouraging them to introduce the brand to new potential clients. A focus on earned and shared media allows user-generated content to mint micro brand ambassadors. Employ CRM (Customer Relationship Management system) for tailored interactions that evolve ordinary habits into treasured rituals.

There are advantages to the OmniChannel approach.

TV, once the dominant mass media, is seeing its influence wane among millennials and even more so with Gen Z. Integrating digital with TV not only extends reach but also intensifies frequency, making campaigns more memorable and cost-effective. Nielsen indicates that dual TV and digital campaigns boost brand recall by 74%. Similarly, the IAB found a 15% increase in purchase intent with this combined approach. Furthermore, after a TV ad, half of viewers seek more brand info, with 57% heading to Google.

The long and the short of building a brand

The art of building your brand through media lies in striking the right balance between long-term brand building and short-term sales activation. There's substantial evidence in the marketing world suggesting that half of your marketing efforts should target brand building, with the other half zeroing in on transactions. However, an alarming trend shows many brands gravitating toward short-term sales without laying a solid brand foundation.

To ensure immediate gains and enduring success, brands must deftly navigate their advertising strategies. By prioritizing brand-building efforts at the outset of the consumer journey and harnessing transactional advertising at its culmination, brands can curate a unified experience for their audience. By leveraging personalized messaging to engage loyal brand enthusiasts, brands can inculcate rituals, nurturing a profound, long-lasting bond with consumers and laying the groundwork for sustained brand strength and affinity.

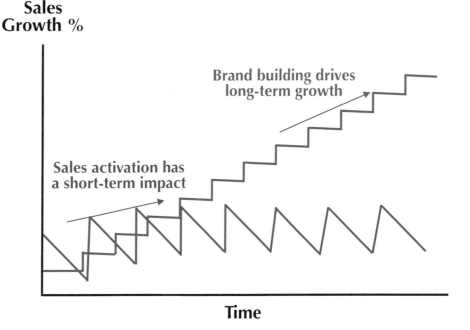

Source: Les Binet and Peter Field, IPA

5. Where and when is your consumer open to engaging?

Place your media on the part of the consumer's life where they will watch, listen, learn, engage, decide, and act. Align with **life moments**, whether they are parts of the day, the week, the year, or even milestone moments in their life. A smart tool for media planning is to map out the day-in-the-life of your consumer, to try to understand what they go through and where they might be most receptive to your message.

Tap into those life moments when people are most willing to reconsider brands. It might be a stage of life, such as going away to university or getting your first job or having your first child. Each life moment is a chance for brands to get consumers to reconsider their current choices.

6. What is the best media to deliver the creative?

The best media to deliver the creative depends on several factors, including the target audience, the brand's objectives, the nature of the creative idea, and the available budget. The brand idea should drive both the creative advertising and the media planning. The optimal media mix should be carefully selected to ensure maximum reach, creative impact, and efficiency.

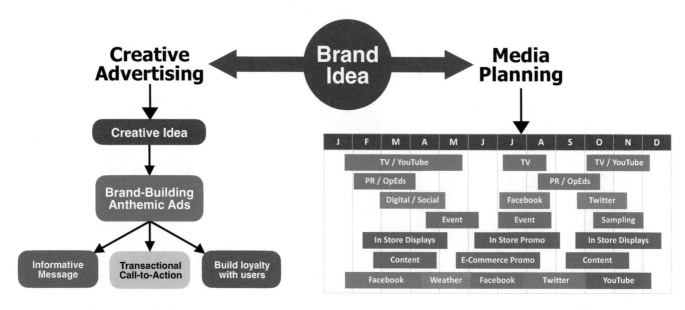

Think of your media as video, billboard and long-copy

- **Video** enables brands to convey their story, trigger emotions, enhance user engagement, and drive conversions via dynamic and captivating content. Platforms for video include TV, cinemas, viral content, YouTube, social media, and your own website.
- **Billboard** excel in achieving visibility when it matters most, grabbing attention, swiftly relaying a brand's core message, and fortifying brand recognition in an easily noticeable medium. This encompasses outdoor, transit, digital or mobile displays, magazine back covers, and in-store promotional signage..
- **Long-copy** aids in elaborating on a brand's core benefits, establishing trust, addressing common questions, substantiating claims, and educating post-purchase clients. Examples of long-copy include websites, PR or content articles, brochures, traditional print, social media posts, and radio dialogues.

By integrating the three media concepts, we unlock the potential of the Omni-Channel approach. Begin with brand building, sales activation, and user-generated content to guide consumers through their journey. Then, employ owned, paid, earned, and shared media channels, seamlessly merging with creative avenues like video, billboard, and long-copy.

Keep your people aligned and engaged as their actions will tighten the bond with consumers

At the **attract** stage, your team should utilize ideal consumer profiles, reinforced by pain points and consumer insights. Use the organizing brand idea to develop new products, packaging, public relations, and advertising that emphasizes the brand's unique selling proposition and distinct features.

At the **inform** stage, ensure all employees understand and can communicate the organizing brand idea, both functional and emotional benefits, and the key features that set your brand apart from competitors. An intuitive website and swift query resolutions are essential. Offer personalized messages tailored to meet the consumer's needs.

As consumers approach making a decision, trust becomes the linchpin to **closing the deal**. Your team should assist consumers, whether in-person or online, throughout their choices and purchases. Continuous data collection and conversion monitoring are paramount for refining strategies.

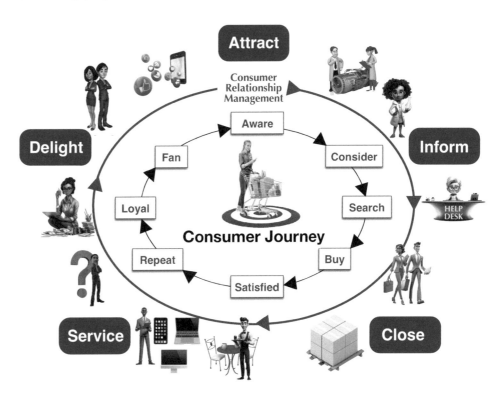

After a sale, delivering high-quality **service** emphasizes the importance of long-lasting relationships. This involves addressing post-purchase inquiries, ensuring smooth returns/exchanges, and leveraging purchase history to introduce targeted promotions, thereby strengthening the bond and cultivating loyal consumers.

At the **delight** stage, it is crucial for your team to prioritize support for VIP consumers. Encourage your people to create 'wow moments' that make it easy for brand fans to share their memorable experiences with their networks.This creates new awareness backed by the endorsement of someone they trust. Prioritizing social media incentives and tracking referrals ensures your brand remains a central topic in consumer conversations.

Elevate your brand strategy presentations using our Beloved Brands presentation templates

Our brand presentation templates reflect the tools you will find in our brand playbooks, Beloved Brands, B2B Brands, and Healthcare Brands.

We offer expertly-designed brand template PowerPoint presentations you can use to build your brand plan, brand positioning, business reviews, monthly reports and creative briefs. We have translated our brand tools from this book into brand templates in downloadable PowerPoint presentations that you can purchase. We include fully completed examples of each slide. And, we include blank versions with definitions.

We have specific brand templates for consumer brands, retail, B2B, and healthcare brands.

https://beloved-brands.com/brand-management-templates/

Our Marketing Training programs will make your team smarter so you can realize their full potential

Investing in your people will pay off. After our marketing training program, you will see them make the right decisions and produce exceptional work that leads to higher growth for brands they work on. We train marketers on the best ways to think, define, plan, execute and analyze. They will learn how to think strategically, define their brand positioning, write a strategic brand plan that everyone can follow, make smart, creative decisions on advertising and innovation, and analyze their brand in ways that set up the smartest strategies to build a plan for the future.

Our marketing training program is built for the real world of marketing.

We want brand leaders to gain added confidence as they head back to their jobs. We get participants to try out each new process, idea, or tool in real time to come up with answers on the brand they work on. We offer our live feedback to help them learn the concepts. Our marketing training program also offers an added coaching program, where they complete a brand plan, brand positioning, creative brief and deep-dive business review.

Our Brand Management Mini MBA certificate program

If you are an ambitious marketer, looking to solidify your marketing skills, our Brand Management Mini MBA provides 36 video lessons for you to learn about strategic thinking, brand positioning, brand plans, advertising decisions, and marketing analytics. We designed our Mini MBA to replicate our in-person training.

Manufactured by Amazon.ca
Bolton, ON

35252250R00133